WOMEN, COMMUNITY, AND THE HORMEL STRIKE OF 1985–86

Recent Titles in
Contributions in Women's Studies

WOMEN, COMMUNITY, AND THE HORMEL STRIKE OF 1985–86

NEALA J. SCHLEUNING

Contributions in Women's Studies, Number 137

GREENWOOD PRESS
Westport, Connecticut • London

Library of Congress Cataloging-in-Publication Data

Schleuning, Neala.
    Women, community, and the Hormel Strike of 1985–86 / Neala J.
Schleuning.
      p. cm. — (Contributions in women's studies, ISSN 0147–104X ;
no. 137)
    Includes bibliographical references and index.
    ISBN 0–313–28976–X (alk. paper)
    1. Women in trade-unions—Minnesota—Austin—Interviews. 2. Women
political activists—Minnesota—Austin—Interviews. 3. United
Packinghouse, Food, and Allied Workers. Local 9 (Austin, Minn.)
4. Geo. A. Hormel & Company Strike, Austin, Minn., 1985–86.
5. Strikes and lockouts—Packing-house workers—Minnesota—Austin.
I. Title. II. Series.
HD6079.2.U52M567   1994
331.4′78′0976431—dc20   93–28037

British Library Cataloguing in Publication Data is available.

Library of Congress Catalog Card Number: 93–28037
ISBN: 0–313–28976–X
ISSN: 0147–104X

First published in 1994

Greenwood Press, 88 Post Road West, Westport, CT 06881
An imprint of Greenwood Publishing Group, Inc.

Printed in the United States of America

∞

The paper used in this book complies with the
Permanent Paper Standard issued by the National
Information Standards Organization (Z39.48–1984).

10 9 8 7 6 5 4 3 2 1

Dedicated to the women and men of the
Austin United Support Group,
and people everywhere struggling to survive

To have nothing in common is impossible,
for the city is a community.

Aristotle, Politics

Contents

Preface

In 1987 I went to nearby Austin, Minnesota, to interview the "women of P–9" for a videotape production on the lives of rural women. Nearly everyone in the United States had heard about the 1985–86 packinghouse workers strike against the Hormel Company. The striking union, Local P–9, had become a household word. But nobody knew about the role that women had played in this historical event. Nobody had heard of the Austin United Support Group.

The contributions of the women and men of the Support Group were significant, as this study will attest. They came together in love and anger, in "tender solidarity" (a term for which I am indebted to my good friend Fred Whitehead), to stand side by side with P–9 and confront a powerful corporation. They fought on many fronts: for their families; for their community; for their own dignity.

Four women were interviewed in 1987 for that video (*I Always Believed It Was a Beautiful Town*): Patricia A. Higgins, Vickie Guyette, Carole Apold, and Barbara Collette. It was one of the most moving experiences of my life to hear their stories and the larger story of the hundreds of women who participated in the Support Group. That initial contact was all too brief, and I dreamed of one day returning to Austin to document their stories in greater depth.

Nearly three years later, in the fall of 1990, Patricia Higgins and I renewed our acquaintanceship when she started graduate school at the university where I work. About that same time, the Minnesota legislature authorized the Minnesota Historical Society to fund the collection of women's history materials. We began developing plans to gather the oral histories of the women in the Support Group. I submitted a grant on behalf of our project, and it was funded.

We developed a brief open-ended questionnaire, and began conducting the interviews in the offices of the Support Group just before Christmas in 1990. As an "insider" in the Support Group, Patricia felt she could get the women to participate in the interview process. The selection of individuals to be interviewed was based on her contacts. While the offer was made to interview anyone regardless of their views on the strike, no strikebreakers volunteered, and most of the women who were interviewed had been strong supporters of the strike. They didn't always agree, however; so a cross section of viewpoints is represented. I was present for about half of the interviews; and because of the travel and scheduling difficulties, Patricia conducted the balance alone. She was trusted, and her involvement in the interviews made the women feel comfortable and probably contributed to their openness and candor. From December 1990 through the spring of 1991, a total of forty-two interviews were conducted, representing more than sixty hours of material.

We then contacted Sharon Fiala, who undertook quite a challenge transcribing the tapes. The sound quality varied; and in those instances when more than one woman took part in the conversations, sorting out the voices was tricky! After the interviews were transcribed, copies were sent to the individuals and they were asked to make any changes, corrections, or additions.

Once the material for this book was selected, a minimum of editing was done—condensing long passages; removing extraneous verbal material (the ums, ahs, and you knows); minor changes in tense and grammar. The reader will note that in several places the word *Hormel* has an "s" at the end. This was a commonly used verbal form of the Hormel Company name. In addition, Hormel was usually pronounced with the accent on the first syllable, and giving the last syllable a shortened "e"—Hor'-mls. After editing, the material was returned to the women once again for their final approval.

Thirty-three women agreed to be identified for this book: Carole Apold, Mary Arens, Joyce Ball, Jeannie Bambrick, Cindi Bellrichard, Susan Benson, Barbara Collette, LaVonne Ferguson, Barb Frandle, Billie Goodeu, Vickie Guyette, Shirley Heegard, Michelle Hendrickson, Patricia A. Higgins, Judy Himle, Bev Huston, Jan Kennedy, Carol King, Carol Kough, Judy Kraft, Madeline Krueger, Dixie Lenz, Marie Loverink, Mary Machacek, Linda Novak, Rietta Pontius, Cheryl Remington, Carmine Rogers, Jean (Victor) Schiesser, Donna Simon, Zetta Simpson, Carmel Taylor, and Julie Wilson. An additional nine women participated, but chose to remain anonymous. The anonymous quotes are identified in the text; all others are either noted in the text or footnoted.

The interviews took place nearly five years after the strike activities began. Most of the leadership of the Support Group agreed to be interviewed, and all of the women interviewed were active in some way. All were still very protective of the image of the Austin United Support Group. So, in some sense, their comments were filtered through a desire to put their best foot forward.

Five years was time enough for the women to have had an opportunity to reflect on their experiences, and they were anxious to tell their story. The pain, anger, and frustration over the outcome of the strike were still sharp and clear. Some wounds will never heal. But in the intervening years, the women had come to understand the changes they had undergone and the meaning of those changes in their lives and in their community.

As I looked back on the interviews, I was impressed with several things: the strength of the women and their vision of economic justice; how deeply committed they remain to their ideals and their struggle; and sadly, how little the passage of time had diminished their pain and anguish. I was reminded of the women in the nineteenth century who struggled eighty long years for the vote. Many of them died before they saw their vision achieved, but their apparent failure did not diminish their efforts throughout their lives. The women in the Austin United Support Group had, and have, a similar big vision. I can only hope that this work does their vision the honor it deserves. I stand humbly before such fierce love and passion.

ACKNOWLEDGMENTS

I am indebted to all the following:

Patricia A. Higgins for being my guide into the culture of the Austin United Support Group. Patricia clarified questions about who was who and what was what that would have been difficult to track down without her intimate knowledge of events and people.

The Minnesota Historical Society for their financial support and their vision of preserving women's history.

To all the librarians at Mankato State University, especially my good friend Kellian Clink. I received additional guidance and assistance from the Austin Public Library, the James J. Hill Research Library, Dave Rademacher in the Minnesota State Demographer's Office, and the Minnesota Department of Trade and Economic Development.

For help with editing and their necessary and always brutally honest criticisms, Sharon Addams, Eric Steinmetz, Fred Whitehead, and a wonderful anonymous editor-reader.

To Sharon Fiala for her excellent transcriptions.

For fine-tuning and tracking on all aspects of the manuscript, my daughter-in-law Lyn Yount and friend Chemutai Murgor.

To Greenwood Publishing Group acquisition editors Cynthia Harris and Lynn Flint for supporting this work. For copyediting at Greenwood, I wish to thank Pat Merrill for her careful scrutiny, and Diane T. Spalding for her work as the project's production editor.

For use of his poem "A Tree Fell," Eide Cardel, and for use of the lyrics to "Lefty's Bar Tonight," John McCutcheon/Appalsongs (ASCAP).

Thanks to friends one and all who sustained me through their faith and interest in this work: Sharon Addams, Suzanne Bunkers, Diana Gabriel, Lynda Jacobson, Phil Kendall, and Sandra Loerts.

All royalties from this book will be dedicated to a scholarship endowment fund at Mankato State University in Mankato, Minnesota, on behalf of members and families of the Austin United Support Group/P–9 who did not cross the picket line. Anyone wishing to contribute to the endowment is urged to contact the university.

Timeline of Events

October 1984	Hormel Company announces wage cuts from $10.69 to $8.25 per hour and retroactive benefit cuts.
October 1984	First meeting called in Todd Park to form the Austin United Support Group.
January 1985	P–9 hires Ray Rogers to organize Corporate Campaign against Hormel.
July 1985	Hormel makes contract offer.
August 14, 1985	P–9 rejects Hormel's offer.
August 17, 1985	The strike begins.
December 20, 1985	Civil disobedience begins at plant gates.
January 13, 1986	Hormel reopens the plant with replacement workers and strikebreakers.
January 20, 1986	The plant and the corporate offices are blockaded and shut down. Governor Rudy Perpich sends in the National Guard. Demonstrations continue through the rest of the winter, spring, and into the summer.
January 31, 1986	National Guard leaves. Plant is shut down again by protesters.
February 3, 1986	National Guard returns.
February 15, 1986	Rally of thousands of supporters in Austin.
February 21, 1986	National Guard leaves.

March 20, 1986   More than 100 people arrested in civil disobedi-
                        ence. Women spend the night in jail.

April 12, 1986   Another rally of thousands of supporters.

April 13, 1986   Jesse Jackson visits Austin.

May 8, 1986   UFCW places P–9 in trusteeship.

Early June 1986   UFCW takes over P–9 offices. P–9 ceases to exist.
                        The Austin United Support Group sets up new
                        offices, continues the strike.

WOMEN,
COMMUNITY,
AND THE
HORMEL STRIKE
OF
1985–86

CHAPTER 1

"The Whole World Is Watching"

Austin is a typical Midwestern small town set in the rolling prairies of south-eastern Minnesota. In 1985–86 a great violence was done to the working people of this serene community—an economic violence that changed their lives forever. In the fall of 1984, the George A. Hormel Company made a series of decisions to reduce the compensation package to its workers. It arbitrarily cut the hourly pay, and retroactively reduced medical benefits. In response, the local Austin packinghouse workers union, P–9, voted to go on strike beginning in August 1985.

In the fine print of its corporate annual report, the Hormel Company's decision might have been named a cost cutting, or a restructuring, or a streamlining of the organization. Others might have identified those same actions as union-busting, holding a community hostage, or yet another example of the dismantling of the American economy. Whatever its name, similar phenomena occurred quietly all across the United States throughout the 1970s and 1980s as companies lowered wages, reduced the number of employees, reorganized, or recapitalized their businesses in a slow and relentless downward economic spiral. The reasons for the assaults against labor were familiar and predictable: we must be competitive, we must be more efficient, we must make sacrifices. After years of cutbacks and concessions, the workers at Hormel made the decision to stand their ground, refusing to give up their hard-won standard of living. What resulted was a long and bitter strike—only the second against the company in more than fifty years.

Many of those voices raised in protest in Austin were women's voices. In the fall of 1984, in response to the cuts implemented by Hormel, the spouses, families, friends, and supporters of P–9 workers came together. Calling themselves the Austin United Support Group (hereafter referred to as the ''Support

Group''), they called a meeting to meet the dual needs of mutual support for one another and for the workers in the plant.[1]

Initially, the Support Group's objectives were informal and quite modest: to bring women together and talk about how they could be supportive, and to raise money to help the families that had lost benefits. As Vickie Guyette, one of the founding members, recalled,

I think there were two groups who were actually thinking about doing something. I remember talking to Jim[2] one day, saying that there has to be something the women can do, and a lot of us were friends already. It was just a matter of getting together and figuring it out; and that very afternoon another woman, Jeannie Bambrick, had called. I didn't have any idea who she was—I had never met her before—and she had the same idea. Then I got together with Michelle Hendrickson, another P–9 wife, and we met for dinner and made up a leaflet. At the next big meeting of the union at the high school, we passed the leaflet out, just to tell women to meet at the park. That's how it got started. Five of us met early at the park, and made coffee and just met each other, because there were some of us that didn't know each other. I'll bet you there were close to 300 women that showed up that night.

That founding group of five women included Vickie Guyette, Jeannie Bambrick, Michelle Hendrickson, Billie Goodeu, and Diane Swanson. Word of those early meetings spread quickly. The meetings were held in Todd Park because, initially, the women were not allowed to meet in the union's building, the Austin Labor Center. They continued to meet in the park on the cool Minnesota fall nights until, as Billie Goodeu recalled, ''one night Floyd Lenoch came out and said, 'You are as entitled to be down there as anybody,' and from then on we moved into the union hall. This was quite an emotional thing for all of us—to be told no, we couldn't, then all of a sudden, we could be there.''

From the beginning, the number of women involved in the Support Group was impressive, reflecting the breadth and depth of commitment to the issues involved as well as a growing and sustained sense of community and mutual support. For almost a year before the strike was called in August 1985, this organization played a major role in developing strategy, organizing support, fundraising, and educating first the Austin community and ultimately the whole world about the economic issues of the strike. Although not all of the members of the Support Group were women, the organization was clearly a ''women's organization.'' Women were the major decision-makers and activists; and even when P–9 joined the Support Group after their formal union structure was outlawed, women continued to provide the leadership.

This book is about the women of the Austin United Support Group and the development of their organization and its goals and objectives, its economic and political agendas. It is also the story of women working together to change their lives and to care for one another and their families. It is a story of strength and vision, a story of anger and action. At times, it is a story filled with great sorrow—the sorrow of lost opportunities, betrayal by friends and family, alienation and destruction of the fabric of community. It is mostly, however, a story of grit and determination, a story of women changing their community, the world, and themselves.

This is also a story of hope, a message of the abiding strength of the human spirit. It is the story of how people responded creatively to major changes in their lives—by creating new economic and political structures, new cultural expressions, and new social networks that revitalized community. It is the story of one community lost and another found.

A BRIEF HISTORY: LOCAL P–9 AND THE HORMEL COMPANY

The George A. Hormel Company was founded in 1891; and for many decades, labor relations were congenial in Austin.[3] George Hormel was generally perceived to be a "benevolent dictator" who worked alongside his employees and socialized with them after hours.[4] Although a union was formed in 1915 and lasted until 1922, George was so well liked by his employees that the union was not very effective in organizing the workers against the Hormel Company. During its early years, the company relied on a largely transient workforce. Packinghouse workers came to Austin on a seasonal basis to conduct the kill and pack of the harvest of meat. They lived on the margins of the community, doing some of the hardest and least pleasant work in the economy. According to historian Fred Blum, these were rough men, unwelcome in the town, social outcasts: "People did not like their daughter to marry a slaughterhouse man . . . a packinghouse rat."[5] Their work was skilled work, but intermittent. They were paid an hourly wage; and when work was slow, they were laid off. After the turn of the century, job security did improve somewhat in the industry, but the Hormel Company was one of the last packinghouses to make a commitment to an annual wage.[6]

In 1929 when George Hormel stepped down and his son Jay took over the leadership of the company, labor relations grew more strained. Jay did not have his father's management skills nor his easy way with the employees, and the distance between management and labor widened. In 1931, Jay undertook an experiment to reduce employee turnover and cut training time. He placed the men in one department on an annual wage. Jealousy on the part of workers in other departments, coupled with an across-the-board wage cut, resulted in further deterioration of labor–management relations.

In 1933 the workers began to organize themselves around labor principles inspired by the revolutionary ideology of the "Wobblies," the Industrial Workers of the World (IWW).[7] Hormel workers like Frank Ellis who early in the century had carried the IWW union card in their pockets provided strong organizational leadership. Rather than organizing workers by traditional guild or craft structures with their implicit hierarchy of work, the Wobblies advocated "one big union" of all workers across an entire industry, regardless of level of skill and type of work. They also advocated for the reorganization of the workplace along participatory and democratic lines: nonauthoritarian, worker-controlled production; a guaranteed annual wage; the decision-making power to set their own work pace; and a strong union structure. Their agenda was a revolutionary one, with its demands for worker control and its attacks on the capitalist class.

The Wobblies were often creative in their organizing efforts. Frank Ellis urged the new union—the Independent Union of All Workers (IUAW), or Local P–9—to organize the whole community of Austin; and "store clerks, cooks, waiters, waitresses, and even some farmers" soon joined the One Big Union.[8] Organizing the whole community was tactically brilliant for a variety of reasons: it expanded the base of support for the striking workers' issues; it raised consciousness in the town about the economic interdependence of workers in a company town; and it left the company isolated from a support base close to home. In fact, the union efforts were so successful that, by the 1950s, "nearly every establishment in town was unionized."[9]

Later that same year, after years of unresolved grievances over a variety of issues, a strike erupted in the hog-kill section of the plant. It was sparked by resistance to a required insurance plan. Some of the most militant workers came from the hog kill—the most difficult and unpleasant task in the industry. They were also the most skilled workers, and their participation was critical to the success of the strike overall.[10] After months of failed negotiations with Jay Hormel, the IUAW members took up more militant tactics. Upon hearing rumors that nonunion workers were doing their jobs, more than 400 men stormed the plant and refused to leave until Jay Hormel agreed to their demands.[11] Their tactic of sitting-in at the plant, and thereby claiming their own work, proved highly effective.

Hormel management personnel responded to the occupation of the plant with a variety of strategies and countermoves. They considered calling in federal troops to protect government-owned meat stored in the now occupied plant, and they took initial steps to organize strikebreakers in Minneapolis. Finally, they put pressure on the local police force, which in turn demanded that Governor Floyd B. Olson send in the National Guard. Despite dire warnings of the threat of "guerrilla warfare with pitiful casualties on both sides," and exhortations to "avoid needless bloodshed," the governor—a former IWW member himself—refused, and instead sent a representative to negotiate a resolution between the union and the company.[12] Olson, who publicly referred to himself as a "radical," was reluctant to call out the troops, and decided instead to come to Austin personally. Jay Hormel warned him that the situation was too dangerous for him to make a personal appearance. Olson disregarded Hormel's warning and—after a quick phone call to Frank Ellis, who told him there was no danger—came to negotiate an end to the strike. Within twenty-four hours of the governor's arrival in Austin, the strike was settled. The workers agreed to turn the plant over to the company in exchange for getting their jobs back without fear of punishment.

The success of this strike had a profound impact for many decades on American labor strike practices, the city of Austin, and the workers in the plant. Although there were no immediate benefits to the workers, the strike set the tone for a series of radical confrontations and sit-downs in the plant, culminating in a "working agreement" that was to characterize union–management relations for the next forty years. The agreement guaranteed steady work at industry-level wages, a year's layoff notice, incentive pay and profit sharing, and the freedom from strikes.[13]

The agreement also guaranteed democratic work processes. In effect, IUAW workers had control of the shop floor. The achievements of worker control of the process of production and democracy in the workplace were two truly revolutionary gains. Under industrial capitalism, workers lost control of the process of their work. The factory system—the organizational controlling mechanism of industrial capitalism—alienated individual worker from his or her work through two primary techniques: a division of labor that broke tasks down into their simplest units, severing control of the work process from the individual worker and placing it in the hands of managers; and a hierarchy of decision-making overlaid onto the work process. The result was an isolated worker who had only part of the process under his or her direct control, whose work was often repetitive, and who was unaware of how that task connected with the overall process. Gaining control of the process of work throughout the plant, then, was both a political and an aesthetic success for the Hormel packinghouse workers. The company benefited as well, according to historian Larry Engelmann. As workers participated more directly in decision-making, they began to exhibit a greater sense of responsibility, gradually taking on the attitudes and agendas of their former managers.[14]

Fred Blum's study supported this insight. Blum attributed the success of the Hormel Company to employee job security and the workers' feeling they were in charge of the process of work through the plant. This meant that the employees were also in charge of their income to a great extent. Decade after decade, the workers negotiated for a set wage based on a mutually agreed production output. Once minimum production quotas were completed, workers could decide as a work group whether they wanted to go home for the day or stay and earn incentive pay. This process of negotiating the workload probably also contributed to a high level of democratic decision-making skills and greater participation generally on the part of the workforce.

Needless to say, the workforce was so satisfied with this arrangement that for nearly fifty years the company, the union, and the community experienced unprecedented economic stability and an environment of good management–labor relations. A good wage and job security benefited everybody in Austin: the company saw ever increasing profits; the workers maintained a very high standard of living; and the town prospered. In 1974, after forty years of labor peace and economic growth, Larry Engelmann was moved to remark: "Today, meat means money in Austin. And it is impossible to distinguish the homes of workers from managers along Austin's clean, well-lighted streets."[15]

Because of the strong role of the union, Austin was an exception to the rule for company towns. In most one industry communities, the wealth flowed into the hands of a few owners or stockholders. In Austin, however, the whole community benefited from the good wages. Jack Chernick's study of Austin's economy in the late 1930s reinforced the commonly held belief that what was good for Hormel was good for the town.''[16] During the 1930s, Austin's population had increased 49 percent—a sign, for Chernick, of the success of the new arrangement between management and labor. In particular, he attributed economic growth in the community to the implementation of the year-round wage and the job stability resulting from the one-year layoff notice. Economic expansion in the Austin community was fueled by the good relationship between the company and the union, Chernick concluded:

Austin's growth in population was due less to the increase in employment at the plant than to the augmented purchasing power and stability of earnings that resulted from the firm's employment policies. These made it possible for Hormel employees to buy more goods and services and thus to open additional employment opportunities.[17]

According to Chernick, people in Austin felt comfortable enough to take greater risks and make long-term financial commitments. Job security translated into expanded consumer expenditures, installment plan buying, an increased number of loans, and housing purchases. Banks and businesses were, similarly, more likely to extend long-term credit because they were assured of payment. The more freely money circulated, the more the community prospered, Chernick noted.

The proportion of purchases made on an installment basis was greater among Hormel employees than in the rest of the state and in various other centers in the United States. It may also be seen in the fact the percentage of homeowners and the frequency of automobile ownership were greater among Hormel employees than among the residents of 29 small cities in four regions of the United States.[18]

In 1951, three out of four workers in Austin owned their own homes, and the population of Austin peaked in 1960 at 30,000.[19] In the 1960s, however, the company began to limit the compensation package; and year after year, beginning in 1963, the workers made one concession after another. According to labor historian Fred Halstead, "In fourteen of the twenty years between 1963 and 1983, significant concessions were demanded by the company and accepted by the union."[20] Over the same period of time, the company periodically raised the specter of relocation. Fear ran deep that the largest employer would leave town, and the workers were often urged by their community to help save the town. Concessions included such things as cuts in pay and losses of control over the organization of work.

In 1978, Hormel came forward with its most serious threat to move the plant out of Austin. In exchange for the company's agreeing to stay in Austin and build a new plant, the contract that year carried many significant concessions on the part of the workers—among these concessions, an agreement to increase production once the new plant was opened and to give up voluntarily their incentive earnings. Instead of going into the pockets of workers, the incentive pay "would be put into escrow to provide a $20 million loan to help the company build the new plant. . . . This amounted to $12,000 per worker,"[21] and it was to be repaid to those individuals once the new plant was built, as an add-on to wages. Further, when the $12,000 was repaid, the incentive would continue for those workers still working in the new plant. In effect, the workers helped underwrite building the new plant. The union further agreed "not to strike for three years after the completion of the new facility."[22]

Some of the members of P–9 were upset with these concessions, however. In 1981, after many conversations with his co-workers, Jim Guyette challenged the union leadership for control of P–9 and won. His challenge was based on serious criticism of several decisions by P–9 leadership—especially, the many concessions they had made; the incentive pay "loan" to Hormel; and the international union's plan to merge Hormel workers at all plants. In 1980 the previously independent P–9 had merged with the United Food and Service Workers Union (UFCW), and there were still many tensions between the local and the international. There was a brief and confrontational power struggle between Guyette with his "night-shift radicals" and the union leadership and UFCW negotiator, Lewie Anderson. Anderson and his supporters tried to deny Guyette and his supporters the right to make motions, for example; but the majority overruled Anderson's leadership and allowed Guyette to bring his proposals forward. At the close of 1981, Guyette won election to the executive board and gained a platform to present his more radical agenda. The new plant opened in 1982, and a host of new issues faced the revitalized, though now divided, P–9.[23]

1984: STRIKE TALK[24]

Jim Guyette was elected president of P–9 in 1984. He barely had time to get settled in his new role when that fall, in a surprise move, the company announced major cutbacks to "remain competitive." The election had been very close; and the results continued to reflect the union's internal disagreements when the membership elected pro-company John Anker as vice-president.[25] The new plant was up and running with a smaller workforce, and the company was now well positioned to process meatpacking in one of the most efficient plants in the country. The union was stunned when, despite high profits that year, Hormel management cut wages 23 percent from $10.69 to $8.25 an hour and made deep cuts, retroactive six months, to health benefits. Those workers who had undergone major surgery, for example, found that they were now personally responsible for medical expenses that had previously been covered. Because the company had already paid those bills, they now began deducting them from workers' paychecks. As a result, some workers received no income after working forty hours. Others received such small checks they were eligible for food stamps. Other company demands included the right to unlimited use of part-time workers; refusing workers the right to sharpen their own knives, and the time on the job to do it; and transferring the costs of uniforms and other work-related expenses from the company to the individual worker.

Under the more militant leadership of Jim Guyette, the workers were, according to Halstead, "fighting mad." Further antagonizing the situation was the fact that P–9 was not free to strike. The 1978 agreement bound the members to continue working until 1985. The wage cuts were difficult to accept, and the retroactive cutback in benefits seemed incredibly unjust. Safety in the new plant was also an issue. The production line was speeded up, resulting in increased injuries.[26] In 1984, according to Halstead, the Austin plant had a 202 percent injury rate, with a loss of work time for nearly one-third of the workforce. The average rate for all industries is 10 percent; for the meatpacking industry, 33 percent.[27]

In the fall of 1984, P–9 began to gear up for a strike. Its activities did not have the support of the UFCW. Nationally, the meatpacking industry had undergone major restructuring. In the new leaner industry, workers lost ground: concessions included plant closings, work speed-ups, and losses in wages and benefits. Located largely in small one-industry towns throughout the Midwest, the labor policies of these meatpacking companies had created economic havoc. Communities and workers bent over backward to keep their livelihood, but company after company either left town or reduced pay levels. A common pattern in Minnesota was one corporation closing a plant and moving out of a town, and a different corporation reopening the same plant six months later with anywhere from 25 to 50 percent lower wages. To further complicate the negotiation process, plants and workers in the same company in different locations negotiated independently of one another. In this climate of reductions, the UFCW—under the leadership of Lewie Anderson, who was director of the Packinghouse Division—was attempting to make the best of a bad situation. The UFCW strategy had been to make concessions in order to keep plants open, and they had already negotiated lower wages at other Hormel plants in the Midwest. In 1984, their objective was to bring the Austin contract into line with agreements already signed throughout the industry.

P–9, however, was not interested in concessions. The workers persisted in their stubborn commitment to stand up to Hormel. Two decisive events had a significant impact on Local P–9's effectiveness. The first was the formation of the Austin United Support Group. The second was that, in January 1985, P–9 hired Ray Rogers and his Corporate Campaign to develop a public relations and fundraising plan. Rogers had successfully coordinated strike campaigns for the Amalgamated Clothing and Textile Workers Union against the J. P. Stevens Company, and had developed campaigns for such diverse unions as the Air Line Pilots Association, the paperworkers, and machinists.[28] The P–9 leaders felt that they needed a national audience for their issues, and Rogers's skills and connections could help win a very tough strike. The tactic of publicly embarrassing major corporate investors and urging them to apply moral pressure on companies that treated their workers poorly had met with mixed success, but P–9 felt Rogers had the organizational ability and the national network to make things uncomfortable enough for Hormel that it might be pressured into withdrawing its cutbacks.[29]

Rogers set about developing a multipronged strategy. From January 1985 until the strike began in August, Local P–9, the Support Group, and Corporate Campaign worked day and night to raise awareness of the workers' issues. Corporate Campaign tied the coalition's strategy to putting pressure on the First Bank System, a stockholder in the Hormel Company. While this pressure failed to influence Hormel directly, demonstrations against First Bank in the Twin Cities and other places served to raise awareness of P–9's position.

In activities reminiscent of Frank Ellis's community organizing tactics, the workers felt it was important to seek the help of the Austin community as well. They initiated a strong educational outreach campaign in the community. According to one chronicler, more than 50,000 flyers were distributed, and P–9ers went door to door in Austin to talk with people about the importance of the union's issues to the town as a whole.[30] Although the workers actively sought to rally the support of the community, by and large they were not successful. The campaign was further undermined when Hormel filed a complaint with the National Labor Relations Board (NLRB), accusing P–9 of conducting a secondary boycott against First Bank.

Negotiations throughout most of 1985 failed to make any significant changes in Hormel's proposal. If anything, the company hardened its position. In its contract offer of July 17, 1985, in addition to the wage and benefit cuts, the company now proposed the elimination of two important hard-won agreements in the 1933 contract: job assignment by seniority, and the one-year layoff notice. Further,

Hormel wanted to add a new clause prohibiting strikes for the duration of the agreement and allowing the company to discharge workers who engaged in job actions. The contract also provided for a two-tier wage system, a thirty percent reduction in pensions, a common labor wage of $9.25 with no increases over three years, and eliminated maternity leave.[31]

The union and the company could not come to agreement. Finally, on August 17, 1985, with 93 percent of the membership voting to support, the 1,500 members of P–9 struck. Once again, the highly skilled hog-kill workers were the most committed to the strike.[32] The issues of money, safety, and control of the work process were too important to bargain away. The workers were especially incensed when Hormel announced that its profits were up 30.9 percent in 1985 over the previous year. They found it difficult to believe that, with such high profits, the company had to cut wages.[33]

Both the company and the union took their messages to the public. To counteract any negative impact on sales from the strike, the Hormel Company spent $70 million on advertising in 1985—up 50 percent from 1984.[34] In addition to relying on the high visibility of Rogers's Corporate Campaign, throughout the fall of 1985 the workers and Support Group members crisscrossed the country with their message of resistance to Hormel's unrealistic contract offer. They talked about how the wage cuts had already created hardships, about the poor safety conditions in the new plant, about the small humiliations such as having to ask permission to use the bathroom. They talked, too, about the need for working people in the United States to begin resisting concessions. They went in large caravans of roving pickets to other Hormel plants throughout the Midwest. Support for the strikers came flooding into Austin from every state in the union and from around the world—despite the UFCW's efforts to discourage giving direct assistance to the local.

Hormel refused to negotiate seriously; and in December, P–9 turned to more confrontational tactics. On December 20, picketers began a series of demonstrations, blocking the plant gates. Hormel went to court to limit the number of pickets. Everywhere, it seemed, P–9 efforts were being stymied by restrictive labor legislation and an indifferent union bureaucracy: the strikers were barred from picketing First Bank; they were locked out of the plant; they could only do token picketing; and their international was urging them to go back to work.

Less than a month later, on January 13, 1986, Hormel decided to reopen the plant with replacement and strikebreaker labor. In the weeks prior to the reopening of the plant, Hormel had advertised widely for replacement workers. Men and women flooded into Austin from Iowa—where, rumor had it, welfare recipients from Mason City were being told to go to Austin to apply for work or lose their benefits—and from the farming communities surrounding Austin. The Midwest was in the middle of a major farming economic crisis, and the rural economy was in a shambles. The $8.25-an-hour wage looked good in an area where minimum-wage jobs were the rule and farmers were losing their land. Several hundred P–9ers also crossed the picket lines and became "scabs" in the eyes of their still striking co-workers.

The strikers, now working closely with the Support Group, responded with months of massive demonstrations, picketing, and civil disobedience. Since union members were forbidden by law to picket, the bulk of demonstrating activities were coordinated by the Support Group and labor unions and other groups from around the state and the nation. On January 20 the protesters organized a blockade involving hundreds of cars from the Twin Cities, and shut the plant down. In fact, entrance into the Hormel plant was easy to block, it being located at an exit of Interstate 90. The highway bisects the Hormel property, with the plant on one side and corporate headquarters on the other. Demonstrators also blockaded the corporate headquarters.

The protests were relatively violence free—despite the fact that media images tended to highlight shouting, angry people who were shown blocking cars and occasionally waving their fists or pounding on vehicles. The Hormel Company played on community fears of the stereotype of a strike as violent—more than on actual incidents—and demanded extra police protection. The local police force and county sheriff's office were pressured into contacting Governor Rudy Perpich; and at their urging, the governor called out the National Guard to protect the plant.

In the following week, with the plant surrounded by members of the Guard, the tensions heightened. P–9 and Support Group members were restrained on all sides, and there was a growing sense of frustration as it appeared that some laws were being selectively enforced or simply ignored. Labor historian Peter Rachleff noted, for example, that, despite state law prohibiting state troopers from interfering in labor struggles, the troopers played an active role against P–9 members.

When mobile pickets try to block the I–90 exit ramp that leads to the plant's north gate, state highway patrolmen break the windshields of their vehicles, pull them out, and arrest them. Several vehicles also suffer transmission and body damage, as the police drive them into ditches and over snow banks. The strikebreakers get through again. For the next several days, drivers cannot use a stretch of I–90 early in the morning unless they have passes which identify them as Hormel scabs.[35]

P–9 and the Support Group never let up their political pressure on Hormel. Throughout the winter and spring of 1986, they mobilized and protested through-out the community—from simple bannering and letters to the editor in the news-paper, to civil disobedience. Vandalism increased dramatically, with the union receiving most of the blame. State and national media took an intense interest in the activities in Austin, and strike-related events were part of the nightly news for many months.

Behind the scenes, tense and bitter discussions continued between P–9 and the UFCW. Lewie Anderson tried over and over again to undermine P–9 President Jim Guyette's leadership by supporting his opponents. P–9ers who wanted to end the strike came to be known as "P–10," and they were highly visible and vocal at union meetings. Efforts to change the minds of the workers were made to no avail, and so the UFCW moved legally to disenfranchise P–9. On May 8, 1986, the UFCW placed P–9 into trusteeship, taking over the books, bank accounts, and management of the union. A series of confrontations and lawsuits ensued, as the UFCW took control of donations flooding in from around the country for the striking families. Many of these donations never reached the families for whom they were intended. According to Peter Rachleff, "The in-ternational retained $1.2 million that other unions had donated to help Local P–9, charging against the funds those strike benefits that it had paid out."[36] On July 3, 1986, the UFCW physically evicted P–9 from the Austin Labor Center; the local merged with its Support Group, and they moved into a rented building several blocks up the street and behind the Hormel plant.

The striking workers and their families were truly on their own at that point, struggling to understand and interpret what had happened to them. The company was attempting to destroy them economically; the community had failed to support them; and now they were faced with the unpleasant task of explaining to themselves and the world why their international union had failed them. Unions, after all, are supposed to represent rank-and-file workers. The UFCW, however, had made it clear that its national agenda of making concessions superseded local agendas.[37] Local P–9 had taken up the fight against union-busting only to experience the irony of being destroyed by its international. P–9 had a new message for unionized workers all across America who were following closely the situation in Austin: watch your back; your own union may work against you.

The UFCW then moved quickly to "settle" the strike. More than a year after it all began—on September 12, 1986—an agreement was reached between the company and the new Local 9 union. The contract was close to Hormel's original offer the previous summer. Some strikers did return to work at this time, but more than 800 were placed on a callback list. Their jobs were permanently lost to the many replacement workers hired during the strike.

In 1988 Hormel closed down the hog-kill portion of its business and began negotiations to transfer that work to a newly formed company, Quality Pork Processors, Incorporated. Hundreds more jobs were permanently lost in this transfer of work to a new corporate entity—a move virtually guaranteeing that many workers will never be called back. The hog kill included some of the best paid and most highly skilled jobs in the plant. In addition, the hog kill had historically been the source of strong strike support. The strike of 1985–86 was no exception, so it was particularly instructive that Hormel chose to rid itself of this arena of worker resistance. Quality Pork promptly reduced wages and benefits to between $5 and $6 per hour.

THE LEGACY

In less than five years, the shape of the Hormel Company had changed, and the nature of work and working relationships there had changed. P–9 and the Support Group lost their economic struggle with the Hormel Company. Their local union, P–9, was destroyed. Many people lost their jobs to replacement workers and were forced to leave town to find work. In 1993, hundreds are still on the callback list. Most suffered major financial losses, and even those who returned to work will probably never recover from the financial setback. There is also a legacy of bitterness and sorrow in the community, as workers who are still out of work avoid meeting the eyes of former friends and relatives who crossed the picket line. Several men who died during the struggle have become martyrs. All in all, the fragile web of interpersonal relationships that made up the Austin community has been ripped apart.

Although the strike is officially over, there is another important story to tell: the story of the members of the Austin United Support Group. They first came together as an auxiliary group, a support group for their striking husbands and wives. They did most of the hidden work of the strike—cooking, stuffing envelopes, keeping spirits up. They also did much of the public work—speaking, bannering, civil disobedience. They went to jail; they talked back to Hormel executives. They were seldom identified or given credit for their work. Their role was assumed, glanced over, ignored by the media. To date, the half-dozen books written about the strike mention them only in passing. They were mostly women.

Their story is important for a variety of reasons. In the long run, what we learn about the Austin United Support Group may be instructive for the American people as they seek ways to interpret and act on their economic environment. The activities of the Support Group and the experiences of the women and men in Austin give us a unique opportunity to study the intersection of some of the most important economic and social phenomena in contemporary history: the ways in which women develop and effect a women's economic perspective; the relationship between women and the labor movement; how people go about the process of developing an analysis of economic events in their lives; and how people respond creatively to social and political change.

People interested in studying the experiences of women will be especially interested in the Austin United Support Group. First of all, the Support Group falls into a long tradition of women's auxiliary activities. These auxiliaries provided an excellent organizational vehicle for effective integration and cooperation between men's and women's labor movement groups. Auxiliaries were initially developed to provide logistical and moral support for largely male union activities; but as women have achieved greater independence in the culture generally, these auxiliaries occasionally developed and pursued their own agendas. Increasingly, the activities of women's auxiliaries are critical to labor movement success.

Labor historians will also find this study of the Austin United Support Group to be of interest. This strike, like others in recent years, finds unions and their supporters taking up broad social, economic, and political issues. For many years, partly in reaction to fears born during the McCarthy era, labor unions have shied away from major political confrontations with U.S. corporations over economic policy. The unions were content with negotiating contract language, vacation schedules, and an expected modest increase in wages. In the past twenty years, however, major shifts in corporate policy at both the national and international levels have forced unions to undertake a more militant and political stand on many issues of major economic impact. For the first time in many decades, the viability of the American standard of living is being challenged. Jobs are disappearing into the global economy, and competition among free trade zones serves to lower wages worldwide to the subsistence level. As the American job market erodes and unemployment increases, the link between family survival and these larger economic issues brings together the agenda of workers in the wage system and the agenda of the family. This situation also brings the worlds of men and women together through shared economic concerns and the need to develop cooperative economic strategies. At this point in history, the labor movement can ill afford to ignore women's half of the economic equation. Distant economic abstractions such as structural unemployment, union-busting, free trade zones, and concessions are now a part of an expanded women's agenda. In the activities of the Support Group, the labor movement's economic agenda and the family survival agenda come together.

Perhaps most important, however, the Support Group can teach us about the building and maintaining of meaningful community. All across the United States we see the breakdown of traditional community, and we have few models for reversing that trend. The Support Group provides an excellent model for understanding how people go about building new systems of mutual support and communication when traditional community fails. We will see how this small group moved from a place of profound alienation and despair to create a vital alternative culture. The strike culture they created was true community, created out of a deep abiding confidence in one another, in the dignity and worth of their work, in love and concern for their town.

The legacy of the Support Group is, finally, the shining tale of a mighty struggle for the deeply held beliefs and passionate dreams of working people of the United States. Their legacy is a story of hope and solidarity, of love and commitment, of passion and pride. Their economic agenda went beyond individual desires and need to focus on the quality of life in their community. They drew a line below which they would not go: their community would fight to maintain a decent standard of living. They drew that line for all of us to see, and raised the questions we all need to answer. How much of a pay cut would we take? How far will we go to fight for our way of life? What do we need to pay mortgages and light bills? To sustain community?

NOTES

1. An anonymously written mimeographed history of the Support Group is available from the Austin United Support Group. The group is also discussed briefly in books and articles on the strike.

2. Jim Guyette, Vickie's husband and president of P–9.

3. For background on labor relations between P–9 and the Hormel Company, see the following items of special interest: Fred H. Blum, *Toward a Democratic Work Process: The Hormel-Packing House Workers' Experiment* (New York, 1953); David G. Bronner, "Changes and Trends in Labor–Management Relations at the Geo. A. Hormel & Company, Austin, Minnesota," M.A. thesis, Mankato, Minn., 1968; Jack Chernick, *Economic Effects of Steady Employment and Earnings: A Case Study of the Annual Wage System of Geo. A. Hormel & Co.* (Minneapolis, 1942); Richard Dougherty, *In Quest of Quality: Hormel's First 75 Years* (St. Paul, Minn., 1966); Larry D. Engelmann, " 'We Were the Poor People'—The Hormel Strike of 1933," *Labor History* 15, 4 (Fall 1974): 483–510; Roger Horowitz, "Behind the Hormel Strike: The Fifty Years of Local P–9," *Against the Current* 1, 2 (March 1986): 13–18; Doniver Adolph Lund and V. Allan

Krejci, *The Hormel Legacy: 100 Years of Quality* (Austin, Minn., 1991); Gerald Francis Neunsinger, "A Study of Management's Attitude toward Labor in Two Minnesota Pack-inghouses," M.S. thesis, Mankato, Minn., 1961; among others.

4. Engelmann, " 'We Were the Poor People,' " 483. I am especially indebted to Engelmann and Fred H. Blum's history for background information on the relationship between P–9 and the Hormel Company.

5. Blum, *Toward a Democratic Work Process*, 158.

6. Engelmann, " 'We Were the Poor People,' " 488.

7. Background on the Industrial Workers of the World (IWW) can be found in the following selected works: Rosalyn Fraad Baxandall, *Words on Fire: The Life and Writing of Elizabeth Gurley Flynn* (New Brunswick, N.J., and London, 1987); Paul F. Brissenden, *The IWW: A Study of American Syndicalism* (New York, 1957); J. R. Conlin, *Bread and Roses, Too: Studies of the Wobblies* (Westport, Conn., 1969); Melvyn Dubofsky, *We Shall Be All: A History of the IWW* (New York, 1969); Elizabeth Gurley Flynn, *The Rebel Girl: An Autobiography* (New York, 1973); Joyce L. Kornbluh, ed., *Rebel Voices: An IWW Anthology* (Ann Arbor, Mich., 1964); Salvatore Salerno, *Red November Black November: Culture and Community in the Industrial Workers of the World* (Albany, 1989); *Songs of the Workers to Fan the Flames of Discontent* (Chicago, 1974); Philip Taft, "The IWW in the Grain Belt," *Labor History* 1 (1960): 53–67.

8. Engelmann, " 'We Were the Poor People,' " 491.

9. Dave Hage and Paul Klauda, *No Retreat, No Surrender: Labor's War at Hormel* (New York, 1989), 38.

10. Engelmann, " 'We Were the Poor People,' " 490.

11. Ibid., 497.

12. Ibid., 500.

13. Hage and Klauda, *No Retreat, No Surrender*, 31.

14. Engelmann, " 'We Were the Poor People,' " 509.

15. Ibid., 510.

16. Chernick, *Economic Effects*. Despite the fact that Chernick gives to the company all the credit for the successful economic environment in Austin—with hardly a mention of the union's role—he reflects fairly on the success of Jay Hormel's version of welfare capitalism.

17. Ibid., 66.

18. Ibid., 70.

19. Hage and Klauda, *No Retreat, No Surrender*, 37.

20. Fred Halstead, *The 1985–86 Hormel Meat-Packers Strike* (New York, 1986), 13.

21. Ibid., 7.

22. Horowitz, "Behind the Hormel Strike," 14.

23. See especially Hardy Green, *On Strike at Hormel: The Struggle for a Democratic Labor Movement* (Philadelphia, 1990), ch. 2, for a discussion of P–9 internal politics as they influenced the strike and its outcome.

24. There is a growing body of literature concerning the 1985–86 Hormel/P–9 Strike. Some of the more important sources include the following: Robert C. Divine, "Turmoil in Austin: Hormel Strike of 1985–86," M.B.A. thesis, Mankato, Minn., 1988; Michael T. Fahey, *Packing It In! The Hormel Strike, 1985–86: A Personal Perspective* (St. Paul, Minn., 1988); Green, *On Strike at Hormel*; Hage and Klauda, *No Retreat, No Surrender*; Halstead, *1985–86 Hormel Meat-Packers Strike*; Horowitz, "Behind the Hormel Strike"; Barbara Kopple, producer, *American Dream*, film (New York, 1991); David Moberg,

"Austin City Limits, Strikers on Guard," *In These Times* (January 29–February 4, 1986): 3, 8; Peter Rachleff, *Hard-Pressed in the Heartland: The Hormel Strike and the Future of the Labor Movement* (Boston, 1993); Peter Rachleff, "The Hormel Strike: Turning Point for the Rank-and-File Labor Movement," *Socialist Review* 16, 5 (September/October 1986): 71–98; Peter Rachleff, "Turning Points in the Labor Movement: Three Key Conflicts," in *Minnesota in a Century of Change: The State and Its People since 1900*, ed. Clifford E. Clark, Jr. (St. Paul, Minn., 1989), 195–222; Peter Rachleff, "Art and Activism in the American Labor Movement," *Artpaper* 10, 8 (April 1991): 12–13; William Somplatsky-Jarman, "Bringing Home the Bacon: The Real Hormel Story," *Christianity and Crisis: A Christian Journal of Opinion* 46, 1 (March 3, 1986): 56–58; *Support Report*, newsletter of the Austin United Support Group, 4 vols., 1986–90.

25. Green, *On Strike at Hormel*, 53–54.

26. Old footage of the Hormel production line shown in a recent film about the strike portrays workers moving at a much slower, more realistic pace. The line in the new plant moves far too quickly, according to P–9 members. The work pace is further complicated by the fact that the plant is kept at a consistent temperature of 45 degrees. People's hands get so cold, they fumble. Accidents are the result. Kopple, *American Dream*.

27. Halstead, *1985–86 Hormel Meat-Packers Strike*, 5.

28. Green, *On Strike at Hormel*, 14–20.

29. Peter Rachleff notes in "Hormel Strike," 85n: "The idea of a 'corporate campaign' is simple: research a corporation to find out what powers, particularly financial, lurk behind it; then, mount public pressure on those financial powers through demonstrations, creative use of the media, massive literature, and consumer boycotts." It is essentially a public relations campaign.

30. Horowitz, "Behind the Hormel Strike," 14.

31. Ibid., 16.

32. Ibid., 14.

33. Lund and Krejci, *Hormel Legacy*, 188.

34. Ibid.

35. Rachleff, "Hormel Strike," 79.

36. Rachleff, "Turning Points in the Labor Movement," 216.

37. Rachleff, "Hormel Strike," 79: "January 21, 1986. UFCW International releases a 43-page 'Fact Book on Local P–9/Austin, Minnesota.' This document attacks Ray Rogers and the elected leadership of Local P–9, and argues that Hormel has been reasonable in its bargaining all along!"

CHAPTER 2

"I Always Believed It Was a Beautiful Town"

It is unfortunate that this strike against the Hormel Company should bear the name of the corporation it challenged. Many strikes are known by the communities in which they occur or by the unions that inspire them: Homestead; Pullman; Calumet; the Minneapolis Teamsters Strike. In many ways, this particular strike is more appropriately the "Austin Strike," because the community of Austin, Minnesota, was so central to its successes and its failures, and because its outcome had such an obvious impact on the community as a whole.

What is community? And why would community be central to this labor struggle? Community is experienced at many levels in the personal and cultural lives of people: it is the places they shop, the neighbors greeted across the counter in the hardware store, the bartender who listens to the sad tale of broken romances. Community is the churches people attend on Sunday morning, the local newspaper brought to the front door by the girl who lives down the street, the local city council, the police. Community is the workplace—co-workers, the way decisions are made on the assembly line, the unions that negotiate pay and rules and regulations, the forms and structures of an economic and work culture. It is also the color and texture of our individual lives: our gender, our values, our personal histories. Community is what we experience and share in common; it is our shared sense of the meaning of our collective lives. Community is people—and systems—we can count on.

Some of the most important community ties are economic ones—especially in small towns. In her study of a widespread miners' strike in southeastern Kansas in 1920–21, historian Ann Schofield described the close relationship between small-town social and economic life: "First, there was the nature of the mining community itself. Small, isolated, and highly homogeneous, it formed an unusually cohesive social unit in twentieth-century America. In many respects, its cohesion resembled that of the preindustrial village more than that of the modern town.'' According to Schofield, the mining community—like other economies dominated by one industry—was ''characterized by the active participation of all members in a distinctive work culture.''[1]

This work culture was built up around respect for mining as a dangerous occupation and the primarily male institution of the labor union. During the strike in 1920–21, women relatives of the miners took an active role, focusing their efforts on the link between the world of work, the family, and the community.[2] These women respected the dangerous work of mining and knew the uncertainties of a husband's job, but they also knew that this job meant the difference between life and death for themselves and their children. As wives of miners, the women endorsed the basic assumptions of the male work culture; but this ''army of Amazons,'' as they were referred to at the time, also redefined and expanded that culture to include the economic and social life of the community as a whole.

Austin, Minnesota, is a typical small Midwestern town—not unlike the small towns of southeastern Kansas. People know each other, or about each other. Everyone knows where everything is, how everything works. Like small-town and village life everywhere, it is a personal and intimate community—oppressive to some who would prefer more anonymity, more freedom; or a warm, supportive environment for others. Austin has a fairly stable, though slightly declining population. In 1980 the population was 23,020, down from a peak of 30,000, and ten years later it had declined further to 21,907. Mower County, the site of Austin, showed a net outmigration of 2,400 people from 1980 through 1986.[3]

Austin is located about 100 miles south of the Twin Cities, and its economic life is fairly isolated and self-contained. Living in Austin has meant either living in the shadow of or basking in the sun of the Hormel Company, but there has been no escaping that central economic force. Hormel is the largest employer in Austin. In 1983, out of a total employment of 11,950, there were 2,360 people working for Hormel. This number declined to 1,737 by 1987, out of a total employment of 16,651. The second largest employer in 1987 was the school district, with 600 employees.[4] Surrounded now by a barbed wire fence, Hormel's plant physically dominates the center of town. At one time the plant even supplied Austin with its electrical power. From the late nineteenth century onward, Austin created its community around Hormel—its social and political life, its economic life, its workplace culture. People in Austin were proud to have Hormel as their flagship company. Over the years a few people may have grumbled that Hormel was discouraging other companies from relocating in the town, to keep community wages low; but by and large the community made every effort to keep Hormel in Austin.

The work at the plant was hard and often unpleasant, but everyone benefited. The community of Austin prospered—more than many other one-industry towns. For more than fifty years, Hormel employees were some of the best paid packinghouse workers, and the community had a high standard of living—one of the highest in the country. In 1984, one in ten Austin workers earned more than $30,000 a year.[5] Class differences were less perceptible in Austin because of the high wages at Hormel. Seventy-five percent of the working class, for example, was able to own comfortable homes. Both the company and the workers in the plant felt that they made strong contributions to the quality of life in Austin.

The importance of a viable economic community became a central issue in the strike—especially for the women in the Support Group. Accessing the networks of culture and community in Austin began with understanding the economics of a one-industry town. The women in Austin quickly came to see that a single-industry economy interpenetrated with community on even the most intimate levels. Even though there were other forces operating to shape community life—the power of the media to shape images of the strike; the power of the churches to withhold support from the strikers; the power of government at both the state and local levels to use force to advance the company's agenda—economic forces and institutions served a central function in defining community life. In small towns generally, there are few options for good-paying jobs, and the level of militancy in labor struggles is probably directly proportional to the perceived threat to those quality jobs. The Support Group's initial outreach efforts focused on identifying and educating others to the centrality of economics to community in general and to Austin's economic community and its close connection to the two cultures of work and family, in particular.

The women's tactics grew directly from this concern for the community: the personal quality of their confrontations with strikebreakers whom they saw as stealing their families' livelihood; awareness of their economic vulnerability in a one-industry town; the direct relationship between their standard of living and a job at Hormel; and their strong identification with the work of the men in their lives. The strike, they argued, was about all these things: jobs, children, homes, and the economic stability of Austin. Their arguments formed the basis for a belief in a moral economy—the belief that the right to survival is an issue of justice.[6]

With so much at stake for the community as a whole, people in Austin quickly took sides. According to Support Group member Barbara Collette, the strike split the town into three factions: those who supported the company; those who supported P–9; and those who remained neutral—or what Barbara called "neutralized." There were some unpleasant surprises for the Hormel workers as people in Austin took up their political positions on the strike. They knew that Hormel didn't support the strike, and that there were other individuals and institutions heavily dependent on Hormel who would side with the company. They were not prepared, however, to find friends and neighbors critical of the strike—or a large segment of the community that was hostile to the "good life" enjoyed by Hormel workers.

The strike destroyed the community of Austin. It changed the people, the institutions, the fragile web of relationships that serves as the vital life force of a small town. What's more, it destroyed the community and everybody could *see* the destruction. People avoided one another on the streets; the strikers changed shopping patterns to avoid Hormel Company supporters; strikers' children were threatened. Plant workers saw people from out of town take their jobs. Businesses closed; homes went back to the bankers; acts of petty vandalism left everyone suspicious and fearful.

Faith in the town's major institutions was shaken—and for many, shattered. The story of the Austin United Support Group begins with the story of the women's confrontation with the community of Austin. It must be an account of the tensions and splits that occurred, the women's struggles with institutional power, the loss of friends and relatives. This chapter concentrates on the breakdown of relationships between the strikers[7] and the Hormel Company, the business community, and community-based financial support systems.

COMPANY TOWN

Austin literally became a one-horse town. Hormels was the horse that fed it, and it pulled all the strings. We saw it all happen when that strike happened. The loyalties of the town were for Hormel, and the town fathers were standing behind the company. They just wanted those workers to do their job and not moan and groan. They had no idea what the company was doing, and what the company was doing was unbelievable. Hormel counted on that—that people wouldn't believe if the truth were told. And they were right. People said, I can't believe that's happening. So they didn't, and the community didn't support the strike.[8]

When the workers in a company town go on strike, it means, as it did in Austin, that they must risk not only their personal livelihood, but the life of the community as a whole. It also means that all the townspeople have an economic stake in a strike whether they like it or not, and whether they believe in it or not. Survival at the very deepest level is threatened—for the worker in the plant, for the businesses in the community, for everyone. A deep fear pervades the town—fear for self, fear for the very life of the whole town.

From the very beginning, the economic health of Austin was important to P–9 and the Support Group. As one woman proudly recalled, she made a conscious effort through her shopping habits to buy products that contributed to enhancing the local economy: "When my husband was working, I shopped for Austin. I was not allowed to go out of town and shop. I ate Hormel products, and when you bought meat you bought Hormel meat. It kept the town going. I say one feeds the next."[9] This sensitivity to buying power has historically been associated with women's economic strategies.[10] The women were anxious to align the community on the side of the workers. As part of the Corporate Campaign, for example, they went door to door with leaflets and informational brochures discussing the issues of the strike. One of the arguments in their analysis was how the community would suffer with the reduction in wages. Over and over again, the Support Group emphasized the importance of bringing the issues back to the impact on the community. In fact, the support of the community was far more important to the women than picketing the distant and indifferent First Bank System. Many of them were critical of Corporate Campaign's strategy on just those grounds.

P–9 and the Support Group began their outreach efforts with the expectation the community would recognize that what was good for the Hormel workers was good for Austin. After all, in the strike of 1933 the community had sided with the strikers, and for many decades Austin was a strong union town.[11] More important, unlike many corporations, the Hormel Company was deeply tied to the Austin community. The Hormel Foundation, established in 1941, held a significant portion of Hormel stock (more than 45 percent), and in conjunction with rights over family-owned stock, exercised virtual control over the corporation. Under guidelines set out by Jay and George Hormel, the proceeds of the foundation were contributed to the community of Austin in recognition of the workers' contributions to the company's prosperity. Millions of dollars were channeled annually to local community development projects, and the Foundation played an active leadership role in the community. In addition, the founders of the company required that the Foundation be headed by local leaders.

George and Jay feared that after they died, outsiders might gain control of the company, leaving the town that had been so good to them with nothing. They . . . wrote articles of incorporation establishing a foundation board of five to fifteen members, all of whom had to be Mower County residents whose chief financial interests were in Austin.[12]

The Hormel Foundation's presence was felt throughout the community, influencing decisions at the YMCA, at the local golf club, in the schools, the parks, and even the Salvation Army. Many of the recipients of the Foundation's funds also sat on the Foundation's board of directors. The Foundation contributed immensely to the "good life" that the residents of Austin experienced. But according to Patricia Higgins, it was not without a price: "Over the decades it's become a power used to control Austin: 'we'll help you, but things are going to be done our way' type of thing. We do get that assistance but there always seems to be these little strings attached."

With the death of Jay Hormel in the 1950s, new management came on the scene, and the cooperative relationship between the company and the union deteriorated. The workers referred to the new bosses as the "Nebraska Mafia," for their former place of employment; and as management attitudes hardened, the gulf between the workers and management grew. The incentive pay system came under increasing attack,[13] and class differences widened. Management grew more and more arrogant and indifferent. This feeling was epitomized in a now legendary story about the new management's perception of what the workers' standard of living ought to be.

The story is told that M. B. Thompson, former Hormel Company president, was overheard at the country club complaining that the workers in Austin lived in nice homes. "Before

I'm through they'll be living in tar-paper shacks,'' he is said to have declared. The story is legend now and P–9 demonstrations often feature a tar-paper shack.[14]

Other accounts claim that Thompson never made this statement, but that he did make it was widely believed by the workers. The story entered P–9 folklore, and contributed to a growing sense of class schism and alienation between the workers and the company.

By the time of the strike, the company's attitude toward the workers was increasingly adversarial. According to one woman, the president no longer mingled with the women and men on the line, and it seemed to her that callousness increased as profits became more important than workers' health and safety: "The Workmen's Comp claims piled high like this. I don't think there was any call for that, had things been taken care of properly. I think they could have avoided a lot of injuries" (Anon.). It was difficult for the workers to accept that the goals of management and labor were no longer cooperative. When that awareness came, it was accompanied by a sense of powerlessness; and under it smoldered a growing frustration and hostility.

My uncle said to me, "You know, some day you are going to know that the Hormel Company has got you right under their thumb. If they tell the town to squat, they'll all squat." It turned out to be the truth, the whole damn town squatted when Hormel said, "Squat." It's a shame. My granddaughter said the other day she knew five Hormels. She gave them the finger twice. That's about all we were getting from them, she said. (Anon.)

The company had always played a strong political role in Austin; and as the distance between the workers and the company grew, so too did resentment of that political power. Direct pressure on the community and local businesses was sometimes subtle, sometimes blatant, but the overall result was that Hormel permeated and shaped the community at all levels. It was not easy for people in Austin to appreciate how much control Hormel really did exercise over the community. Carol King described her sense of disbelief when she went out to solicit support from the business community.

We all knew this was a company town, but I don't think any of us were aware of how much control they really had and were demanding through the town. Some of the merchants were very quick to put up our boycott signs in their stores; but then when the Hormel Company pressured them, they were very quick to withdraw them, too. Another business owner took the Hormel merchandise out of his store, and he was really pressured by the Hormel salesman to put it back in. It did stay out for a long time, but he has it back in now.

As another woman explained, "That's the hard part about living here and staying here. What can you do in this town that isn't connected to Hormels?"[15]

When the strike started, the company began flexing its political muscles through the Hormel Foundation. The Foundation board worked actively to undermine the strike by bringing direct political pressure to bear on the union and by using its role in the community to shape public opinion. Robert Divine, in his study of the strike, reported that the Foundation was quite open and public about its views. In a July 11, 1985, letter to Mayor Tom Kough (who was also a striking worker), the foundation supported Hormel's position in the strike.[16]

The presence of the Hormel Company was felt everywhere during the strike. People in the Support Group worried about company spies, and there was a general environment of distrust and fear about how much the company knew and what they would do to the striking workers. The women felt as if their every movement was being noted and that there would somehow be consequences for their support of the strike: "If you went within two blocks of the Support Group you were blackballed in town. I think that everybody felt that the company had their eyes, or everything was being recorded, license numbers, the whole ball of wax."[17] This atmosphere of fear and intimidation was a strong deterrent to potential supporters in the Austin community. Billie Goodeu recalled how it made the work of the Support Group more difficult: "I think people were scared. I think they believed in what we were trying to do, but were afraid to speak out because this is a one-industry town. This is Hormel town." Billie described a phone call her husband received years after the strike, from a man who "was on the company side; he wasn't a union man. He is now retired and he was telling my husband that there was so much he wanted to do for us, but he didn't dare."

Some of these fears were borne out in fact. Hormel continued to harass workers—even several years after the strike had ended. No detail was too small for the company's attention. A manager sent a threatening letter to one of the P–9ers on the recall list, for example, complaining about a "Boycott Hormel" bumper sticker on the worker's wife's car.

You may recall that by letter dated October 27, 1986, all employees were warned that participation in boycott activities would subject them to appropriate discipline. This is to notify you that vehicle registered in your wife's name with License Number 414 AQX has been observed on public roads in and around Austin, MN, displaying a "Boycott Hormel" emblem. . . . Failure to comply . . . will be considered grounds for discipline up to and including discharge, which in this case, could require removal of your name from the Preferential Recall List.[18]

In addition to its open threat and and blatant hostility, the letter reflected Hormel's belief that Marie Loverink's behavior should be controlled by her husband. Marie, however, had her own ideas about the situation. Her response was printed in the Support Group's newspaper, the *Support Report*.

I have removed the Boycott Hormel sticker that was on the vehicle that *is owned by me and is in my name*. You might also like to know that I have replaced my old sticker with a brand new removable sticker in my back window so I can remove it from my vehicle before entering my husband's property and place it alongside my mailbox. In the morning when I leave my husband's property, I can easily grab my sticker and put it back in my vehicle. Mr. Novak, I will continue to boycott Hormel products in any way I see fit. . . . This is still America and I will stand up for my rights.[19]

The dynamic of corporate paternalism so carefully cultivated by Jay Hormel no longer masked the true nature of the company–union relationship. The company had failed its employees; and as the battle lines were drawn, the union members turned to the community for support in their struggle against the company.

THE COMMUNITY DIVIDED

Perhaps the greatest disappointment for P–9 and the Support Group was the failure of the community to support the strike. They expected the company to be hostile, but they were not prepared for the community's indifference and even open hostility to the issues of the strike. Initially, P–9 was not aware of the latent economic divisions in the town. Early strategy had paid special attention to the role that a decent wage played in the community's economic health, but had overlooked the politics of intraclass tensions. When strikers went out on the picket line with posters demanding a return to the $10-per-hour rate, they were surprised at the level of resentment they found among people who worked at jobs paying the minimum wage of $3.35 an hour. Austin was not only a company town; it was a town characterized by a two-tier wage system with a significant differential. In 1983, the average earnings of packinghouse workers in Austin was $11 per hour, and assemblers were making only $7.50 an hour. In 1987, the median wage for Austin's "food processing" workers (probably all at Hormel) had dropped to $9.75 per hour, and assemblers were making $7.85 per hour. Minimum-wage workers, who outnumbered Hormel employees, were concentrated in the retail trade.[20]

Susan Benson felt that this hostility could be traced to jealousy over the high standard of living of the Hormel workers.

People were jealous of the Hormel workers. They were ones that always had the campers, always had the bikes, always had the cars—because it was such a good wage. There was almost a sense of vengeance or satisfaction, like meaner, leaner—"Now you're where I've been all these years." I didn't grow up in Austin, so it's hard for me to understand how someone can be jealous of their neighbor for having a secure job. The whole community was envious of anyone who got a job there. It did pay well enough for those people to live a good upper-middle-class lifestyle.[21]

Another woman recalled how indifferent the strikers had been to those intraclass feelings.

Some of the signs we carried in the beginning caused a lot of bad feelings. One alluded to how the pay cut might mean my child won't be able to go to college, and how wives might have to go to work. There were people already in Austin that can never see how they could pay for their kids to go to college, and their spouses were already working, so that was bound to rub them the wrong way.[22]

According to Patricia Higgins, in the minds of many townspeople the Hormel employees had—in addition to their high wages—a privileged position in the community and received many informal benefits directly related to having a job at Hormel.

If you worked at the Hormel Company they rarely fired anybody; so if anybody lost their job, it was because they died. So if you had been there for ten or fifteen years and you wanted to buy a new house, you'd just go to the bank and say, "I need money to buy a new house." And they'd say, "Where do you work?" And you'd say, "Hormel Company." "No problem"—and they'd give you the loan. Austin is a community that always lived way above the national standard for income. So there was always this stigma in town that the Hormel people were just a little bit better; they were treated a little bit differently.

The year the strike began, the Midwest was in the midst of a major farm depression. P–9 found little sympathy in the farming communities around Austin or from farmers who were in the process of losing their farms. Hostilities between the farmers and the plant workers had been fueled for years by the Hormel Company, according to Patricia Higgins.

Every time the farmers wanted a better price for their hogs, Hormel would tell the farmers, "Look, we'd give you more money, but we have to deal with this union, and these people are overpaid, and we just can't pay you any more because we have to pay all these high wages." Then, when the union would come to negotiate their contract, it would be the reverse: "We'd pay you more money, but we've got these farmers out there, and we have to overpay them." This went on all the time. And the sad thing is that the union and the farmers could never get together and realize what was happening to them.[23]

For these and other reasons, the community split into those supporting the strike and those against it. There was also a significant bloc of people who attempted to stay neutral. But Barbara Collette, for one, believed that neutrality soon came to mean the same as supporting Hormel.

By mid-October 1985 it became very apparent to me that the company was trying very hard to keep people neutral. Neutral, to the company, meant on their side. In total frustration, I think, I became involved. Maybe out of defiance to the company. Austin really wanted us to believe that, if you stayed neutral, life would go on; there wouldn't be a fight. But it was more like being neutralized. The office I worked in, for example, was a company office; our livelihood was dependent on the company. And yet they prided themselves in being neutral.

Although they were initially stunned by the lack of support from the community, the Support Group members quickly swung into action, made a few changes to their messages, and shifted from an informational and educational mode to more political and confrontational strategies. As the community became increasingly polarized, reactions were immediate, and individuals took to challenging one another directly. The political became personal with a vengeance.

We had stickers on our truck—"Boycott Hormel" and "Cram Your Spam." In Austin we received glares, and the middle finger. I have a Support Group jacket that has my name on one side and just says "Justice for All" on the other side. Very noncontroversial. And yet every time I wore that jacket in this town, I felt like I was Hitler or some other terrible person.[24]

As the community grew more politicized, the women in the Support Group became more aware of just how alienated they were. The polarization was apparent in the smallest interpersonal exchanges.

I sell gambling tickets down at the Legion Club on Thursday and Friday nights, and there were people that didn't buy tickets from me just because they knew I was a P–9 supporter. When we started the military support group last year [1990] for soldiers in the Gulf War, a woman called me and gave me their son's address. We were going to send boxes to Saudi Arabia. Her husband called another so-called friend of ours and said he didn't want his son's name connected with ours because we were P–9ers. So the hate hasn't quit and it will never quit.[25]

It was especially difficult for the Support Group and P–9 when the community appealed to the workers' strong sense of commitment to Austin. Many people in Austin felt that P–9 should just give in to save the community. According to one woman,

It was shut up, get back to work and save the community, take what the company offers you. So I mostly kept my mouth shut. You knew the community didn't support you, so if you had a discussion with them it wound up being hostile. The only thing they thought about was going back to work—or, tuck your tail between your legs and come and line their coffers, come and do business at their stores. They didn't seem to realize that the strike was for their benefit, too. (Anon.)

The Hormel workers were especially sensitive to this argument because they felt that, through many years of concessions, they had already contributed a great deal to their community. The failure of the community to recognize and appreciate their prior sacrifice was a strong source of bitterness. One woman recalled, for example, that many women in Austin had supported Hormel during World War II.

If us women wouldn't have gone over and worked, the plant would have collapsed because you could get better jobs in other plants with military contracts. People said, "This is our plant, this is our town"—back to that again—so we stayed and made the food that went over to Europe. Women kept that plant open for Hormel, or they wouldn't have had a plant. They were on a split wage over there: women were paid less. I went down on the dock and did a man's job. (Anon.)

Dixie Lenz felt that the community was just plain indifferent. "It was not their fight, after all," went this line of reasoning.

They wanted us to just sit in a room and support each other and not go out and fight, not expect anything of the community. In other words: "Don't back us up against the fence. We can't do anything to help you—or we don't want to. It's not my problem; don't bother me."

Over the long months and years of the strike, all of this conflict and tension left Support Group members with intense feelings of isolation and alienation. After all the politics was said and done, what was left was the pain and discomfort between people.

I felt alienated. If you had your button on when you went shopping, it was the people from the Support Group that you would run into that would talk to you. The other people, they would just shun you. I really felt like an outsider in my own town. You just never knew how people felt, how your friends felt. They would keep quiet, maybe, about their true feelings.[26]

For others, the bitterness was profound: "I was born and raised here. My childhood was spent here. My family was and are union people. I still feel the whole town turned on me and I still treat them accordingly and I probably always will."[27] Overall, the women had a hard time coming to grips with the rejection by their community. One woman described people in Austin as living in a "Disneyland type of world"—unable to cope with the realities of the strike.[28] Other feelings ranged from anger and sorrow, to dismay and uncertainty: "I have a problem every time I ponder on the way a community can treat human beings with less dignity, respect and gratitude than you would give dirt on the bottom of your shoe. And an even bigger difficulty as to how they accomplished this feat."[29]

THE BUSINESS COMMUNITY

An influential, and vocal, sector of the community was that of small business owners. Thanks to the high-profile vehicle of the Chamber of Commerce, they were perceived as leaders in the community. The strikers placed high hopes on actively involving the business community in the workers' behalf. With this support they could accomplish two objectives. First, the business community represented a strong political force in Austin, and it could bring pressure to bear on Hormel. Second, the strikers hoped to use local businesses as another vehicle to educate and influence the community at large. Businesses were frequented by everyone, and their highly visible support could hasten a quick resolution of the strike.

The strikers appealed to the self-interest of business owners, arguing that a 23 percent cut in wages would seriously undermine the local business economy. The business community benefited directly from having a good wage at the plant and, historically, had recognized this fact. In 1948 when a national strike in the meatpacking industry threatened to involve the Austin workers, the Austin Chamber of Commerce and community businesses contributed to a strike fund. Although the strike never came about, the small businesses had quickly allied themselves with the workers.[30] Supporting the 1985 strike was clearly in the best interest of small businesses, if they believed that a high level of personal income at the plant contributed to their profits.

There were other factors, however, that went into political decision-making in the Austin business community. One factor may have been the hostility of the small businessperson toward unions generally. Most likely, however, the power of the workers' income notwithstanding, the purchasing power of the Hormel Company and its other financial influences on the success of a given business—either currently or potentially—were more important. There existed a fear—whether real or perceived—of what the company would do to individual businesses.

The very nature of business life in a small town may have played a role in the refusal of the business community to support the strike. Radical economist Thorstein Veblen provided us with a perceptive but slightly cynical analysis of the nature of the small-town business culture of his day. In a 1923 essay entitled "The Country Town," he argued that, because small towns have a captive population, businesses do not have to be competitive with one another—a situation he called a "relative monopoly."[31] Veblen believed further that small-town life creates a unique political personality in the business community. In order to succeed in a small town, the small businessperson must cultivate a noncommital, neutral role. A whole culture of neutrality results, shaping morals and customs and even political behavior. This culture is driven by a particular style of salesmanship: "Circumspection. One must avoid offense, cultivate good-will, at any reasonable cost, and continue unfailing in taking advantage of it." According to Veblen, this meant adopting a deferential personal style that avoids controversy: "So one must eschew opinions, or information, which are not acceptable to the common run of those whose good-will has or may conceivably come to have any commercial value." Success is based on keeping the customers coming, and it requires adopting a very conservative approach that soon comes to characterize small-town business life: "The country town is conservative; aggressively and truculently so, since any assertion or denial that runs counter to any appreciable set of respectable prejudices would come in for some degree of disfavour, and any degree of disfavour is intolerable to men whose business would presumably suffer from it."[32]

As Veblen might have predicted, the small-business people of Austin tried to stay out of the controversy. Their hesitancy, probably fueled by a sense of self-preservation and fear of losing customers, only served to alienate the strikers from the business community. Instead of supporting the striking workers, the business community chose to adopt a position of neutrality. Unfortunately this decision was made in a political environment that was already highly charged. When Carol Kough asked the owner of a drugstore to post a flyer in his window supporting P–9, for example, he put the flyer up. It was gone the next day, however, and the owner said that he wanted to remain "neutral."

Not only did the business owners not support the strikers, they soon blamed the strikers for a real downturn in business. It was not a good time for a strike. The Austin economy was already stressed with two additional pressures: a serious farm crisis; and a general erosion of small-town economies as big warehousing centers—dominated by the likes of Walmart and Target—attracted buyers away from local business owners.[33] Either actively or by default, the business community needed somewhere to lay the blame for declining revenue, and the strike only made matters worse.

Very few of them supported us. Probably not because they thought we were wrong, but because the strike hurt them. They wanted to believe we were wrong. They had to blame somebody and they weren't going to blame the Hormel Company, so the people who were on strike got blamed.[34]

Some businesses aggravated the already tense environment by actively supporting the company with pro-Hormel signs and symbols in their windows. The Chamber of Commerce took a strong position against the strikers—saying "We don't need the workers' money"—and actively discouraged its members from supporting the strike. Businesses who might have supported the strikers were intimidated into silence by the Chamber's aggressive stance.

We really got into it with Larry Haugen [president of the Chamber of Commerce]. In fact, we refused to go into his office because he had put up a bunch of material with Hormel promotions on it on the walls. Some of the business people did talk to us privately. They felt that if they said something they would be blackballed by the rest of them.[35]

When support from the business community was not forthcoming, the Support Group responded by calling for a boycott of local businesses. It was a decision born of frustration: "people didn't boycott the local merchants until they felt they were being boycotted against. It was a two-way street."[36] In a classic consumer action, the women asked supporters to use their buying power to send a message. It took special effort and extra time to drive to the nearby communities of Albert Lea or Rochester, but many families began shopping out of town. They collected the sales receipts to present to the Chamber of Commerce as evidence of their economic power in the community.

We went down to the Chamber office—the guy got real mad and threw the receipts we brought in in the wastebasket. I told him, we're the ones that put the businessmen's kids through college and now they're not behind us, why should we trade with them anymore? He said that we were being childish. (Anon.)

In 1989, the *Support Report* reported that a total of $528,620.01 in receipts had been collected.[37] According to one woman, businesses tried to pretend that the boycott hadn't really affected them, claiming that they were going out of business or that they had planned to retire anyway (Anon.). Others were equivocal or lied about their true opinions and allegiances. Vickie Guyette caught one of the businesses in a deception.

I remember going into Godfather's Pizza and asking them if they belonged to the Chamber of Commerce—because the Chamber was speaking out against us and all. He said no, but his sign was up on the wall saying he was a member. If you'd call to order a pizza, he'd lie and say, no, he wasn't a member. Or they'd say no, we don't use Hormel meat, but then they really did.

The boycott did receive some support in Austin, but there was disagreement and debate among the women about its overall effectiveness. Carol King and others felt that, since the community as a whole hadn't supported it, the boycott had not had much of an impact. She compared the community response in Austin with that in the nearby town of Albert Lea, which was also struggling with a plant closing: "If we had had people that were not directly involved in the strike standing behind us like the people of Albert Lea stood behind the Farmstead workers, then I think it would have made a difference." Some felt the boycott only alienated the community further from the strike.

It could have been that we angered people by asking them to choose between one side or the other. We put them on the spot. You might have had a manager in a store that was 100 percent behind us, or the workers might have been 100 percent behind us, but they didn't dare take sides openly.[38]

There were many other reports, however, that the boycott *had* been effective and had made a serious impact on businesses: "You could find people that would tell you, 'Well, I got my hours cut because [we] just didn't have the traffic coming through the store.' "[39] Most women in the Support Group thought the boycott was a good idea, although several worried that it was unfair to the business community: "I guess the only thing I have trouble with is: by hurting store owner 'A,' does that really get back at Hormels? We were suffering. Why make other people suffer?"[40] Another woman mentioned the lack of support among the striking families as well: "The only people that boycotted were the people on strike and nobody had any money anyway. Too many people went right back, as soon as a special would come out. And it [the boycott] should have been called much sooner" (Anon.).

Despite the nonsupportive climate, some businesses actively supported the strikers. They put signs in their windows, or placed cans on their counters for people to throw in their spare change. Others went out of their way to donate goods and services: "George's Pizza used to bring pizzas out to the guys on the line. They are a working-class pizza place, very much oriented toward working-class people. Mr. Donut donated stuff too."[41] Others gave anonymously, "because they were afraid of making the Hormel Company mad, or making their next-door neighbor mad, or making other people mad if they took that stand."[42] Patricia Higgins never forgot those businesses that did support the strikers.

There are places where I shop today because I know anonymously those people donated money or were supportive. But to this day I can't say anything, because they asked the Support Group to keep their mouths shut. Hormel's arm can be quite long, and they don't want to get themselves in a position where they might lose money.

The Support Group also called for a national boycott of Hormel products. There was universal agreement among the women that this was a good tactic. Even though there was no real way to assess its impact other than speculating on declining profits of the Hormel Company in general, it did give people a strong sense of personal empowerment.[43] According to one woman, Hormel supporters were quite aware of the boycott. She was harassed by First Bank, a major stockholder in the Hormel Company: "We sent a boycott sticker on a Visa card payment and we got a letter back two days later. They insisted full payment be made within ten days" (Anon.). Many women reported hearing from people around the country who continue to boycott Hormel products, five years after the strike. Overall, the women felt that the national boycott was an effective strategy.

When people refuse to boycott Hormel products, to me, that means they're taking a stand and they're on the side of Hormel, saying that we don't deserve this wage, or what we were fighting for. I am boycotting Hormel products to this day. I probably never will buy another Hormel product. The things that happened to people during this strike, the families that were torn apart—I don't think any amount of Hormel products could ever bring back some of those terrible things.[44]

FINANCIAL SUPPORT SERVICES

Initially the Austin United Support Group sought only moral and political support from the community. When it became clear that the strike was going to continue indefinitely, the striking families looked to government programs and private agencies within their community for financial support to meet their basic needs. Most of the strikers had never needed community financial support; but survival needs quickly overcame any discomfort about asking for help, as they looked for alternative sources of income.

At the beginning of the strike, P–9 members received token payments of $40 a week from the UFCW strike fund. These payments continued up until the time P–9 was placed in trusteeship. Although P–9 and the Support Group raised some money during the most active period of the strike, those dollars only served to hold off major financial disasters. Most families were hurting. Once the strike was "settled," those 800 workers still not recalled and unofficially still on strike became eligible for unemployment benefits, which helped somewhat. There was concern at one point that they would be denied the unemployment benefits. Hormel had filed a lawsuit to deny payments to sympathetic workers at their plant in Ottumwa, Iowa. In April 1986 the State of Iowa ruled that Hormel had to pay benefits to 500 fired workers who claimed Hormel had locked them out of the Ottumwa plant.[45] The settlement cost Hormel nearly $4 million.[46] The threat of the loss of government benefits was an effective strategy on the part of the company. It was another example of Hormel's callous tactics to break the spirit of the striking workers and inhibit labor activism. Denying workers their jobs was one thing. Working to deny them unemployment benefits was another. Had Hormel won its suit, this would have set a legal precedent for intimidating workers in future strikes. Hormel went too far in its efforts to control individual workers' lives, and the courts were forced to remind the company of the limits of its power.

When the strikers turned to public programs for assistance, they did so with mixed feelings and a mixed response. Because of their standard of living, most of the striking families were not eligible to receive any Mower County welfare benefits. To get on welfare, people had to "spend down" their assets. Those families who either had nothing or lost everything in the strike were eligible for some benefits, providing they met the eligibility requirements. Most people were not anxious to strip themselves of all their worldly possessions, and some were too proud to receive welfare: "I didn't feel real comfortable. For one thing, you're brought up that it was a lower-type person that took welfare. It was a shameful thing."[47]

Nevertheless, public financial-assistance programs did exist as potential sources of income, however distasteful the accepting of those dollars might have been to individual workers. Those few people who were eligible, though, ran into other more immediate and personal political and moral roadblocks. There is no anonymity in a small town, and people had to endure varying levels of microscopic inspection and even harassment. According to Patricia Higgins, "there were people working in the welfare offices that either had husbands or family members that crossed the picket line. P–9 people who went to apply were told, 'You have a job—all you have to do is cross. Just because you choose not to, don't come in here and ask for money or help.' " These comments were illegal; but people unfamiliar with the welfare system went away frustrated and empty-handed.

A few families did manage to receive some benefits. Donna Simon's son was one of the lucky ones.

Our son had only been at Hormel a year, so he was cut to $7.25 an hour, not $8.25. His daughter had been in the hospital with pneumonia, and Hormel had paid that bill. When they retroactively cut the medical benefits, they started taking $40 a week out of his pay to repay the hospital bill. He got a check that qualified him for food stamps. I told them to go get them. I said that's one of the worst black eyes Hormel can have is for one of their workers to qualify for food stamps. I'm glad he went and got them, because he kept those benefits all through the strike. But if you didn't have them before, you were just out of luck.

There is a certain poignancy in Donna's comments. She makes the implicit assumption that the company should feel a moral responsibility for the plight of its workers. This paternalism is a common expectation in many company towns. In general, however, the striking families were not eligible for public assistance, nor did they seek it. Two women did report receiving some minimal benefits to help meet their energy needs. One family got two windows replaced and some insulating materials, and the other family had a hot-water heater replaced.

Unable to find support from government programs, the increasingly desperate families turned to private charity sources.[48] Here, too, they came away disappointed—and in some ways, more distressed. While very few of the women expected the public assistance programs to help, and while some of them were reluctant to use those public services, most made a special point of mentioning the failure of the Salvation Army to treat everyone in the community equally and to come to the strikers' aid. The women were upset about this for several reasons: because they perceived that the Hormel Company was controlling the decision-making at the Salvation Army through the charity organization's representative on the Hormel Foundation board; because the Foundation was a major contributor to the Salvation Army and probably influenced policy; and because the charity's programs were supposed to be open to anyone in need. The women expected more from the Salvation Army: "The first year, the Salvation Army didn't give the strikers Christmas baskets. The second year they were given baskets but—if I remember right—they had Hormel hams in them."[49] That first year, Mayor Tom Kough and his wife Carol tried to talk to the Salvation Army. According to Carol,

We were at the city officials' Christmas dinner, and after the party, we stopped outside and talked to the head of the Salvation Army and Mary Francis from the Social Security office. And Tom and I spoke our feelings about the baskets and what they were for. Tom said he'd always donated. We stood outside for a good hour, freezing to death, and the head of the Salvation Army said, "I promise I'll check, but I was told this, and I was told that." We said, "Why don't you come down and talk to us?"

Another woman bitterly recalled other unpleasant incidents.

When Christmas came, some people went down to the Salvation Army to apply for the Christmas basket and they were told to tell the union to take care of them. One time the

Food Shelf had extra sweet corn, and we took that down to the Salvation Army to give it away. They let us hand it out on the truck, but we weren't allowed to tell people who we were or where it came from. You got that attitude all the time from town.[50]

Although local financial support was not forthcoming, nationally there was broad support—primarily from other unions—despite efforts by the UFCW to paper the country with correspondence condemning P–9.[51] Surprisingly, few of the women mentioned that flood of support from other unions—not because their gifts were unimportant, but more likely because the union culture had not been part of their culture, but of P–9's. Although they handled the money when it came in, and helped raise it through speaking tours with P–9ers, the money came from the world of national and even international brotherhood, the world of union solidarity. When the women did comment on other unions' giving, it was generally to mention incidents of local support: money from the workers at Farmstead in nearby Albert Lea; from the UCAW, the local carpenter's union; and from the many individuals who did offer their moral support: "The men at the utility company were real supportive. I know one that personally got into a lot of trouble simply because he got caught waving and honking at some pickets. He got called on the line for that" (Anon.). A few women also mentioned local unions that refused to support them: the schoolteachers, the police, and the textile workers. This attention to the significance of local support reflected the women's sense, in general, of the importance of the community. Not that the more distant support wasn't appreciated—it was. But even more important was how their friends and neighbors helped or didn't help.

Many other individuals and institutions in Austin helped in whatever way they could to ease the financial problems of the striking families: "The Post Office used to bring down leftover samples of soap or shampoo, whatever"; "The VFW supported us, the Legion. K-Mart was very good to us. They gave us toys at discount, one Christmas."[52] When strikers got behind in their bills, they sometimes found an understanding environment.

The utility company—for a while they were really good about not turning your utilities off, but they would pressure you. And I was getting strange phone calls all the time, especially when my husband was gone, about the phone company taking our phone away. Lynn Huston looked into it at the phone company and they said it was somebody else doing it. The Hormel Credit Union—they didn't make us move out of the house right away. The utilities didn't shut off until after the strike was supposedly over. That's when things started getting even nastier.[53]

Counseling services were clearly needed, with all the stress and hardship. One individual committed suicide, and several women noted that the incidence of alcoholism and family violence increased dramatically in the community. But gaining access to low-cost psychological support from the county mental health service was problematic: "We should have interacted with the Mental Health Clinic a lot closer, but we couldn't, because the man involved with the Mental

Health Clinic was an avid supporter of Hormels who spoke out against the strike.''[54] Larry Maier, director of Mower County Mental Health Services, personally paid for a full page ad in the *Mower County Shopper*, on December 3, 1985, sponsored by the "Committee for Positive Action," which he headed.[55] The headline on the ad was "RAY ROGERS MUST GO.''[56] Maier's controversial stand kept people from seeking the county services.

Recreational activities in the community also ground to a halt. The strikers avoided former friends and acquaintances. In a small town like Austin, it was hard to avoid coming into contact with strikebreakers and Hormel management. Many strikers denied themselves the release from stress that these activities could have provided: "I think community activities suffered because nobody wanted to go where there might be somebody from the other side. They didn't want to mingle. So community activities were either company type or they were places where the workers would go. The two no longer mixed.''[57]

COMMUNITY DENIED, COMMUNITY DESTROYED

How are we to explain the profound sense of betrayal that the women in the Support Group articulated in their interviews? They began the strike with high expectations: their town would support them, their town would stand behind them. After all, they believed, the community stood to gain from a successful strike. The workers had already given many concessions over the years for the sake of the town. So where was everybody? Why didn't the town see the obvious? Why didn't they believe the union rather than Hormel?

The men and women supporting the strike based their expectations on a series of implicit values—values that formed the framework of their idea of community. A core value of belonging in Austin was the belief that Hormel was "our" company. As a long-time resident of Austin, Barbara Collette believed in this overriding mythology, even though her parents never worked at the plant. It was a common perception throughout the community.

A lot of us truly believed what Hormels told us. When I was a young girl growing up in Austin, I really believed that what was good for Hormels was good for our community—because Hormels would make it good for us. We blindly followed that and believed that. We were all blind. We allowed them to destroy our town. We need to get it back—we should have; our parents should have. Our grandparents never should have given control to that company. We should have been watchdogs; but we really, really believed they would do what was right.[58]

This feeling that "we're all in this together" was reinforced by a strong worker culture whose roots lay in Frank Ellis's IWW philosophy: a strong sense of worker independence; control of the work process; the team concept on the shop floor; and a tremendous pride in hard work that is well rewarded. Prosperity for Austin, the men and women of P-9 believed, began with their good work. Their pride in their community was based on their pride in their work. Because of this sense of connection and closeness in the community, the lack of support was all the more keenly felt. Over the years, the community had either become indifferent to, or had lost sight of, the fact that the root of prosperity was in the productive labor of the men and women who worked at Hormel. The community now attributed the source of that value to the company, instead.

Attitudes within the community itself worked against the workers. One key institution in Austin that actively undermined the importance of labor's role was the Hormel Foundation. Over the years, its main task was the maintenance and perpetuation of the image of Hormel as the "good company" that made Austin what it was. This perception, so carefully cultivated, worked against the P–9ers. Gradually the town came to see Hormel as the giver of wealth and prosperity, not the workers.

Ironically, the workers, too, believed that Hormel was acting in their best interest. The roots of this belief were probably twofold: first, a carryover from paternalistic management styles; and second, the fact that the workers had control of the work process for so many decades. The more ownership they had over the process of their work, the more they felt a strong sense of identification with "their" company, because they had a lot of control within the company. There had been decades of labor peace, as well.

Another reason the community may have failed to support the strike was the general anti-labor bias in contemporary American culture. In Minnesota, the southern part of the state in particular had a history of hostility to labor unions— unlike the nearly universal support for unions in the well-organized northern mining communities and the supportive climate for unions in the Twin Cities. The pattern of corporate economic development in southern Minnesota was like that in many rural areas: lower wages, no unions, and a dependent labor force with few alternatives. Austin was an exception to that general rule. Frank Ellis and Local P–9 had organized the whole community of Austin. They were also challenged by George Hormel to organize the meatpacking industry throughout the Midwest, and they made good on that challenge. But by the mid–1980s the climate in Austin reflected a growing antipathy to labor unions: unions were linked with denying people the "right to work," they were perceived as communistic, or they were controlled by the Mafia, went some of the criticism.

Fear also played a role. The dynamics of labor struggles in a small town are different from activism in an urban industrial area. Small towns today are similar to communities in the nineteenth century, in the sense that they are often held hostage to the vagaries of one employer. Aside from some notable work deriving from the Appalachian coal-mining communities, we have few contemporary studies of the dynamics of labor relations in small communities. Even today, workers in small towns are captives of the dominant industry. Helen Lewis, for example, has argued for the application of a colonial model in analyzing labor relations in Appalachian coal-mining communities. Because people in small isolated communities have few options for alternative sources of income, a culture of dependence based on exploitation of resources and people results: "Those who control the resources preserve their advantages by discrimination. The people are not essentially passive; but these 'sub-cultural' traits of fatalism, passivity, etc. are adjustive techniques of the powerless."[59]

The severance of work from issues of survival in the larger community was another major factor inhibiting P–9's ability to convince the town to support the strike. Because it is difficult in an urban society to conceive of community as an intimate web of economic-political-social activities, we fail to connect labor issues with our own individual survival. Americans in the early labor movement saw this connection because they lived it. In the transition to an urban society, the greatest failure of the American labor union movement may have been its inability to sustain the link between the issues of the individual wage earner and the economic health of families and communities. The changing nature of community itself in the first half of the twentieth century probably contributed to this narrowing of vision, but in any case the unions were unable to respond to urbanization's massive social dislocations and realignments that destroyed community. As unions became more "modern" after the 1930s, they organized the workers in the workplace and did not connect those labor struggles to the larger community. Unionized workers gradually narrowed their vision, and their labor agendas became self-serving. They were not interested in larger social issues— just in getting "theirs." This attitude served to alienate the general public even further from the union agenda. Increasingly, labor union advances were perceived as coming at the expense of other workers.

But in Austin, the women of the Support Group made no neat distinctions between the individual worker, the needs of their families, and the health of their community. They cared about their community, and their politics grew out of that caring and connection with friends and neighbors. Out of the mixed feelings of love and sorrow, bitterness and betrayal, they took a good long look at Austin. For Barbara Collette, the world would never be the same again.

I always believed it was a beautiful town, and I always wanted to come back here. That was my goal for twenty-one years: to come back to Austin, where things were so beautiful. And all of a sudden I had to face the fact that Austin wasn't a beautiful town. That it was a whole town of people wearing pink sunglasses, or wearing blinders—that wouldn't talk about bad things, because someone might find out that there's a problem in this town, so shut up. And we all shut up. All those years. And then the strike came. It wasn't just the issues over the strike, but so much more, I think. We had all become complacent. But just because it's always been like that, it doesn't make it right. I personally hope it never goes back to what we call "normal."[60]

NOTES

1. Ann Schofield, "The Women's March: Miners, Family and Community in Pittsburg, Kansas, 1921–22," *Kansas History* 7, 2 (Summer 1984): 160.

2. See Louise A. Tilly, "Paths of Proletarianization: Organization of Production,

Sexual Division of Labor, and Women's Collective Action," *Signs: Journal of Women in Culture and Society*, 7, 2 (Winter 1981): 400–417.

3. *1990 U.S. Census of Population and Housing*, U.S. Department of Commerce, Bureau of the Census, Washington, D.C., 1990.

4. *Austin Community Profile*, Minnesota Department of Trade and Economic Development, St. Paul, 1984, 1986, 1988.

5. Dave Hage and Paul Klauda, *No Retreat, No Surrender: Labor's War at Hormel* (New York, 1989), 37. "By the late 1960s a two-income union family brought home a staggering forty thousand dollars a year with full medical coverage, spent weekends at a lake cabin near Fairbault, MN, drove new cars, and played golf at the country club"; ibid., 135. I am indebted to Hage and Klauda and to Hardy Green, *On Strike at Hormel: The Struggle for a Democratic Labor Movement* (Philadelphia, 1990), for background on Austin.

6. The concept of a "moral economy" was explored in depth by English historian E. P. Thompson in his characterization of a "pre-class" consciousness on the part of working people. See E. P. Thompson, "The Moral Economy of the English Crowd in the Eighteenth Century," *Past and Present* 50 (November 1971): 76–136.

7. Throughout the book I will use the terms "strikers," "P–9," "Support Group," and "striking families" to reflect a variety of contexts and meanings. When I use the term "strikers," I am referring to both P–9 and the Support Group as their agendas coincide and they act together. I tend to use the term "striking families" in a similar generic manner. The difficulty comes when choosing between the very specific "P–9" and the "Support Group." Sometimes these terms are mutually exclusive; sometimes they are parallel. My choice of terms is also driven by the interviews themselves. Most of the time the women spoke from the perspective of their participation in the Support Group, even when they were involved in activities generated by Corporate Campaign or P–9. In addition, there are clearly turf issues here. Books already published about the strike, for example, mention the Support Group only occasionally, and never in a policy or decision-making role. The interviews that form the substance of this study tell a different story. Clearly the women saw the Support Group playing a major role. Finally, to further confuse terminology, when P–9 was placed in trusteeship by the international union, all the P–9ers (both male and female members) "joined" the Support Group. From that point on, the Support Group was speaking for both.

8. Susan Benson.

9. LaVonne Ferguson.

10. See Dana Frank, "Gender, Consumer Organizing, and the Seattle Labor Movement, 1919–1929," in *Work Engendered: Toward a New History of American Labor*, ed. Ava Baron (Ithaca, N.Y., and London, 1991), 273–95, for a discussion of the role of the boycott and strategic buying in women's economic actions.

11. Hage and Klauda, *No Retreat, No Surrender*, 38.

12. Ibid., 157.

13. Ibid., 44.

14. Fred Halstead, *The 1985–86 Hormel Meat-Packers Strike* (New York, 1986), 11.

15. Mary Arens.

16. Robert C. Divine, *Turmoil in Austin: Hormel Strike of 1985–86*, M.B.A. thesis, Mankato, Minn., 1988, pp. 29–30.

17. Carol Kough. The author personally experienced this hostile and intimidating climate when she went to Austin in 1987 to make a video production about the Support

Group. Everywhere the crew went, they were observed from a distance by the local police department. The crew staged one scene where Support Group members passed out leaflets on a downtown public street. Many passersby went out of their way to avoid taking the leaflets, or even being videotaped. Among those who were taped, one individual turned out to be a lawyer with a law firm that worked for the Hormel Company. A week later, the author received a letter warning that, if his image was used in the video, he would sue her.

18. "Unethical and Anticonstitutional Hormel Co. Is at It Again!" *Support Report* 2, 18 (May 20, 1988): 3.

19. "Unethical and Anticonstitutional Hormel Co.," letter, *Support Report* 2, 19 (June 3, 1988): 2.

20. Compiled from *1990 U.S. Census of Population and Housing* and from *Austin Community Profile*, 1984, 1988.

21. See Karl Polanyi, *The Great Transformation: The Political and Economic Origins of Our Time* (Boston, 1957), for an analysis of intraclass jealousies.

22. Julie Wilson. Julie and others made several comments about the wives of Hormel workers not being in the workforce. Data to confirm those perceptions are not available. Census data indicate that, in 1980, 45.2 percent of women over the age of sixteen in Austin were in the workforce. This had risen slightly to 48.6 percent by 1990. No breakdown is available, however, on just who those stay-at-home women were. *1980 U.S. Census*; *1990 U.S. Census.*

23. Patricia Higgins.

24. Judy Himle.

25. Carmine Rogers.

26. Cheryl Remington.

27. Jean (Vietor) Schiesser.

28. Jeannie Bambrick.

29. Marie Loverink.

30. Fred H. Blum, *Toward a Democratic Work Process: The Hormel Packing-House Workers' Experiment* (New York, 1953), 33.

31. Thorstein Veblen, *Absentee Ownership and Business Enterprise in Recent Times: The Case of America* (Boston, 1967), 147.

32. Ibid., 159.

33. Retail sales in Mower County in 1984 were $172,405,062 and $169,583,680 in 1986. It is difficult to determine whether the decline can be attributed to the strike or the collapsing farm economy. *Austin Community Profile*, 1986, 1988.

34. Shirley Heegard.

35. Carol Kough.

36. Carol Kough.

37. *Support Report* 3, 7 (April 7, 1989): 9.

38. Shirley Heegard.

39. LaVonne Ferguson.

40. Jan Kennedy.

41. Mary Arens.

42. Shirley Heegard.

43. Historian Peter Rachleff believed that the boycott was effective: "Though company claims sales are up over 1985, if one takes into account the sales of newly acquired FDL [Foods, Inc.], Hormel sales are actually down by 25 percent. Company admits earnings

are down 25.7 percent. Firsthand reports from Ottumwa, Fremont, Dubuque, and Beloit report workweeks significantly below 35 hours. All are indications that boycott is having major impact.'' Peter Rachleff, ''The Hormel Strike: Turning Point for the Rank-and-file Labor Movement,'' *Socialist Review* 16, 5 (September/October 1986): 83. Green, *On Strike at Hormel*, 279, agreed because ''both the company and the UFCW have worked hard to stamp it out.''

44. Judy Himle.

45. Green, *On Strike at Hormel*, 255.

46. Ibid., 278.

47. Jan Kennedy.

48. See Franklin Folsom, *Impatient Armies of the Poor: The Story of Collective Action of the Unemployed 1808–1942* (Niwot, Colo., 1991), for an account of the failure of private charities throughout American history to ameliorate the plight of unemployed workers.

49. Patricia Higgins.

50. Mary Arens.

51. See Peter Rachleff, *Hard-Pressed in the Heartland: The Hormel Strike and the Future of the Labor Movement* (Boston, 1993), for a detailed account of national and state union support.

52. Mary Arens; Donna Simon.

53. Rietta Pontius.

54. Barbara Collette.

55. According to Hage and Klauda, *No Retreat, No Surrender*, 143: ''What started to push him toward getting involved was Rogers's very first speech and the emphasis on fighting power with power. Maier sensed right away that the idea was out of place in a town like Austin.'' His ad (see below in the text) called for a community response to Rogers's tactics, ''since our community is being held hostage.'' The ad included a coupon for people to respond with their criticisms of Rogers. More than thirteen hundred were returned.

56. Divine, ''Turmoil in Austin,'' 43.

57. Cindi Bellrichard.

58. Barbara Collette, quoted in Neala Schleuning, *I Always Believed It Was a Beautiful Town*, videotape, Mankato, Minn., 1987.

59. Helen Matthews Lewis, Linda Johnson, and Donald Askins, *Colonialism in Modern America: The Appalachian Case* (Boone, N.C., 1978), 15.

60. Schleuning, *I Always Believed It Was a Beautiful Town*.

CHAPTER 3

"I Really Know What Betrayal Feels Like"

A deep respect for social, political, and moral order runs through small-town America. Until the strike, Austin was a community where people seldom questioned the existing power structures in their community; the media, churches, the courts, and the police were like the descriptions in high school civics courses. But then everything changed. When the strike got under way, the women in the Support Group expected their government, their police, their media, and their religious institutions to support them—or if not support them, at least apply the rules equally to everyone. They were stunned, therefore, when the traditional institutions of power and influence in Austin failed to support them. The women responded at first with disbelief, then anger; and as they struggled to overcome the feelings of betrayal and alienation, some of their energies were transferred to confrontations with these institutions and their leadership.

Although the women never participated in overt acts of personal violence or property destruction or demanded changes in the system as a whole, their close encounters with the power structure in Austin forced them to reexamine the nature of power generally in their lives. Political activism is often the occasion for people to become aware of their own political strength and power, their own sense of themselves as political actors.[1] Some of the most radicalizing experiences for the women in the Support Group came as a result of direct confrontations with the institutions of authority in Austin—the government, the church, the media.

Other experiences helped to solidify the process of radicalization: the women discovered—and used—their voices to speak their minds; they forged connections and combined their power with others of like mind; and they created alternative political and social institutions to advance their agenda of justice and fairness. The encounters between the Austin United Support Group and the power structures of Austin provided the occasion for this process to develop, and the experience left the women—and Austin—changed.

THE GOVERNMENT

From the very beginning, the weight of public opinion was against the strike. One of the first disappointments the women experienced was the refusal of the Austin City Council to support them—or at least remain neutral. In an attempt to keep the council as unbiased as possible, for example, P–9er and council member Gerald Henricks had introduced a resolution urging both sides to submit to mediation.[2] With the council's support, the women believed, the strikers would be in a position to apply public pressure on Hormel to settle the strike in the best interests of not just the workers, but the whole community. But on May 6, 1985, the council sided with Hormel and passed "unanimously a resolution calling for Local P–9 to discontinue the Corporate Campaign."[3] The failure to gain the council's support was difficult for the women to accept: "It got to the point of helplessness. It made me mad. These kids—nobody was really helping them; the town wasn't doing anything. You'd expect something like this in other countries—dictatorships" (Anon.).

Carol Kough recalled how quickly the city government became a political battlefield—much of the debate centering on the potential conflict between her husband Tom's dual role as mayor and a striking P–9 member.

They kept saying to Tom, "You're biased. You're on the side of the union. You're not staying neutral." Yet there were two other councilmen that worked for the Hormel plant: the police chief's son and his brother. For all those people it was never a political issue. It was only Tom that was the issue. Tom tried to stay neutral when he was doing his job as mayor. But when he was being himself as a private citizen working to keep his job in his private life, he was told by many he could not do that. He had every right to his privacy; and when he was being Tom, my husband and P–9 proud worker, he was all for the union position he took. When he was acting as mayor, he held up his obligations to be neutral, which caused him much name-calling by union members. He kept the two jobs separate as best as he could. Especially with the Guard situation. Tom wasn't given the true facts on that. In fact, we followed up on information that I would love to make public in Austin. Some legal stuff.

At one point, Mower County Sheriff Wayne Goodnature even sought a restraining order against Mayor Kough's involvement in law enforcement matters relating to the strike.[4]

Even after the strike was officially over, the city council apparently felt the need to exercise its authority over the strikers. Clearly aiming to silence the strikers' First Amendment rights, in May 1987 the city council passed an amendment to the Austin city Code, outlawing unnecessary and undesirable noise. In the eyes of the women in the Support Group, this was a direct attempt to limit their right to hold marches and demonstrations. The proposed legislation included—among many other restraints—prohibitions against "yelling, shouting, hooting, whistling or singing on the public streets . . . at any time or place so as to annoy or disturb the quiet, comfort, or repose of persons in any office, or in any dwelling, hotel or other type of residence, or of any persons in the vicinity." Apparently this particular choice of wording did not pass constitutional muster; but in September 1987, a simplified version was passed.[5]

The women in the Support Group organized a petition drive to have the legislation overturned, and the issue was hotly debated in the columns of the local press. On October 5, 1987, Barbara Collette wrote a letter to the editor of the Rochester, Minnesota, *Post-Bulletin*, charging that "the mayor of Austin and the City Council are again trying to create mistrust and division in the city of Austin." In addition to the noise ordinance, a second law was passed on September 8, 1987. There was little question that it was targeted at banning the distribution of Support Group literature: "No person shall leave, throw or distribute or cause to be left, thrown or distributed any placard, handbills, posters, advertisements, circulars, leaflets, pamphlets or other printed or written materials or papers upon the public streets, alleys or public grounds of the city or in or upon any vehicle left or parked thereon."[6] Barbara Collette's letter went on to criticize this ordinance as well:

This one does not even deserve to be addressed, because in my opinion, and in the opinion of a number of attorneys, this ordinance is a blatant violation of the Constitution. . . . What happens if a local church wants to let the citizens of Austin know they are having a fundraiser? What happens if a new business comes to Austin that may not be able to afford the high cost of advertising in our local papers? What about a person who may want to run for public office and does not have a large budget for advertising?[7]

The city attorney did not agree with Barbara's claim that the ordinances were unconstitutional, but she and members of the Support Group remained convinced that the legislation was targeted at denying the strikers their constitutional rights.

Despite the hostile environment in Austin, most of the women reported that, in general, they felt free to speak their minds. But a few women—some of whom were the most vocal in their community—felt that some of their basic constitutional rights had been abridged: "You thought this was a free country, until you voice your opinion and then you found out you didn't have rights" (Anon.). Believing abstractly in constitutional rights was a lot different from what could happen when you tried to exercise them, Mary Machacek warned.

I think we were afraid to say a whole lot and do a whole lot. I felt like we lost our freedom of speech, our freedom of action, here. We could speak; but in some way, we were going to suffer for it. It was going to come back to haunt us at some time.

Despite their disillusionment with local government, the women expected to find a more supportive audience at the state level. After all, in 1933 Governor

Floyd B. Olson had come personally to Austin to settle the strike then. In addition, Minnesota had a long tradition of support for labor and an appreciation for a hands-on, personal style of politics.

My husband always said that if [Hubert H.] Humphrey were alive, he'd be down here and doing something. Governor Rudy Perpich wouldn't even see the guys when they went up to see him. They wrote letters—they didn't answer. You figure you vote them into office, and you figure they're fair, and you find out all of a sudden they're really not fair. (Anon.)

Democratic Farmer-Labor (DFL) Governor Perpich was from the northern Minnesota town of Hibbing, a community with a long history of militant labor union struggles against iron ore–mining companies. People in the Support Group were incredulous that he was insensitive to their cause, given his background and his populist tendencies in general. The Iron Range region was in a long period of economic decline, and Perpich had been elected largely by northern working-class supporters who looked to him for an economic revitalization plan.

It was widely known that in the 1930s Olson had resisted Hormel's requests to bring in the National Guard. So, when Perpich sent the Guard into Austin with little discussion over whether that show of force was really needed, some women felt betrayed by their community—and others, by their country. Although the Guard was a state organization, it took on greater significance as a symbol of national military force and the use of power against citizens. The Guard's presence symbolized the total breakdown of communication and the failure of local political institutions to mediate the tensions. As Barbara Collette recalled, the day the National Guard arrived was a painful moment in her life; but as a result of that day, her political awareness was transformed.

The National Guard coming to Austin was the hardest, most hurtful day of my life. I'm not sure I'll ever recover from that. My husband had just retired from the military; and when I saw those men and women get off the backs of those trucks with the military uniform on and stand against me—who had been part of the military for 21 years—I really know what betrayal feels like. My government betrayed me; the military betrayed me. I truly understand what greed was all about, because they were only there to open the gates for the Hormel Company so they could make money, so they could break the union, so they could do whatever they wanted to do or felt they needed to do.

Vickie Guyette also had a chilling memory of that day: "The fog and the yellow lights at the Hormel plant and the eerie feeling of seeing all those men jumping out of trucks. Seeing the National Guard climbing out of trucks, it was like it can't be happening here in Austin. We're being invaded." Although the Guard was supposed to maintain a neutral role and was strictly barred from taking police action, Robert Divine witnessed Guard assistance in making arrests during acts of civil disobedience.[8] The damage was already done, however; and the credibility of governmental power structures at all levels was undermined.

THE POLICE DEPARTMENT AND THE COURTS

Throughout the strike, the P–9s and Support Group members were involved in repeated confrontations with the city and county police. Therefore, along with the National Guard, the police became the symbol of all the powers in the community that were arrayed against the Support Group. In fact, encounters with the police were some of the most radicalizing experiences people had during the strike, because they occurred during conscious acts of civil disobedience. The Support Group was heavily involved in direct action as a primary means of expressing its new political consciousness. Such action brought many women into the political arena for the first time. Early in the strike, P–9 members were barred from picketing, and were loath to be arrested because they hoped eventually to return to work; so the bulk of direct confrontation with the police— who were perceived as agents of Hormel—was undertaken by the women of the Support Group and by out-of-town supporters.

When Hormel reopened the plant with replacement workers, the protesters undertook a variety of mass actions over a period of several months with the goal of shutting down the plant. Many of these actions occurred in January, when temperatures in Minnesota fall well below zero. The protesters organized moving barricades of cars when the number of walking picketers was limited by court injunction. They blocked exits from the freeway to the plant entrance. When the National Guard was brought in on January 20, 1986, the tension escalated, as the women became even more determined to challenge the array of power aligned against them. After some training received from the Twin Cities chapter of Women Against Military Madness (WAMM) in traditional nonviolent civil disobedience tactics, they went out to lie down in front of the plant gates. When one person was arrested and carried away, others would step in and take their place. The goal was to fill the jails with hundreds of protesters and overwhelm the local community's ability to feed and house the detainees. On March 10, for example, 122 people were arrested while blockading the plant.

As the sense of bitterness and frustration mounted, the women increasingly lost respect for the authorities. They were especially disturbed by what they perceived to be the selective application of the laws. Even when both sides were victims of random violence and vandalism, the strikers were blamed for all the violence going on in town. According to Vickie Guyette, "I got a letter from the police department, encouraging me to use my influence with the Support Group to stop criminal activity in town. I mean, like they think that we're just bad people." According to another woman, the Hormel Company could do things no one else could—such as putting a barbed wire fence around the plant, when it was illegal to have barbed wire in town.[9] According to Barbara Collette, the city covered up a significant dumping of waste that looked like lard and that polluted several miles of the Cedar River. Despite eyewitness accounts and photographic evidence, the authorities refused to act against Hormel.

Many incidents of unequal enforcement of the law occurred on the picket line and in violent confrontations between strikebreakers and strikers: "My husband had a scab pull a gun on him, and nothing was ever done to that scab. Had he pulled the gun on the scab, you know darn well what would have happened."[10] In other cases, the women felt the law was manipulated to charge them unfairly with criminal acts.

I was arrested for "tampering with a motor vehicle." I saw a car coming down off the freeway in front of the plant, and it was my sister-in-law. She was a scab. I rapped on her window and asked if I could talk to her, because they had been sending us harassing letters and telephone calls. At that moment a hand came on my back and said I was under arrest. I had touched a motor vehicle, so I had tampered with it. (Anon.)

According to many of the women, there were crimes committed by replacement workers and strikebreakers that were never reported or prosecuted. For example, many of the replacement workers crossing the picket line removed the license plates from their cars so they couldn't be identified. Also, there was a reckless-driving incident in which a child was even hurt. Carol Kough witnessed these and many other criminal incidents where police looked the other way. The unfairness was so blatant that Mayor Tom Kough at one point ordered the police to enforce the law equally. In response, Carol recalled, "the policemen's wives signed a petition to have Tom removed from office because he jeopardized their husbands' lives!" Carol and Tom were regularly harassed: "I got a phone call every night for two weeks—and this character was cussing me out, calling us all evening saying, 'Ha ha, we're going in without a fight.' " The police did nothing, according to Carol: "How many officers absolutely turned their heads! One day, I threatened to make a citizen's arrest, so the police finally went down and they hollered to stop the guy, and he got so nervous he hit that stop sign, and the thing on the bottom of the sign blew his tire. After that he never called again." On a more serious note, she recalled an incident where a strikebreaker had a gun in his car: "we told the officer, and asked him what he was going to do about it. This was a sheriff's deputy, and he said, 'Carol, you've got to understand. These people are scared.' And I said, '*I* can't drive with that gun on my seat. You'd have me arrested!' " On another occasion, the police allowed the employees who worked in the corporate offices to carry baseball bats to defend themselves, but the Support Group members were not allowed to have any similar "weapons."

On more than one occasion, the local and county law enforcement people were overwhelmed by the strikers. They requested backup; but, by law, the state patrol was barred from getting involved in labor disputes. Witnesses reported, however, that the state patrol officers were especially active in trying to clear motor blockades. In one case, a patrol officer drove a car into a ditch to get it off the road and prevent it from blocking the highway—and, in the process, endangered the woman who was sitting on the passenger's side.

Sometimes, people connected with the police went out of their way to provoke antagonism. At the July 4 celebration in 1986, Sandy Goodnature—the wife of the Mower County sheriff—wore a T-shirt bearing the message "Put Your Heart in Austin, or Get Your Ass Out of Town." One woman recalled another incident, in April 1986, when Lynn Huston was arrested for no apparent reason.[11] This provocative behavior on the part of the police caused one woman to reexamine her attitudes toward the law and the police generally.

We were down at the courthouse trying to find out why somebody was arrested. Some of the police came out and lined up in front of us and said that if we didn't disperse they'd have to start arresting us. So somebody went inside and the rest of us stayed out. It wasn't against the law to be there and the cops weren't in any danger, but it really made you think. How many times have you told your kids that, if you're in trouble, go to the police? Well nowadays I'm not too sure. They should run home to me if they're in trouble. (Anon.)

Incidents of unnecessary roughness on the part of the police were also noted by several of the women, particularly during civil disobedience actions. Some of the women were handled roughly when they were picked up and carried to police vans. In another incident, Mary Arens noted, "I remember getting slammed up against the fence real bad by a cop. He told me to get the hell out of here. He was my friend here. He used to be."

Although there wasn't much to laugh about during these days of stress and tension, there were a few unforgettable moments where the women had fun at the expense of the authorities. One of the most common ways to "get even" when you feel powerless is to ridicule your tormentors publicly. This small gossip item appeared in an issue of the *Support Report*: "At a hotel Halloween party in Albert Lea, can you guess what sheriff was seen with his new girlfriend—obviously tipsy—and making a fool of himself?? You only get one guess."[12] There were even some light moments in the midst of very tense situations: "I remember the day in January. We were out at the gate. Goodnature [the sheriff] was there; and the gate was padlocked, so he called somebody in to have it sawed off. They sawed it off—but it was their own lock! It was Hormel's lock, not ours!"[13] Sometimes the confusion generated by mass acts of civil disobedience would create interesting opportunities to even the score. One of the women recalled several occasions where the strikers had an opportunity to practice a little creative confrontation.

When the cops threw the tear gas, some of the guys picked it up and threw it back at them. They were downwind. The second time they really had us, though. They held the canisters as long as they could before they threw them. One day we pinned Simonson, one of the cops, up against the fence. We took his gun, took his buttons, anything that was loose. Here was this great big guy, six-six, and they had him hanging up there. I can still see him hanging there in mid-air. (Anon.)

The judicial system also came under criticism; faith in the neutrality and objectivity of the law was shattered after the arrests for civil disobedience began.

It was not easy for the women to break the law and find themselves standing in front of a judge, but they felt compelled to challenge their community on many levels. Women like Cheryl Remington learned that the courts could interpret the law selectively, and that the rules were different, depending on who you were.

I was a firm believer that if you were right you would win, and I found that if you have money you will win. To this day when someone says they're going to court or whatever, I just can't help but laugh. Because you'd better have a lot of money. By having a lot of money you have a lot of power. If you're a penniless person, no one really cares about you, whether you're right or wrong.

Several women reported being especially incensed with the behavior of District Judge William Nierengarten, who heard many of the civil disobedience cases. Vickie Guyette expected judicial impartiality, but what she found was something else: "The whole courtroom was full of P-9 people, and he just told us to get out of *his* town. It was his town!" Far more disturbing to the Support Group, however, was Judge Nierengarten's blatant disregard for basic constitutional rights. As Jeannie Bambrick recalled bitterly,

I want my children to grow up respecting the law, but it's really hard to teach this to them when I have a hard time believing it myself. I sat in the courtroom and I heard a judge say, "Well, I know I'm taking the people's First Amendment rights away from you, but I'm going to do it anyhow." And then say, "Yes, I did confer with the Hormel Company to see what they wanted done with you people." I lost all respect. I'll bet, too, if you went to the files of these court proceedings you probably won't find that statement made in there, but it was made.

It seemed to the women that the courts were acting on orders from the Hormel Company, not on behalf of justice. When the courts used video footage gathered by the Hormel Company as evidence against the strikers, for example, it lent a certain believability to that charge.[14] The police would, at their leisure, review Hormel's videotapes of protests and demonstrations, and then would mail out arrest warrants when they could identify people.

These and many other incidents of unequal treatment and blatant disregard for the law gave many of the women their first deep insight into how the town of Austin was run. The power structures they had previously counted on to be behind them, and to act on their behalf, suddenly became their enemies. Cheryl Remington recalled with dismay the day her eyes were opened.

I'm one of those people that never had a traffic violation in my life, and here I was up against the National Guard and the police. The day of the so-called riot was unbelievable. We weren't even doing anything. Just to see the power! It was scary to know that you were on your hometown street and could be arrested for doing absolutely nothing.

THE CHURCHES

In a striking indictment of religious institutions in Austin, every woman who was interviewed expressed a profound sense of anger and disillusionment over the failure of the community's churches to support the striking families. The high idealism of the strikers raised expectations for both spiritual support and political endorsement of their issues. For many families in Austin, the churches represented the one institution that would certainly concern itself with issues of rightness, of community suffering, of compassion—with the very essence of community and ethics. The reality turned out to be just the opposite.

From the very beginning, the churches were caught up in the politics of the strike. Initially, the P–9 executive board had gone to the Pastoral Association and specifically asked the churches to stay neutral and not take a position one way or the other. Patricia Higgins felt that the board's reasons for making this request were probably good; but in the end, the move backfired.

I think they had a bad experience in 1978. When the Hormel Company decided to build a new plant, they wanted the workers to donate part of their wages toward building the new plant. The churches were real instrumental in getting up in the pulpit and saying, "We think these people should take a cut in their wages for the betterment of Austin." Well, the workers didn't necessarily feel that way, so there was a lot of bad feelings. So, I think the executive board just didn't want to deal with the churches this time around.

Unfortunately, this position of neutrality only served to further confuse the situation and, in retrospect, was probably a tactical error. After the strike began and it became apparent that families needed both ideological and spiritual support, the Support Group recontacted the Pastoral Association over a period of several months. Patricia Higgins personally went to the clergy and tried to talk to them, but "they felt the strike was wrong and the union made a lot of mistakes. But I felt that really wasn't their place. Their role was to show support for the people, not to place judgment on them."

Most of the churches either supported Hormel or sided with the institutions of law and order—against the strikers. St. Edwards Catholic Church, for example, housed the National Guard when it was called in to help the strikebreakers cross the picket line. From then on, the church was referred to as "Fort Edwards" by the women.[15] Ministers used the pulpit and Sunday church bulletins to influence and comment on the strike situation and urge neutrality: "I wouldn't even go to my own church, because every Sunday it was the same thing: pray for both sides and don't help anybody."[16] The following item appeared in a church bulletin as late as 1988; it was reprinted in the *Support Report*, and reflected one minister's hostility toward the strikers:

Your faithful people. Satan has done his best to harm us, the majority of you have endured, have cooperated, have been loving and supported the church and its elected leadership. . . . In our recent years the peaceful leaders are the ones fixed in history. Haters, strikers, brawlers, the like are soon forgotten. (They ought to be.)[17]

The message was quite clear: the strikers were doing evil, and those people who stayed on the side of the company were doing the right thing. His comments were also telling in that apparently the strikers had not supported the church financially. It was probably the case that they weren't able to, but nevertheless they were taken to task for failing in that regard. Some families were publicly shamed and held up for ridicule by their congregations for their failure to support their churches. It was a particularly blatant attempt to bring the power of the church to bear on the strikers and force a resolution of the conflict.

They would bring up the strike in church. In one of the bulletins, they listed "missing members" of the church. About 15–20 of us had our names printed. There was really a stink about that. They called us "missing people of the church—missing contributors." We didn't give to the church at that time because we were supporting our son. It was very embarrassing. (Anon.)

The women also were upset that the churches refused to help the families economically. They felt that the churches had a moral obligation to respond to need: "I know different people who belong to my parish and needed things. They could have helped them. The church is the richest organization in town. I don't think there was any excuse."[18] When her church didn't support the strike, one woman's reaction was swift and direct: "When my church told me they weren't going to help with food and things, I told the minister right out that the money we would have given the church we were going to give to the Support Group" (Anon.).

Some churches did help. But by and large, their support was anonymous and on an individual basis: a contributor paid tuition for strikers' children at the Catholic school; there was help at Christmastime with gifts; and small bills were often paid.[19] One woman commented ruefully, "The Catholics did more for us, and we weren't even Catholic."[20] Individual ministers also reached out from the religious community. A woman minister from the town of Lyle brought in some food baskets. And several of the women mentioned two very supportive priests from the Austin diocese: Father Charles Collins, a very outspoken supporter of the strikers who was transferred to another parish because of this position; and Father Daniel Murray.

The women were especially dismayed over the failure of the churches to minister to the emotional needs of the striking families: "People were hurting—not only financially. But they [the clergy] didn't come even just to talk to them."[21] The Support Group felt that some of the churches were either indifferent or actually punitive to their striking parishioners. It was especially devastating because the strikers had neither the funds nor the access to secular counseling resources and had to rely on the ministry for emotional support and advice.

Some families were even denied spiritual support: "Our minister came to our place and said that my husband was just totally sinful. It was just horrible. We left the church that day" (Anon.). Jim Guyette was censored and expelled from his strict congregation—St. Peter Lutheran—for his union activities. The church objected in particular to his civil disobedience, which ran counter to biblical injunctions for Christians to submit to the civil authorities. His union activities were seen as "doing the Devil's work." The Guyette family held religious services at home after that. But the pain was, and still is, very real.[22]

Many families voluntarily left their churches, citing not only the lack of support from the churches, but also the decision by some churches to become directly involved in the strike.

After Father [Donald] Zenk allowed the National Guard to bunk out in their school gym, I haven't been back since. In fact, I called him three different times to tell him how disappointed I was. I don't know that they were actually taking sides, but I'm sure they made good money allowing the National Guard to camp out. (Anon.)

Barbara Collette believed that the churches had caved in to pressures from Hormel, partly as a result of watching what happened in her own church, St. Olaf Lutheran: "Our church wasn't neutral; it was a big supporter of the company. Some of the really big heavyweights at Hormels went to church there, and the church was under some real stress financially—so I think the church made an economic decision to support the company." Barbara wanted her church to take a political stand in support of the strike.

I went to the pastor, and I told him I was very angry that the church was not there when I was arrested and that the church did not have anything to say about conditions that people were placed in the jail, that the church didn't stand up and scream bloody murder because of the tear gas that was thrown during the strike, and that the church didn't say anything about the National Guard being used against the community to save profits for Hormel.

When I was done, he was obviously as angry as I was, and he started yelling and screaming at me that I was brainwashed by Jim Guyette and Ray Rogers. It was such an insult to my intelligence. I reacted very unkindly and screamed and yelled back. Anyway, it became a shouting match. It came to me walking out of the church and me not going back to the church for probably two years or maybe longer. The church had always been very important to me, so it was very difficult for me to do.

Although Cindi Bellrichard tried to maintain a separation between the politics of the strike and her spiritual life, she too—like other women—found it was impossible.

I told my minister I had a hard time sitting next to Mr. [Charles] Nyberg [Hormel senior vice-president] and I couldn't concentrate on what was going on in church because as soon as I saw Nyberg I'd get so angry. He told me that, as long as I was feeling that

way, there was really no point in my coming to church. And that was the last time I
went.

Some of the most painful accounts came from women who had difficulty
coping with the presence of strikebreakers in their congregations.

I talked to my pastor about it, and he said, "I noticed you'd signed up for Communion
on Sunday morning and you didn't receive it." I said, "when I looked up and saw a
scab standing up there to give me Communion, I said, 'No way.' " He said, "Next time
just come up and walk to my side." I said, "No, thank you, I just won't be back." And
I didn't go back. That's how I feel about it. Somebody lies to me once and sells me
down the river, hey, I don't give them a second chance.[23]

The bitterness is almost palpable in Carol King's account of her struggle to
remain active in her church and reconcile her religious beliefs with her political
position:

A lot of people in the Support Group dropped away from their church, but we never
considered it. The scabs, the company made us withdraw from so many things—they
were not going to win with our church. I had a call from our minister because, one
morning when a scab was greeting people at church, we walked on by, we would not
say hello. This was a very difficult thing, as a Christian, for me. I hope someday I'll be
able to. I told our pastor that, and I said, "I shouldn't have to ask his forgiveness—he
should ask mine." And he said, "Well he'll be glad to do that," and I said "He's not
welcome in my home."

Another woman who chose to remain active in her church—despite her discomfort—recalled,

I know a lot of people cut their contributions down, and others even stopped going to
church. I talked once with Father Murray and I told him I can't do that. Why should I
deny myself my God? God didn't have anything to do with this. It was those SOBs over
at Hormel that did it.[24]

THE MEDIA

As the story of the strike developed, the media—primarily print and television—became major players in the politics of the strike and in the city of Austin.
They had a pivotal role in the analysis, interpretation, and dissemination of
information about events as they unfolded. The Support Group, like many other
groups that challenge the status quo, had a love/hate relationship with the media.
Ideally, the strikers hoped the media would be sensitive to their story and be
supportive of their point of view, because they needed to get their message out
to a national and even international audience. At minimum, they hoped for an
objective telling of their story. As events unfolded, however, it quickly became

clear that the media brought to their analysis a set of attitudes and beliefs that, in the eyes of the women in the Support Group, were not only not objective, but in fact supportive of the company.[25]

The media have an important function beyond mere reporting of news and events within a community. It is the role of media to reflect the happenings of collective life and to analyze and interpret the meaning of those events. The media function as institutions in a community; and because they are part of that community, they are never really able to stand outside of it and be objective, be truly neutral. Like other institutions, the media are subject to political and economic factors operating around them, to culture-bound stereotypes, and to limitations and other factors unique to their craft.

The more divisive the Austin community became, the more the women perceived the media to be biased against the strike. Although the Support Group was fairly satisfied with the Twin Cities and national coverage, at the local level they felt that the media clearly supported Hormel. They also believed that the media had not come to their interpretation independently or objectively. Behind the newspapers and television stations, the women saw the long arm of the company: "It was a very biased media. You might get a good interview one time and then a terrible one. It just depended on how far the arm of Hormel could reach, and it reached pretty far."[26] Billie Goodeu echoed her daughter-in-law's analysis: "It was Hormel's media. The TV people were Hormel's people."

The perception that Hormel controlled the media was based on a variety of observations. For example, Robert Divine reported that the company was able to use the local media to communicate strategy to nonstriking workers: "Announcements on the local radio station, which had become common practice, warned Hormel workers to stay away while the entrances were blocked."[27] Money was identified as another factor shaping public opinion. Income from advertising is important to all forms of media and, according to Patricia Higgins, may have been a factor in the Austin media's behavior: "I think at the time of the strike the Hormel account for the radio was over a third of their financing. They also did a lot of business with the newspaper."

Several of the women were skeptical of the media's agenda in general, believing that the way a story got told was probably self-serving: "They told what they wanted to tell, and how they wanted to tell it," as Jan Kennedy put it. Barbara Collette felt that profit was the major motivation.

The media had its own agenda. As far as I'm concerned, you can flush the newspapers and TV down the toilet and we probably wouldn't be missing much. They told their side quite well—and I'm not even sure it was Hormel's side. They did what they had to do to get people to turn on their channel and read their paper.

Like the average TV viewer, the women in the Support Group had seldom questioned the construction of the nightly news. Most of what appears on the news occurs outside our immediate experience; and we have been educated to appreciate the results of visual construction, rather than examine how or why it is done. We have no cause to question the veracity of what we see when it is presented as "news," because we have been taught that the news is "real." Through their insights into how the media interpreted and presented events they had personally observed or participated in, the women were forced once again to reexamine cherished beliefs and expectations about the nature of institutional power in their community. They quickly became experts in the techniques the visual media, in particular, uses to manipulate audiences. They concluded that what they were seeing bore little resemblance to the reality they were living, or even to their motivations.

The media wasn't in our favor at all. The way they put it, we were radicals. I mean us sixty-year-old people, we were radicals! My cousin called from Washington D.C. and wanted to know what was going on—that we were rioting in the streets! This isn't true. And then, later on, they just kept showing the same scenes over and over of the people beating on the cars. They didn't just show us. (Anon.)

Most of the women felt this manipulation by the media, which "had a way of twisting the things that we said and leaving out a word here or there, and then it ended up making it sound completely different from the way it was intended."[28] One of the women taped the six-o'clock TV news for two years straight. Her suspicions were confirmed: no matter what the news event about the strike was, the same images of a few initial hostile confrontations were shown night after night, perpetuating the stereotype that labor was violent.

The media also contributed to the invisibility of the Support Group. Whether it was because the Support Group was made up primarily of women, or because the media was unable to deal with the subtleties of a strike culture and the need for a support infrastructure, the Support Group never was clearly identified. According to Shirley Heegard,

The media never could separate the Support Group from the union. I don't ever remember them coming down to the office to do a story about us. They could have come down. I don't think the media ever supported the Support Group or the strike. I had a conversation one time with one of the men from the media and he was very, very negative and very rude.

Carole Apold felt that the women were ignored "because the media wanted the strike to look violent, so they tuned in on the men. They kind of more or less overlooked the women." There is much merit in Carole's insight. Strikes have traditionally been portrayed as male events, even though many striking workers are female. If the Support Group had been presented as a "women's organization," the media would have had to incorporate a "women's perspective" into their analysis of the strike. This, in turn, might have led them to see the strike in a broader context—that of family and/or community.

Because the media sensationalize news events and are attracted to high-intensity incidents, the coverage of the strike ignored the day-to-day struggles and overlooked the pedestrian, but necessary, activities of the Support Group. Portraying the activities of the Support Group might have humanized and contextualized the events of the strike in their commonness—food distribution; fundraising to pay someone's light bill; cooking up a pot of soup for tired protesters. These acts don't sell newspapers or cause people to turn on a particular channel for the nightly news, however.

On a few occasions, the Support Group was able to use the media for its own agenda, because they were sensitive to the media's insatiable need for events involving a lot of visual action. Often, however, this meant that the only time they got coverage was when large numbers of people were involved. Shirley Heegard recalled that part of the rationale for civil disobedience was to attract media coverage.

We got a lot of press with the civil disobedience. We had to do it to get the message out to other people what was going on in the little town of Austin, Minnesota, and that we were fighting a big corporation. We also got national news that people ought to boycott the Hormel products—that was the main thing at that time.

In addition, the strikers had limited access to the Austin *Daily Herald* newspaper to air their views, although "they did publish a tremendous number of letters in the *Herald*. They had to restrict the number of words, and then you could only have your letter published once a month, because people were writing every week and every few days."[29]

The Support Group was more successful in reaching a broadly representative audience on a national basis. In general, the women felt that, the further away from Austin the media were, the more accurate was the picture painted of the strike's events and issues, even by the mainstream media. P–9 and Support Group activities were well documented in the alternative, labor, and political progressive press—although, again, the Support Group's role was marginalized or ignored. Articles sensitive to the P–9 perspective appeared in everything from traditional academic journals to publications like *The Progressive, In These Times, Labor Notes*, and many, many others. Sometimes the strikers even felt like they were having a major impact.

One highlight for me was being on the Peter Boyle talk show in Denver. It was an hour long. And then eight days later, Nyberg had to come out of the woodwork in rebuttal to our show. If nothing else, the company had to spend the money and the time for this expensive trip for him. We have part of a tape of what he said. Nyberg said that they could have given P–9 what they asked for, the gist of it being that down the line maybe it wasn't a good idea. The idea was that they could have given us the money but they wanted to get us for less because Austin was a one-industry town.[30]

There was one last lesson that the women of the Support Group learned from their many interactions with the media. The perceived failure of the media to be "objective" in Austin led, in turn, to skepticism of coverage of political events in the media in general. The women's insight into the subjectivity of the media was a powerful radicalizing experience.

You looked at everything you saw on the media differently. You stopped and realized, "Okay, the media is covering it this way—but what is the real story?" The media's saying this is the way it is. And what's really behind it? Are the people that are being beat on the line by the cops because they deserve it? Is that what's really going on? Or is it just the cops being mean again? We have had so much of that in town—they'd look at us like we deserved to be tear-gassed. Now I look at everything on the news—the political protests and everything—wondering what the real story is behind it.[31]

THE MEDIA: SUSAN BENSON'S STORY

At the time of the strike, Susan Benson was a reporter for the Austin *Daily Herald*. She was also the wife of a P-9er. In the summer of 1990, P-9 had organized a picnic and gathering to celebrate the fifth anniversary of the strike. Susan asked her editor if she could do a story on the event. Her editor agreed. But when Susan arrived at the picnic, she quickly realized how difficult her task would be. No matter how she looked at it, the politics of the strike would inevitably enter in; and she was afraid her article wouldn't be published.

I know what the meat of this picnic is. I know it's camaraderie. It's getting back together. It's that feeling again, and that support again. This issue is not resolved, and those of you who feel angry about it—that's me too. But I knew that if I went and reported the news which I should be reporting, that it wouldn't get printed. So I thought, "Okay, I have the opportunity to get something in the paper on this—some exposure. But how do I go about that?" My answer to myself was that if I fluff it enough to get it past the editor, it'll get printed, and then at least people will know that those people got together at that five-year picnic and there was a multitude. If I kept it light, I thought it might go.

The new editor of the *Herald* was not from Austin and hadn't been there during the strike. Susan told her that originally the paper hadn't supported the strikers. She wanted the editor to know the political realities of her decision: "she said, I see what you mean. She knew right away what could happen. But then she said, do the story. Tell what you've got to tell. Just do what you've got to do."

Susan decided to do a whole series on Austin—before, during, and after the strike. She proposed a series of interviews talking to scabs, the men and women still out, the business community. Susan believed that, if it was sensitively done, the series could contribute to healing the divided community.

The only way this town is going to mend is for each person to understand why the other did what they did. So I said, "That's what I'd like to do." And she said, "All right.

Tuesday we're going to talk about this to the managing editor.'' She wanted to be there with me so she could offer her support, to say that I could really be unbiased in this.

Susan Benson's account of what happened next is one of the most compelling stories rendered in all the interviews conducted for this book. As her story unfolded, it exposed the subtle and not so subtle relationships that shaped the role of the press in Austin. It also brought into sharp relief the question of neutrality and objectivity in a free press. It is one of the most courageous stories of the strike, for its exposure of the manipulation and raw power endemic to a company town. But even in their ethical failure, the characters in this mini–morality play are touching. The economic survival of a newspaper in a company town is the ghost haunting the shabby tale.

Susan began her story by outlining some of the problems she encountered. One of the first was whether people would even feel free to be interviewed. She anticipated resistance from the strikebreakers, but was surprised to find none. The workers still out were a different story. They were afraid—especially those people still looking for work.

They were very leery of giving me their names, about going on the record. It was because, "If Hormel finds out, I will be banned from any job in town." They weren't worrying about getting back into Hormel. It was, "I'm up for a carpenter's job—or I'm hoping to get on at the highway department—and if they find out that I said something bad about Hormel, I'm not going to get that position."

Getting information from the Chamber of Commerce about the impact of the strike on the economic environment in Austin turned out to be quite a challenge. Susan called the president of the Chamber for background data, trying not to be too obvious about her intent.

I knew he was going to catch on, and I wanted to be able to do as much research quickly and fast before people found out what I was doing, because the doors would close—I wouldn't get the figures that I needed to compile. So when I called I said, "Do you have figures maybe ten years ago, five years ago, seven years ago, and maybe more recent?" Something like that.

The president agreed to give Susan the data, and they made arrangements for her to pick it up at the front desk of the Chamber office. Susan then called the manager of the Oak Park Mall for data about the mall's economic situation. The interview did not go well.

He became indignant when I asked about 1985. He knew that I was comparing what the strike had done, even though I had never mentioned it. So he proceeded to give me a lecture, a verbal and abusive lecture, about how digging all this up is not going to help the community, and how dare I, and who did I think I was? As professionally as possible, I had to remind him that I was a news reporter, and this is news—whatever happens in a town is news, and the economic situation of the town is definitely news. I said, "If the town is coming back, if there was no significant problem during the farm crisis or during the strike, then why not tell me?" So he just completely painted a rosy picture. "It's always been good," he said, "and it's getting better."

According to Susan, the mall manager must have then called all over town, because she got much the same lecture in subsequent calls to other business owners. She continued,

Then I went to get the figures. I went during the lunch hour. He [the Chamber president] had said it was going to be right on the front desk, so I went in and asked the secretary for it. She said, "Oh yeah, it's right here." She looked around and it was gone. She found it on his desk. Well, I knew he had been contacted by this time, and that he wasn't going to give me those figures; but the secretary didn't know that. She said, "Oh, he must have pulled it back in here. Maybe there's some more figures he's got to add in here before he gives it to you." I said, "That's okay." I snatched it from her hand. "He can call me with the figures," I said. So out the door I went.

Susan went back to her office "and started pouring over unemployment rates. There was a significant parallel to the strike, and two years later, and I was trying to correlate the data with the farm crisis, too." Then her phone rang, and

it was the most exciting call I ever had, because Mr. Nice had suddenly turned into a raving maniac. He started off very poised. He said, "Can I ask you why you're asking for those figures?" And I said no—it was none of his business as far as I was concerned. I told him that I was doing research for a story, that I could tell him that much, but other than that he'd have to read it in the paper. He proceeded to go into detail that he knew exactly what was going on, and that he wasn't about to put up with this. This kind of reporting didn't help the community. I had to remind him that I wasn't in PR work, nor was I in advertisement. I was in news. Keep the things separate. I think they were used to having the newspaper be an advertisement piece for them. I told him I wasn't writing propaganda. "You gave me the facts. I'm going to put these facts down. I'll let people decide for themselves what they want to know, or hear, or read into it." At the very end of the phone call, I said that he hadn't been interviewed yet, and that I had intended to interview him. He's a significant part: he's the one that swept all those little receipts into the wastebasket and said he didn't need P-9 people in his town. Well, the figures show that maybe you did. Maybe you should have had those P-9 people buy a few things in town.

Susan proceeded with the interview, and they ended the conversation on a fairly even note. But the story had only begun to unfold. The managing editor was confronted the next day at a local meeting of the business community.

Unbeknownst to him (he's only been here a year or so), he had no idea of the significance that Hormel has in this town. I explained it to him before he okayed the assignment, and I told him he'd get repercussions, and he said, "No way. News is news. We're not bought out by anybody.'' I explained to him that, for some reason, during the strike the truth was not printed in this paper. But he didn't believe it because he was Mr. Macho Ready-to-go Newspaperman, and he had no idea what he was up against when he walked through the doors of the Ambassadors Club at a seven-o'clock breakfast meeting. And he said, in his own words he said, ''Susan, if you think people can be ugly''—he said— ''wait 'til you get them behind closed doors.'' All together it was the ugliest thing that he had ever been through. A newspaper editor, and he cowered.

A series of meetings followed between Susan, the managing editor, and other editorial staff of the paper. Susan was resigned to their outcome: ''I knew what was up. I anticipated that this story was not going to get printed. I knew that deep down in my heart, but I still kept doing it.'' She submitted her drafts of the series, and

the next day I was told, ''Yes, these stories can be printed if you take this out, this out, this out, and this out.'' Well, then all it became was just a PR piece. I was asked to remove anything negative about Hormel, the strike, anything that indicated that there was an economic slump right after the strike happened. I was not to say that the scab that I interviewed said negative things about Hormel management at the new plant. I said, ''No, the story goes in the way I see it.'' Then my editor stood behind me and said, ''Nothing will be printed.'' The article got ''killed,'' it's called—the story got killed in the newsroom. This is a terrible thing for a newsroom to undergo. These people were absolutely outraged. They wanted to quit. They didn't even want to write for the paper anymore, because any newspaper that was going to be bought out because the company, the town company—they didn't want to have any part of it. Everybody was appalled. In fact the other editor went in and made a formal complaint on his record that he objected to this—and if this ever comes up, he has nothing to do with it. He washed his hands of it. The managing editor cowered for weeks. In fact, he still can't look me quite in the eye, because he knows that if this ever does come out, if this story ever does get printed, he goes down as the editor that killed it.

Concern for the image of the company and the town were two of the major reasons for the decision to kill the story. The other was a more pragmatic, and— according to Susan—more sordid reason: money.

There was also a financial aspect to it—advertising dollars. The publisher said that we cannot cut off our nose to spite our face here. Hormel's significant. On top of it, since next year is the 100th birthday of both the paper and Hormel, they're cooperating on a special edition, and the publisher was hoping that Hormel would pay the $150,000 for the cost of this tabloid. They were supposed to split it 50/50, but he was really hedging that Hormel might pick up the whole tab. They were going into negotiations that week.

Although it was not widely known that the story was killed, the editor did receive complaints about the decision, according to Susan. Other staff members were demoralized by the experience, and applied for jobs elsewhere. As for

Susan Benson, "Unfortunately I'm stuck living here and it's the only paper to work for."[32]

On every level of the Austin community—political, social, moral—the striking families encountered denial, hostility, rejection, and indifference. One by one, cherished beliefs crumbled as the alienation grew. The women believed in justice, and the courts showed them vindictiveness. They believed in the police, and police power was used selectively against them. They believed they lived in a democracy, and then they found laws passed to limit their constitutional rights. They believed in the moral leadership of their churches, and found that, according to many religious leaders in Austin, God was on the side of the Hormel Company.

Of all these disappointments, the biggest was the discovery that the churches had surrendered their spiritual responsibilities "unto Caesar." When faith is betrayed, loyalty and support dies—whether it is faith in government or in the media. But when spiritual institutions fail people, the very heart and soul of a community dies. Equally troubling was the virtual denial of the Support Group perspective on the strike, at all levels of the community. This denial was symbolized by the failure of the media to recognize the women's version of events. They suddenly had no voice in their own community, no way of reaching out to tell their story. With nowhere to turn, the women in the Support Group sought refuge and support in those intimate structures of day-to-day living so important to women: co-workers, family, and friends. But as we shall see in Chapter 4, even here they met disappointment and alienation.

NOTES

1. For a good discussion of the nature of political power and powerlessness, see Michael Lerner, *Surplus Powerlessness: The Psychodynamics of Everyday Life . . . and the Psychology of Individual and Social Transformation* (Oakland, Calif., 1986).

2. Dave Hage and Paul Klauda, *No Retreat, No Surrender: Labor's War at Hormel* (New York, 1989), 140–41.

3. Robert C. Divine, "Turmoil in Austin: Hormel Strike of 1985–86," M.B.A. thesis, Mankato, Minn., 1988, p. 24.

4. Hardy Green, *On Strike at Hormel: The Struggle for a Democratic Labor Movement* (Philadelphia, 1990), 326, n.55.

5. City of Austin, Ordinance No. 148, Second Series, Amended Chapter 10, September 8, 1987.

6. City of Austin, Ordinance No. 159, Second Series, Amended September 8, 1987.

7. *Post-Bulletin*, Rochester, Minn., October 5, 1987.

8. Divine, "Turmoil in Austin," 69–70.

9. Carol Kough.

10. Jeannie Bambrick.

11. Peter Rachleff, "The Hormel Strike: Turning Point for the Rank-and-file Labor Movement," *Socialist Review* 16, 5 (September/October 1986): 82.

12. Untitled, *Support Report* 3, 3 (December 2, 1988): 8.

13. Mary Arens.

14. Barbara Collette.

15. Judy Himle.

16. Mary Arens.

17. "Minister's Mouth," *Support Report*, 3, 1 (September 2, 1988): 7.

18. Mary Arens.

19. Rietta Pontius.

20. Jan Kennedy.

21. Mary Machacek.

22. Scott Carlson, "A Hot Coal on Ashes: Guyette Fights On after the Hormel Strike Though the Battle Has Exacted a Toll," St. Paul *Pioneer Press*, November 9, 1987. Reprinted in *Support Report* 2, 7 (November 20, 1987): 2.

23. LaVonne Ferguson.

24. Donna Simon.

25. See William J. Puette, *Through Jaundiced Eyes: How the Media View Organized Labor* (Ithaca, N.Y., 1992); and Marc Raboy, *Movements and Messages: Media and Radical Politics in Quebec*, trans. David Homel (Toronto, 1984).

26. Jeannie Bambrick.

27. Divine, "Turmoil in Austin," 90.

28. Judy Himle.

29. Carol King.

30. Madeline Krueger.

31. Jeannie Bambrick.

32. Susan Benson wrote the following to the author on March 2, 1993: "Since the tussle over my stories occurred, there was a definite decline in morale and respect for superiors. One editor in particular went to bat for my stories, to the point of forcing the publisher and managing editor to putting his objections in writing on his work transcript. Steve Lorenzer was his name. The managing editor became increasingly agitated by Mr. Lorenzer's attempts to force the paper to comply with news ethics. Mr. Lorenzer received so much pressure from his superiors that he contacted an attorney about harassment charges. Other reporters and editors took Mr. Lorenzer's side and supported his efforts. To make a long story short, Mr. Lorenzer was laid off on a Friday afternoon. The department deteriorated shortly after. Editors who had been with the paper for more than 24 years submitted their resignations. Reporters began seeking other job opportunities. Seven of the original eight reporters and editors eventually submitted their resignations over the next several months. None had other employment lined up and all, but myself, were without even the availability of a spouse who could financially support them."

CHAPTER 4

"I Say, 'Once a Scab, Always a Scab' "

The indifference and hostility of community institutions was hard to accept, but it was mild in comparison to the even more painful encounters on the personal level. Some of the most difficult moments for the women came as a consequence of rejection and betrayal by close friends and family, colleagues at work, and co-strikers who crossed the picket line. In the end, the strike was not just an abstract labor issue or a community issue. It was a painfully personal issue; and wherever the women went in Austin, they were forced to deal with criticism, harassment, and even fear for their lives. The political became personal. And with the breakdown of formal structures of order, confrontation moved to the personal level as well.

THE WORK ENVIRONMENT

The offices, factories, and shops where people work are core environments for building and maintaining the collective culture of a community. The give-and-take of colleagues and co-workers serves, over the years, to strengthen interpersonal networks and bring people into one another's lives in hundreds of small meaningful ways. At work, people share birthdays, gossip, and lunch in the back room. They discuss what they saw on television the night before; they gripe and complain about the boss. Over time, they create a web of personal connections that helps make the work flow more smoothly and contributes to a general sense of well-being.

For the women in the Support Group who worked at jobs in town, it was a challenge to maintain the delicate balance between their activities on behalf of the strike and a potentially uncomfortable or even hostile environment at work created by colleagues critical of P–9's actions. Keeping their jobs was extremely important, especially once the strike began. Their jobs often meant the difference between survival and losing all they had worked for.

The pressures were enormous at those job sites where involvement in the strike became an issue. In some places, strike behavior was monitored. A few women were actually fired from their jobs. Thus, some of the women chose to keep a low profile when they were advised against involvement in the Support Group: "My boss had asked me—because of the position I had at the hospital—to stay out of the limelight."[1] Other women found they had to deal with divided professional loyalties.

On my job I'm a supervisor, and I have had direct training against unions and unionizing. Since my husband was no longer working, I needed to keep my job. I had to keep a lower profile. I couldn't always speak up or be involved in some of the things that were highly visible, in fear that I would be seen by someone and then lose my job.[2]

Donna Simon recalled several incidents where women were openly harassed on their jobs—especially if they had jobs that required contact with the general public.

They were harassing those two women who worked in the Hy-Vee supermarket. They had worked there for five years before the strike, but there were two women who complained to the manager that these two P–9ers were rude. I wrote a letter saying that they were not rude, not discourteous, they were good workers. I thought it was the most un-Christian thing I've ever seen done in the city of Austin. The manager didn't fire them. K-Mart also got a complaint. They wanted a girl fired. And the manager at K-Mart said, "No, she's a good worker. I'm not going to fire her." The woman said, "All right, then I'm never coming into K-Mart." And he says, "Well that's fine, then. Have a good time shopping at Shopko."

Women who had jobs that involved close contact with the Hormel Company, like Susan Benson, were especially concerned.

I worked with the public in a local law firm. The people that I worked for were on the Hormel board and the Foundation board. The only security we had at that point was my job. So I had to keep the job, I had to wear two faces. The only sympathizers that I had in co-workers were other people involved in the strike. We almost had to meet in the back room to give thumbs up to each other. We had to keep a professional posture to maintain our jobs, and it was difficult.

Some people lost their jobs or quit them because of the pressures put on them, or because of their own sense of being under a lot of stress. Barbara Collette was given a choice between resigning her position as a real estate agent for Sterling Real Estate or continuing with her Support Group activities. Sterling did regular business with Hormel, and didn't want to jeopardize an important customer. Barbara resigned rather than give up her role in the strike.[3]

Individual women experienced alienation and rejection on many levels. In some cases, as with Barbara Collette, the communications were straightforward. A woman who worked as a cashier in a supermarket recalled more subtle forms of rejection. People would move to another line when they saw her standing there. She quit because she couldn't handle that mute but open rejection, coupled with constant harassment from her co-workers. The workplace had become unbearable for her.

There was no middle ground. You were either for the strike or against it. I ended up quitting my job, just because it got to be so bad. The people I worked with also didn't agree with me. People would make comments—like, "The stupid people out there on strike." Or, "Boy, this sure is a good buy Hormels has on this product." Things like that. It was like, how far can we egg this girl on before she loses it?[4]

Joyce Ball was one of two women who were quietly "let go" from their jobs at a local grocery store. The reasons seemed flimsy to Joyce and had clearly been fabricated because of the womens' connection to P–9 and the strike.

When the strike first started, two of us were working out at Eldon's IGA. We were doing demos of Hormel products. And of course when all this came about, why, they didn't have us doing Hormel products anymore because they knew that we both were P–9 wives. They finally used the excuse that they were remodeling their store so they let me go, and then it wasn't long and they let Shirley go, too. Then they put the Hormel Delicatessen in their store.[5]

Other women weren't at all surprised when they lost their jobs: they worked part-time for the Hormel Company. Despite these pressures, however, many women who worked at jobs still managed to continue their activism, and others even risked talking back: "I was told I shouldn't be over there being involved. I said, 'When I leave this job, what I do is my business.' And I did" (Anon.).

By putting pressure on the women who supported the strike, the community probably hoped to influence the striking workers to return to work and end the strike. The tactic of harassment played on the potential for dividing the women's loyalties between the needs of their families and the more abstract class or union issues. In most cases, however, the battle of wills only served to strengthen the women's resolve. Judy Kraft told her boss, " 'If you don't like what I'm doing, you fire me right now.' And he walked off." In some cases, the Hormel Company itself played a heavy-handed role. Although he didn't even work for Hormel, Patricia Higgins's husband was harassed.

I had to think about my husband's job before I got involved in the Support Group really heavily. The Hormel Company tried to have him fired. He's a state electrical inspector, so he had to go in and inspect their wiring. They went to the head of the state electrical board and said they wanted him removed because of my activities. Thank goodness, the board was smart enough to say, "Mrs. Higgins doesn't work for us; we can't control her actions. Therefore you have to let Mr. Higgins in."

FRIENDS AND FAMILY

During the strike, the town was—as one woman put it—like the Hatfields and the McCoys. Friends and families split and went their separate ways—sometimes quietly and sometimes after violent disagreements and bitter arguments. The whole social fabric of the community was permanently altered as people struggled to realign themselves in their relationships. Sometimes it was just a matter of going out of one's way to avoid people. In other situations where interaction *couldn't* be avoided, there were pain, tears, anger, and—all too often—confrontation. Some of the more difficult encounters were between long-time friends. Billie Goodeu recalled how painful it was to meet and interact with their friends who did not support the strike.

My friendships are very valuable to me. People that had been my friends for years—when they happened to see me on the street—would look at me like I was something that crawled out from under a rock. I was Sunday school coordinator at our church for ten years, and I went to church this one Sunday to make coffee in the kitchen, and three gals came up to me and told me off. Gals that were more my family than even friends.

Billie was hurt and confused by her friends' failure to support her views. It was the last thing she expected, and her dismay reflects how strikes touch all aspects of people's lives: "I guess I wasn't aware of how this part would take place in the strike." It was especially difficult for women to remain friends when their husbands were on opposite sides of the issues. Billie, for example, tried to maintain one such friendship, but it was difficult.

I had this one friend—more like a sister—and her husband was "company." We got together for coffee and we made the agreement that the strike was not going to break up our friendship. But my husband was on TV quite a bit, and she made the statement that when she sees her friends on TV it hurts them. I don't know why—it wasn't done to them personally. I'm still struggling with that friendship.

Hardest of all was how to break off relations with those friends who actively worked against the strikers.

My friend's son went back. We don't really have too much in common anymore to say. She works in the Hormel office there, and I'm sure she talked her son into going across the line. I'm not so friendly with them. I don't say hi. A lot of times they say hi, and you just ignore them. Sometimes you have to be nice, but you don't say any more than you have to.[6]

The harassment wasn't all one-sided. Although in some ways it was often easier to deal with nonsupportive neighbors and acquaintances by just avoiding them, these less intimate relationships in the community also provided an opportunity for an occasional verbal confrontation. These confrontations gave both sides an opportunity to vent their strong feelings.

When I went to Red Owl to shop, I'd run into Keith, the store manager, and we used to have some screaming matches right in the aisle. People would just walk by and stare. Mostly I'd get on him about the churches. I kept shouting at him. We never got so we weren't talking to each other, you know—it was a good discussion. But he'd give his side and I'd yell my side.[7]

Sometimes the women found a way to get even, though the victory may have been small. Carole Apold worked hard to make a strikebreaker feel guilty enough to move out of her apartment building.

After the strike started, a scab moved in upstairs, and we found out after about a month that he was a scab. It didn't take too long—about six weeks later he moved out. Down in the laundry room I started hanging up my "Cram Your Spam" t-shirt. I think that helped him decide to move.

The guilt that strikebreakers may have felt was not enough to make them leave the plant again, however. In fact, since attitudes on both sides hardened so, and with the community of strikers so divided, that guilt may never be resolved.

Dealing with friends and acquaintances was one thing; but when families split over the strike, it was even more devastating. Such families often had to maintain some kind of ongoing relationship, such as getting together for holidays or attending funerals. There were families that tried to convince their striking members to return to work out of concern for them. One family was upset and ashamed when their son was arrested, because no one in their family had ever been in jail.[8] In other families, strikers encountered open anger and hostility.

Families tried a variety of mechanisms to cope with the tensions over the strike and still maintain their social ties. One of the easiest things to do, according to Barb Frandle, was just avoid any strike discussions at all when families got together: "My brother-in-law was kind of a big shot where he worked, and they don't have a union. He couldn't see our side of it anyway, so we just kind of didn't talk about it." In other families, heated arguments resulted. Linda Novak recalled that, when the members of her family took different positions, "it was a blowout." Mary Arens could talk to her mother about the strike, but her brother refused to listen: "If you can get close to bringing it up, he says, 'You did it. It's your problem. I don't want to hear about it.' " Intra-class resentment over the high salaries of Hormel workers also contributed to dividing Mary's family.

My sister-in-law thought we were all crazy. She told me we had no right to be doing this, because she drove by the Hormel parking lot and saw that all the cars were brand-new cars. She said, "If you can afford a brand-new car, you don't need to be fighting for higher wages.'' You couldn't get it through to her that that wasn't what we were fighting for. We talk today, and we get along okay, but that feeling will never go away.

Sometimes family members went out of their way to irritate the strikers, even years after the strike ended.

My sister-in-law ruined my Christmas Eve. After all these years she brought it up and said that her son-in-law said that if he was working over there he would have crossed the line. And she said, ''I can't see why these people can't forget what happened, forget all about it.'' I thought she was for us, and now I found out she wasn't. (Anon.)

Another woman's sister-in-law deliberately provoked her by wearing a ''Spam'' T-shirt to an Amway get-together they both attended: ''That was the end of that. We're just now starting to talk again. I mean that was a pretty cruel thing to do.''[9]

If family members crossed the picket lines, the stresses were often beyond resolution. As Patricia Higgins recalled, in one family ''the mother went back and the daughter stayed out. It just caused huge emotional problems for people.'' In Donna Simon's family, relationships were permanently severed.

My husband's daughter—her husband went back to work and scabbed. To this day she does not speak to me; and I'm not going to beg for her conversation, because I don't feel I have to. My husband goes and talks to her, but I have nothing to do with her. They don't come over for any holidays. They haven't been in our house since he scabbed. My own daughter, and his [Donna Simon's husband's] son, stayed out and lost their jobs.

The hostile environment also had a profound impact on the children in Austin. In addition to the stresses of economic want, they found themselves caught up in strike issues. Children on both sides wore T-shirts supporting Hormel or P–9 until the shirts were outlawed at school. Jim Getchell, Jr., formed ''P–9: The Future Generation,'' an organization of high school students. The strike even affected the academic climate in the schools: high school teacher Bob Richardson resigned because the school wouldn't allow teachers to discuss the strike in their classes. At one point, more than 300 high school students walked out of school and marched to the Hormel offices, where they were threatened with arrest if they didn't disperse.

It was especially difficult for children when they were uncertain about what to do or how to respond to their parents' activism. As the community became more polarized, the children were forced to assume similar positions, or at best try and stay uninvolved. According to Jean (Vietor) Schiesser, there was no easy way for children to handle the conflict among the adults in the community. The divisiveness spilled over into the schools and created tensions between the children and their parents, and among the children themselves.

My daughter was one of the kids that walked out of school. Her dad and I followed her path. She knew we were right behind her in the car and that she wasn't on her own. But later when she could see that the kids at school were nailing each other—especially the boys—then she could see it wasn't a very popular idea. That's when she asked that I not get arrested, because she didn't want to see me in jail with the criminal elements.[10]

Children did worry about their parents' involvement in demonstrations. And one mother was hesitant at first to get involved in the Support Group because she was worried about losing her foster children.

P–9 children were sometimes caught up in conflicts over what relationship they should have to the children of strikebreakers. Vickie Guyette refused to allow her children to play with strikebreakers' children, telling them, "They took your daddy's job." Another woman let her son make up his own mind: "During the strike he sassed kids whose dads were scabs. I told him he could do what he wanted. I didn't want anything to do with the parents; but if my son wanted to play with their children, that's fine" (Anon.). Parents couldn't always protect their children from the tensions in the community, as this letter to the *Support Report* indicated:

Coming from a large city, we always held the notion of quaint small town hospitality and friendliness. . . . However, when my wife and little girl were insulted by a foul-mouthed strikebreaker on a public sidewalk, we woke up. I'll never forget the look in my 3 year old daughter's eyes when she asked me what a f———ing bitch is and why a grown up would call her such things?[11]

There were even threats of violence directed at children. In a series of interviews she did in 1990, college student Jodi Litfin recorded the following frightening story:

They also received threats on the children's lives. One letter in particular showed pictures of the children hanging from trees. The Guyette's received a similar letter, along with many others. One night in the summer of 1985, when Jim and Vickie were at the Labor Center and the daughter of a P–9er was babysitting their three young children, a man called and said he knew she was home alone with the children and he was going to come over and kill all four of them.[12]

Children picked up and internalized many of the messages from the strike. One of the most poignant stories was of a small boy's response to the call to boycott Hormel products.

My daughter-in-law was given a Hormel ham at Christmas last year [1990], and she had gone home after work and picked up the kids and they went out to the mall. She quickly ran into one of the stores. And when she came out, my grandson was standing out in the parking lot, and anybody that came by, he was saying, "Here, Mister, would you like a Hormel ham? We don't eat it." He was trying to give away that Hormel ham. He was nine years old. People looked at him like he was crazy.[13]

STRIKEBREAKERS

After the plant was reopened with the help of the National Guard, a barn on the outskirts of Austin was painted with the slogan "Scab City, 6 Mi.—Boycott Hormel." It was a bitter testimonial to the anger and hatred that striking workers feel for the most intimate enemy of organized labor: the strikebreaker, or "scab." On the first day Hormel reopened the plant, about 350 P–9 members crossed the picket lines to return to work, and Hormel quickly hired replacement workers to fill the remaining positions. While the women in the Support Group had strong feelings about the replacement workers, they reserved their most vehement hatred for their former friends and co-workers who crossed over. On the day the plant was reopened, the women in the Support Group stood across the road from the plant entrance and watched the men and women go into the plant. One woman recalled her outrage and dismay, especially over the way the strikebreakers went out of their way to taunt the strikers.

The day they let those people go through the picket line was just like a bomb. People just drove right on through. We just had to stand at the fence and watch them come in, yelling and laughing at us. That really hurt—that they couldn't see it our way. They were, like, on the other side of the fence. They could care less. We all needed jobs. When they went back first, that did it for the rest of us. If they had stayed out, we all would have gotten back. They're the ones that are the reason my husband didn't get his job back. We had a list of names of those workers that went back. We didn't forget who they were. We never will. (Anon.)

The strikebreakers had seriously compromised the position of their still striking union brothers and sisters—in effect, disenfranchising them from their jobs. Friends and co-workers who had been standing side by side in solidarity now screamed epithets at one another. The union and the Support Group had been "family"; the company, the enemy. And now part of the family had joined the enemy.

Nearly every woman interviewed had a story to tell about the betrayal of the union by the strikebreakers, and how increasingly difficult it became to live in the same community with their now bitter enemies. Chance meetings between individuals were especially awkward, as Madeline Krueger recalled.

One day I went over to K-Mart and, as I walked in the door, here was a classmate of mine who was coming from my left. She crossed right in front of me, and I had my mouth open to speak and she just—I knew she saw me—but she just cut me dead, would not speak. And I thought, "What's the matter with her?"—and watched her walk off. I found out later that, while we were gone out of town, her husband had crossed the picket line. I've seen her numerous times, but we just don't see one another anymore. Or at least we pretend we don't see one another.

The nature of the small-town social environment only served to exacerbate these uncomfortable interactions. It was hard, if not impossible, to avoid running into each other in Austin—at work, in the stores, at family gatherings, even at funerals: "One fellow went to a funeral, and this woman introduced her husband who was a scab. And he said he had to shake his [the scab's] hand, and that he'd been washing it for two days" (Anon.). According to Carol King, there was some small measure of satisfaction in simply ignoring strikebreakers: "I just loved it when they said hello. You could look right through them." Chance encounters could be especially awkward and uncomfortable.

I was out at Hy-Vee one day and a scab saw me and turned around and went three aisles out of the way to avoid me. They won't run into you; they won't look at you. It was especially awkward because you didn't always know who scabbed and who didn't. You had this horrible feeling of not knowing. "Can I talk to you? Are you a scab?" Or rumors were that this one went back, and that one went back. You didn't know who you could talk to. Or if you knew the guy was scab, but you didn't put him together with his wife. (Anon.)

It was easiest, however, to avoid any contact at all: "I had to wait on scabs in my job at the bakery. I could put on the nicest front. But when I'd meet them off work, I didn't talk to them. One of the women I worked with couldn't wait on them, so she'd stay in the back room."[14]

It wasn't always easy to figure out who was a strikebreaker and who wasn't. As a result, people went out of their way to avoid people they recognized, even when they were uncertain about whether the other person had crossed or not. This avoidance behavior further eroded the community, creating a climate of uncertainty and suspicion. Even small decisions such as where to have one's hair done had to be reconsidered: "I used to go to a beauty shop where the wife of a scab worked. I never went back. And when they called and wanted to know why, I said, ' 'Cause you've got a scab's wife working there. And I'm sorry, I won't be back.' "[15]

The *Support Report* regularly carried items warning readers about strikebreakers. The paper named names and included pictures to let people know who couldn't be trusted anymore. One item read: "Scab _____ when asked if he was still a scab—said—'No, I am retired now.' "[16] And one issue ran a column with a picture headlined "SCAB OF THE MONTH." The cut below the picture went on like this: "_____ recently told someone that things weren't so great in the plant. 'There is no union,' she reportedly told someone!"[17] The *Support Report* even printed one strikebreaker's response to harassment from an anonymous striker. The strikebreaker had received a birthday card that included a poem entitled "I'm a Scab." He wrote, in part, "During the strike I put in more time for the union than most. I believe I did my part. Now the strike is over. If I'm a scab, so be it. It keeps my two children and myself fed and clothed." The *Support Report* responded to his letter by running an article entitled "Judas Was a Scab" on the next page.[18]

It was difficult for the women when one of their friends' husbands crossed the line. The closer the relationships were, the more problematic it became to maintain them. Marie Loverink lost her best friend when her friend's husband crossed: "We had a short confrontation and I left and haven't spoken to her since, and I think of her often." Another woman recalled,

I had a phone call from one woman. I just told her I thought her husband was a Judas and that he's betrayed us. She asked me if we could ever be friends, and I said, "I don't know." She's tried to speak to me, but I have not to this day spoken to her. I've been condemned by my friends for not shaking hands with them. But that's a bigger lie. Why would I shake hands and talk to them when I feel so strongly about it all?[19]

Even more problematic were interactions with wives who urged their husbands to cross: "She told her husband to either get across the picket line or there's the front door. A lot of the wives, though, had no control over the decision" (Anon.). The Support Group women were especially critical of those women who encouraged strikebreaking.

I remember one women saying, "Well, we had to look out for ourselves." To me, that really said it all—they didn't give a shit about anybody else. Those are the same people I feel sorry for today because they're really by themselves. They don't really have a lot of close friends, they spend a lot of time at home, they don't go places. They really isolated themselves, because they didn't care about anyone but themselves.[20]

Some of the strongest feelings of betrayal came when women who had worked together for months in the Support Group discovered that one of their own members had crossed. And it was especially tragic when a woman disagreed with her husband's decision. Vickie Guyette remembered one woman who had a hard time making up her mind.

She was always involved, and she felt close to us. I think she was informed. She was an intelligent person. She had to have known what we were saying, and it made sense to her. And then she'd go home and listen to her husband saying he had to cross the picket line. It was ripping her up inside. I don't think, if she would have made the decision, that he would have gone back. Some of those women had a hard time choosing between the Support Group and what their husbands wanted.

Several of the women reserved their deepest loathing and anger for those strikebreakers who consciously exploited the Support Group programs before they crossed the picket line. Jeannie Bambrick recalled one woman in particular.

As soon as they gave us their sob stories and got the free handouts, then their mates went across the line. Those are the ones I'm really bitter towards. Because they took food and money from somebody that really believed in our purpose and lost everything. One woman said she'd never get a job, because she just wanted to stay home and be a mother.

Billie Goodeu echoed Jeannie's contempt: "But shortly after they got the money, he scabbed. Now, *she's* having to work. While she was getting money to make her house payments, my daughter and her husband were losing their house." Billie went on to recount similar stories of people taking money from the Support Group and then crossing the picket line—one of her relatives included.

There's one gal I never speak to to this day. She's a relative. They got money to make not only their house payment one month, but also their car payment. They left the Support Group office and bragged that they had money in savings. Why should they spend their money in savings? Let the Support Group pay. There was another woman who was pregnant who had no insurance. So they went in and worked with the union programs for a little while. I know that the baby's medical bills were all paid, and their fuel was paid for, and one of their farm payments was paid. And then the baby was born and they came in and got their free handout of free food. And then he went across the line. She is one that I felt really used the Support Group and then turned against us.

Some women were not content to just sit passively and complain about the strikebreakers. They put their feelings into actively challenging them, face to face. There were many incidents of harassment and heated confrontation. Billie Goodeu recalled the day she exploded.

I never have been one to speak up for myself. But one day I was out in the parking lot at the union hall, across from the Hormel Credit Union, and nobody was with me—you know, you can do a lot of things when you've got your friends standing with you. But I was standing alone, and all of a sudden I saw these scabs coming out of the credit union and I just had a heyday. I said things I never dreamt would ever come out of my mouth. But it gave me so much satisfaction! And one of the gals came out of the union hall and said, "Billie, is that you? I can't believe you're saying that." And I said, "come on and join me. I'm having a heyday today." But that was not my nature. I can't tell you what I was saying. But I had one of them that was going to come over and slap me, and I was just daring him. "Well, come on ahead," I said. "You're about the lowest thing that ever crawled on the face of the Earth. So come on over—I'm not afraid of you." I couldn't believe I was saying those things myself.

Some of the women in the Support Group became very verbally aggressive and did not hesitate to express their contempt directly to the strikebreakers. There was a tremendous sense of satisfaction in these encounters, according to Carol King.

Going into Penney's one day, I called this one woman's husband a "scab." She just laughed and said, "We're getting a paycheck every week. What are you getting? My husband's working. What's your husband doing?" And I said, "Well, at least he can look in the mirror and know that he isn't a scab. You will be a scab for the rest of your life." As we were walking out, we just said, "Scab!"—and the woman became frantic. She was just so incensed that we would dare call them "scabs." They didn't consider themselves scabs—all they did was go back in and get their jobs!

Sometimes the strikebreakers deliberately provoked the strikers. Relations were still tense in 1990, when Carole Apold and other P–9ers were approached in Lefty's Bar.

Just a few weeks ago we were sitting in Lefty's—quite a few of us at a table—and all of a sudden, John Morrison, R. J. Bergstrom, and Don Stillwell walked in. It went dead silent in there. The jukebox even stopped at the appropriate time, you know. The owner went to put money in the jukebox. They had just gotten their profit-sharing checks. We didn't confront them, so pretty soon they got fed up and left.

Don came up to me that night. Our daughters are the same age, and my daughter's going to be in his daughter's wedding. He came up to me and tells me what a lovely daughter I had. Then he told me how much his wife missed me, and I looked at him, and I said, "Yeah, Don, you caused a lot of friendships to be dissolved." He just walked away.

They try to catch you off guard. They'd drive by and wave, and half the time you wouldn't know who you were waving at until it was too late. John Morrison used to come up behind me in stores and say hi. I'd turn around and start to say hi, and then I'd realize who it was and I'd just look at him and say, "Are you talking to me?" And he'd walk away. I remember one time Tom Cheeta showed up at Lefty's and he got drug out of there by his hair. I tried to rip his beard right out of his face. There were certain times they'd come into Lefty's, you know, just testing the waters. They knew they weren't wanted in there. They would do this after they'd been drinking.

In many of the stories the women told, there was a pervasive sense of longing, a feeling that "if only" things had been done differently, everything would be okay—their families, their town, their lives. Once the sense of outrage had cooled, only analysis and sorrow were left. Carol King blamed the failure of the strike on the shop workers who crossed.

We always thought that, if the shop people had stayed out, Hormel would not have been able to get the plant running. The machinists, the welders, the electricians, the boilermen. A lot of the shop people were scabs. One of them said he had to cross because he had two little girls to feed, and I said, "What do you mean? We have a daughter in medical school that costs $16,000 a year. It doesn't cost you that much to feed those little girls." Every one of them had their own excuse.

In general, there was no sympathy for strikebreakers, although one woman was moved to forgive a woman in especially desperate straits.

When you've got three small children and you're in the hospital going to have your fourth child and your husband crossed the picket line because he has no insurance—I feel sorry for that woman, I really do. If you do it out of desperation, I have no qualms about that at all. (Anon.)

Most of the women, however, felt exactly the opposite. There could never be understanding, nor forgiveness. Several women even suggested that, if they had responded with more violence against the strikebreakers, the strike might have eventually been resolved in P–9's favor: "I always said that the first people that crossed the picket line should have been greeted at their home when they came home from work—and they wouldn't have gone through the second day. I think we should have been more like the coal miners."[21]

By the winter of 1990–91, little healing had taken place in Austin, and the pain of failure was still very real. Some women were able to understand and forgive; but, by and large, people were still embittered. For Carmel Taylor, though, it was important to hold her head up and not let the men and women who had crossed the line win the moral victory.

A lot of pressure was put on you at that time to hate scabs. I know these people took things away from me and did things to my family, and they know, too. I can live with myself. Can they live with themselves? I had to talk to my husband about that. You didn't do anything wrong. You stood up for something you believed in. Why avoid these people, then? You don't have to be their friends, but you don't have to avoid places where they are. Don't stay away from the mall because there's a group of them sitting at their table. You walk by them and let them feel uncomfortable.

SERIOUS TROUBLE/VIOLENCE

Overall, the strike in Austin was nonviolent. There was no overt violence in confrontations between the police and the strikers and their supporters. If there had been, the government probably would have responded with more repression, public opinion would almost certainly have gone against the strikers, and—in all likelihood—the level of violence would have escalated. There were some incidents of pushing and shoving, terroristic threats, and a few shouting matches; but by and large, hostilities between strikers and strikebreakers were limited to acts of vandalism against property and an occasional fistfight.

Throughout the strike, P–9 and the Support Group took special pains to emphasize the importance of maintaining a nonviolent strike. There was concern that some people might want to stir up trouble for the sole purpose of undermining the credibility of the strike. Carol Kough was always on the lookout for potential troublemakers, and worked to keep things peaceful and nonviolent.

We knew they had people in there wanting to instigate trouble. So, every time I'd see something going on, I'd go and try to get in that group. I'd say, "Hey, why don't you guys go and have a cup of coffee." We knew of instigators, informers. Ones that eventually crossed the picket line. Why, they even had a retired Hormel corporate person wiring up the union hall for the security system and CB communication! He even wanted to wire it up to his home so he could help out! Tom went to the union officers and asked them why they were allowing these people into the security system. A couple of them working on the security system were the first ones back in the plant. We had people all about saying that they'd been asked to inform, asking what they should do. I told them, "Do whatever you do. Don't talk to me—debate your own conscience."

Several women believed that the UFCW sent people into Austin to instigate violence purposely. In one case, the women felt their suspicions were borne out in fact: one man who had worked for the UFCW, at the time of the strike, later went to work for the Hormel Company in their Dubuque, Iowa, plant. In another case, the *Support Report* accused an individual of spying on the strikers and trying to discredit P–9 by secretly taping conversations for the police and the FBI. This man, who worked for the UFCW, "according to FBI files has fingered P–9 members as well as members of the Austin United Support Group, as possibly involving themselves in 'organized vandalism in Mower County.' "[22] The article went on to interview Jim Guyette, who accused the man of making provocative statements and "trying to set people up."

Despite extensive peacekeeping efforts, the tension in the community occasionally erupted in incidents of violence against people and/or damage to property. Many of these incidents were between strikers and strikebreakers. In March 1986 at the height of the confrontations, the Austin *Daily Herald* identified a total of 242 incidents over a two-month period as being "strike related" violence. Linking vandalism to the strike further eroded public support. The statistics did not indicate whether the victims were strikebreakers or strikers, but there were victims on both sides. The damage in dollars was relatively small—only $11,515—and most incidents were of an interpersonal nature, rather than attacks on the company, the government or other symbolic institutions. There were many incidents of aggressive verbal behavior: eighteen terroristic phone calls and eighteen reports of threatening letters, for example, and forty threatened assaults or actual assaults, reflecting the highly personal nature of the tensions. Other incidents of a harassing nature, or reports based on a fear of potential harassment, were the twenty-six incidents of people being followed to and from work (probably reported by strikebreakers) and sixty-six requests for extra patrols (probably made by the Hormel Company). There were also seventy reports of criminal damage to property, indicating that many people were acting on their frustrations. There were only four reports of potentially life-threatening encounters—attempts or actual incidents where cars were run off the road.[23]

During the interviews, however, the women reported a number of other serious incidents—such as shots being fired, or people's dogs being hung from trees. People received hate mail, and there were many acts of petty vandalism. Tacks were spread in the parking lot of the Support Group, for example—causing a lot of flat tires. And sometimes, car windows were broken. According to one woman, the acts continue to this day: "They're not leaving it alone."[24] Most of the incidents affecting strikers were never reported to the Austin police, because the striking families felt that justice would probably not be served anyway, according to another woman. Instead, for a long time the Support Group was blamed for all of the vandalism that occurred in Austin. Carol Kough recalled that even peaceful protests were characterized as violent: "Tom and I were still accused constantly of instigating violence. Tom was in the headlines again, accused of leading the rally to close the corporate office. No matter what you did."

Many of the acts of vandalism occurred at people's homes—once again heightening the level of personal fear, and further alienating people from one another. Although these were often acts against property, they were, nevertheless, very personal attacks: Round-Up herbicide dumped on lawns; garbage thrown about; damage to shrubbery. When Carol King moved into a new house next door to a strikebreaker, her family experienced many such incidents, including having their house egged. Patricia Higgins's car was vandalized several times.

When the scabs came out, they put cleaning solution in squirt guns. That stuff is very potent and it took the paint off my car. It's like an acid. I've also had my car vandalized twice at Mankato State University parking lot. Somebody's taken their keys and scratched all over my car and my trunk—probably because of the bumper stickers on my car.

There were also many incidents of face-to-face violence or threats of violence. Carol Kough recalled many verbal assaults: "We've been threatened with being burned out, shot at. I've had a joker calling me for a month. I haven't been able to sleep in that bed. He can tell me which light I got on, in which room of the house." In another incident, Carol was physically assaulted by another woman.

After one of the council meetings, one of the women came out and grabbed me and started to go on me. A police officer stood there; and when I saw him, I said, "Take your hands off me!" And the police officer just stood there. I was getting attacked and nobody moved. Finally my son walked over and told this person, "Get your hands off my mother." And then the officer finally came over. Then these three other women started in, talking against the Support Group, and I said to them, "Wait a minute. What it boils down to is jealousy. You're jealous of what the Hormel workers make and what benefits they had."

Life-threatening incidents were not common, but they were no less frightening for all that. One woman who chose to remain anonymous reported, "My neighbors. I put 'Boycott Hormel' stickers in my window, and my bedroom window was shot out. My scab neighbor across the street—he didn't have anything in his window except a big old rock." Patricia Higgins recalled several harrowing incidents.

My worst experiences have been in my car. Twice I've almost been run off the road by cars that belonged to the Hormel Company. Their salesmen out on the road. They'd come up behind me and see my stickers on my car and they would try and run me off the road, or they'd harass me. This goes on on a regular basis, still today.

Even when there was no direct threat, some people felt fearful and anxious. Carol King was very concerned for her son: "He's handicapped, works at the workshop which has a lot of contracts with Hormel. We wouldn't let him wear his 'Cram Your Spam' T-shirts to work."

The violence in Austin was a very special kind of violence, too—a very intimate and personal kind of violence. It was in some ways like a war, where opposing sides take up strong ideological positions that they are unable, and do not want, to abandon. For some of the women, the damage has been irreparable. For others, the only resolution has been an uneasy truce. When members of a community are driven to violence against one another, that community is probably divided permanently, at least during the lifetimes of the participants. Betrayal, anger, fear, and aggression haunt every wave of the hand, every smile, and every nod in Austin. The bitterness between people is rekindled with each sight of a friend or former co-worker who crossed the line, each petty encounter at the grocery-store checkout counter or on a Friday night in the bar. Like so many little deaths, all the indignities that people suffered, all the homes and jobs that people lost, all the alienation of friends and family—they all simmer beneath the facade of small-town life in Austin.

The deepest wounds resulted from betrayals between people who had worked side by side, demonstrated side by side, voted in solidarity to go out on strike, or washed dishes together in the Support Group kitchen. These betrayals were so personal, so intimate. The hard decisions that people made during the strike still echo back the plaintive question in the song "Which Side Were You On?" It is the only question left in Austin. And in the middle of the town—surrounded now by an eight-foot-high barbed wire fence—is the Hormel Company, literally and symbolically dividing the town in half.

NOTES

1. Jean (Vietor) Schiesser.
2. Judy Himle.
3. Barbara Koppel, "A Company Town Decays," *Progressive*, 53, 2 (February 1989): 12–13. Reprinted in *Support Report*, 3, 5 (February 3, 1989): 2.
4. Jeannie Bambrick.
5. Joyce Ball.
6. Carmine Rogers.
7. Mary Arens.
8. Judy Himle.
9. Linda Novak.
10. Jean (Vietor) Schiesser.
11. *Support Report* 2, 22 (July 22, 1988): 6.
12. Jodi Litfin, "A Community Divided: Austin, Minnesota," unpublished paper, December 17, 1990, mimeo. Copy obtained from Pat Higgins.
13. Billie Goodeu.
14. LaVonne Ferguson.
15. LaVonne Ferguson.
16. Untitled, *Support Report* 3, 3 (December 2, 1988): 8.
17. "Scab of the Month—Delores Novak," *Support Report* 3, 2 (November 4, 1988): 7.
18. "Birthday Greeting" and "Judas Was a Scab," *Support Report*, 2, 20 (June 17, 1988): 4 and 5.

19. Mary Machacek.

20. Judy Himle.

21. Carol King. Coal miners historically have defended the practice of shutting down the mines during a strike, thereby giving the workers a much stronger bargaining position.

22. "Dale Edward Francis: Whereabouts Unknown," *Support Report* 2, 13 (March 14, 1988): 2–3.

23. "Strike-related Incidents Total 242 in 2 Months," Austin, Minn., *Daily Herald*, March 3, 1986, p. 1.

24. Joyce Ball.

CHAPTER 5

"It's Time to Fight Back"

The desire for human community is strong. As the women who supported the strike found themselves increasingly alienated from the larger Austin community, they turned to one another to reconstruct a meaningful world. The center of that world of meaning became the Austin United Support Group, as hundreds of women underwent a process of political and social transformation that changed them and their community. Over the course of several years they evolved from being group members interested in the more personal aspects of supporting one another, to being a well-organized and highly motivated force for social change. The source of that motivation for transformation—politically and personally— is the topic of this chapter.

The membership of the Support Group was broadly representative: it included young and old, single and married, wives, friends, and supporters. The often nightly meetings were lively and chaotic. According to Vickie Guyette, the Support Group actively involved hundreds of people.

Meetings initially were 200 to 300, up until August of 1985. Later on, after the union went on strike, the meetings grew in size—up to 600. The meetings went on regularly and with good attendance for one-and-one-half years. By 1988 they were down to about twenty people. We were used to these large meetings; we expected the union hall to be packed.

From the very beginning, the Support Group was well organized—a fact that surprised and pleased Ray Rogers and the Corporate Campaign when they arrived in Austin to develop a strategy of response to Hormel's cutbacks.[1] The women had started out with modest means and objectives, such as bake sales and bannering and reaching out and educating the community of Austin—both on their own and working with the Rogers organization. Very quickly they developed the necessary leadership skills to expand their outreach efforts to a statewide and national audience.

The Support Group's most important challenge was creating and maintaining the spirit of the new community—bringing people together. The solidarity within the group served to counterbalance the sense of loss and alienation from the larger community.

When other unions would come, and other women from other Hormel plants, they often said they could just feel the solidarity when they walked in the hall. I mean, it looked like one big happy family. They didn't even know anybody when they walked in, but they felt like they were part of it—and that's a really neat feeling to give somebody that comes in from outside.[2]

Hardy Green, author of a book on the strike and a Corporate Campaign employee, also noted the strength and power of the Support Group meetings, calling them "a source of wonder to every outsider who viewed them."[3]

THE IMAGE OF THE SUPPORT GROUP

The Support Group was not well received in Austin, and the community did its best to discredit the women on every front. There was probably a good reason for the community to be concerned about the Support Group—especially as the women increasingly took on a more visible and militant role in the strike. Unlike the striking workers, the women's actions could not be controlled. They could not be threatened with the loss of their jobs, nor were their actions subject to legislation restricting labor union activities. Jan Kennedy remembered some of the more negative reactions to their initial efforts on behalf of the strikers: "They called us troublemakers. I think the town just wanted to forget about what the company was doing to us, and they didn't like the fact that the Support Group kept making them think about it and look at it." Very quickly, the Support Group was cast in the role of violent enemy and a threat to the peace of the Austin community. It was often unfairly blamed for criminal activities in the community: "Any vandalism that was done in this town they attributed to us. We always felt that some of those kinds of things were done by people in the community that wanted to really make us look bad."[4] By making a distinction between law-abiding members of the community of Austin, and the strikers as criminals, the community was able to find yet another way to isolate and ignore the strike. Fears about political violence on the part of the Support Group became a handy excuse to avoid supporting the strikers. Accusations against the women also played on the more general fears about crime and escalating violence in American society. Criminals had no role in "true" community. This perception led Billie Goodeu to comment somewhat cynically, "I kept looking for my picture in the post office!"

As the Support Group shifted toward political activism over the course of the strike, the labels used against the group became increasingly politicized and virulent. Suddenly the women had to be taken more seriously. For example, Austin's Chief of Police Donald Hoffman called them "Communists" in a television interview; they were referred to as "dogs" in the newspaper; and others referred to them as "dissidents" and "radical militants."[5] The women were deeply offended by these epithets.

I am a very good American. But the one thing I remember vividly—and I will never forget until the day I die—was that because I supported a union I was called a "Communist," a "terrorist," a "dog," and I was referred to as "sewage." If I am a dissident, I'm in very good company. Lech Walesa is a dissident; Nelson Mandela was labeled a "dissident." And all the Chinese students at Tienanmen Square that were killed were labeled "dissidents."[6]

Playing on deeply ingrained American fears of communist conspiracies and political radicals was one way of further alienating the Support Group. Other people simply dismissed the women as "crazy": "Our image? The media bent over backwards to make people look like raving maniacs."[7]

References to gender were also used to discount and discredit Support Group activities. As the women were drawn more actively into physical confrontation with the police, several of them reported receiving criticism based on the perceived conflict between their militancy and the "proper" role of women. One of the women felt that this criticism reflected an overall disrespect for women's abilities.

People didn't like the Support Group because they didn't like us sticking together. And I don't think they liked that a group of women had power to do things, that they could do these kind of things. They couldn't believe it came out of us. That we'd go out and organize and get money coming in. (Anon.)

According to Vickie Guyette, "They thought we were a bunch of crazy women, that we should be home." And Cheryl Remington recalled that before the strike, the women were perceived as "more or less a bunch of dumb women,"

and nobody really took us seriously. Then as the strike progressed and we really became one with P–9, then I felt that we were really looked upon as low-lifes and we didn't know what we were talking about. It didn't deter me. I didn't have a bad feeling about myself, but I felt that everyone else probably looked down on me.

In addition to distorting and misrepresenting their position, discrediting the women's work on the basis of gender served in an indirect way to discount by association the strike agenda as a whole. As a result, the community was split along yet another fault line: gender. "Proper" women didn't get involved in labor union activities and politics. Women who did such things lost respect in the eyes of those individuals who were intent on maintaining traditional roles for women.

Once the women took their message outside of Austin, however, the image of the Support Group changed: "we were treated like we were saints. People would wave and give us the clenched fist. It's no wonder we were always glad to get out of town. People would stop and talk to us, and say, 'Isn't it too bad the community didn't stand behind you?' "[8] But even though they were celebrated and supported in other communities, the women still keenly felt the alienation from their own community.

GETTING INVOLVED

What motivated these women, in the first place, to come down to a local park on a chilly autumn night and take part in a major labor struggle? For many of them, getting involved meant going against cherished beliefs about themselves as women and as law-abiding citizens. Involvement required a major shift from the image of themselves as passive and traditional nonactivists, to challengers of the power structure in their community. The process of becoming outspoken and politically active women took place on many levels. For some, it was the very act of coming down to the Labor Center and stuffing envelopes; for others, it meant going out across the country and giving speeches.

The women's involvement began with a commitment to take up the collective effort at the individual and personal level. Believing in the goals of P–9 and the strike agenda was the primary factor motivating women to join and become politically active. The motivation for involvement and activism had several important origins. One important motivator was concern for the economic viability of their families and their community. Historically, this collective concern for others has characterized much working-class political activism. Concern for others also has strong roots in women's socialization. In the Support Group, acting on behalf of others was sometimes articulated as concern for family; at other times, as a call for justice and fairness in their community.

A few of the women specifically mentioned a general commitment to union issues as their primary motivation for becoming involved, indicating a strong working-class consciousness. Although she didn't work at the plant, Patricia Higgins got involved directly because of her family's union involvement. It was her way of expressing working-class solidarity: "I have a brother-in-law that went out on strike and didn't cross. My dad and my father-in-law are retired from Hormel, and my husband is a very strong union person."

A union consciousness was not widely articulated by the women in the Support Group, despite their husbands' involvement with P–9 and Austin's history of being a "union town." It was not that the women were hostile or indifferent to unions; they weren't. "Union" had to do with the workplace, and unions traditionally have been perceived as male arenas. Like unions nationwide, despite the fact that many women worked at Hormel, the leadership of P–9's executive board was male, except for the position of financial secretary.[9] The culture of the union was also the culture of the workplace; and although some of the women knew what it was like to work at the plant, they did not have a strong direct experiential bond with the packinghouse "life." Their corporate cultural realities were their homes or their own jobs or both. In addition, P–9 and the Support Group tried to keep their identities distinct from each other, up until they were forced to merge. As a result, when the women spoke about their primary allegiance, it was to the Support Group rather than the union. Although a few women did mention union rights and their affinity with unions everywhere, most did not identify fighting for the idea of unionization itself as a primary motivating factor.

On a more practical level, the absence of a strong union identity and consciousness on the part of the women probably resulted from several additional factors emerging out of the strike situation. First, the union was limited as a vehicle for strike action. Direct action often fell on the shoulders of the Support Group, while P–9 was caught up in dealing with the UFCW and the Hormel Company. By contract and by federal labor regulation, P–9 was prohibited from many forms of protest. Second, there were constant power struggles with the national UFCW leadership over control of the local agenda. The lack of a strong union consciousness on the part of the women could have resulted from this bitter division with the UFCW. The failure of the UFCW to support the local strike probably contributed to anti-union sentiments at some level and made the women cynical about union activities generally.

In addition to their commitment to a working-class agenda, several of the women may have been motivated by prior experiences in political activism in their community. The leadership skills these women had gained in other political arenas became a valuable resource for the Support Group. Patricia Higgins among others, for example, had been involved in Democratic party politics. Vickie Guyette had been active in several confrontations with local government over a garbage-hauling franchise and an electrical power company contract.[10] Most of the women, however, had only had nominal political experience prior to joining the Support Group. One woman described her limited experience: "I belonged to an animal rights group at one time. There was no protesting, but we wrote letters to Congress."[11]

Involvement in the Support Group was a whole new dimension of politics, as many of the women quickly discovered. It required a serious commitment of time, energy, and risk-taking that was often difficult to make. It was uncharted territory for many of the women. Several women reported being hesitant to get involved at first, believing that the strike wouldn't last long. Others had to limit their participation because they had jobs. The time commitment was significant; and as the strike wore on, keeping their jobs became critical to family survival. One woman noted, "The women in the Support Group—this doesn't look like a group I wanted to hang out with. These were all women at home, who weren't working. I was working nights and sleeping all day, but these women had excess

time. I was only able to participate on weekends.''[12] Still others were reluctant
to make a commitment because they feared Hormel would retaliate: "They were
scared they would get on the list of people that wouldn't get called back. That
was their biggest fear. They were threatened, and that's all it took" (Anon.).
One woman was not comfortable with the Support Group's militant posture.

I think I also stayed away in the beginning because the people in the Support Group
seemed so radical to me. I think we were so desperate to have people understand, and
have people take our side, that they didn't think through some things. And it was real
frightening for people like me—maybe it was more frightening for people who are shy
and quiet—but it was real intimidating. I really thought they were a bunch of raving
maniacs running around Austin throwing leaflets at everybody, yet nobody was taking
time to stop and tell me what the real issues were, and I just labeled them all "radicals"
and stayed away until I couldn't anymore.[13]

For many of the women, family and household responsibilities had to come
first. As Julie Wilson recalled, "It would have been very difficult to be involved
if you had small children—even if you had high school kids." The strike had
also placed an additional workload on the household economy as the women
were forced to spend additional time stretching limited economic resources to
meet their family's needs: "There were so many things to handle to hold your
family together. Everything from sewing clothes and cooking from scratch and
more errands. To maintain some kind of lifestyle took a lot more effort."[14]

Not everyone joined the Support Group. Women who elected not to get
involved were sometimes resented by those who had decided to take an active
role. They were perceived as being just too lazy to come down and do their
share, or they "just wanted everybody else to work so they could sit back and
reap the benefits of it" (Anon.). Active involvement was also a gauge of commitment to the strike. Some of those who stayed away probably knew that they
were going to cross the picket line, or they just stayed away "because their
husbands didn't believe in the strike, or they didn't either."[15]

Throughout its three most active years (1984–87), the Support Group involved
hundreds of women and men in varying degrees. Whatever their individual
motivation—concern for their family's survival, a commitment to union and
working-class solidarity, or the economic health of their community—the women
of the Support Group developed and acted on clearly defined goals that were
ultimately grounded in their commitment to one another. Those goals centered
on mutual care and support for one another, and a demand for a moral economy
based on justice and fairness.

GOAL: A SUPPORTIVE ROLE

Initially the Support Group had a very narrow set of objectives that emerged
spontaneously as a result of the wage and benefit cuts. The women concentrated

on developing a mutual support system for one another; they came together to share information; they supported their husbands as the latter continued working for lower wages and benefits because they could not strike; and the women worked to educate one another and generate support for the union's issues.

Nearly every woman in our interviews mentioned support for husbands, or wives, or P–9ers in general as one of the main goals of the Support Group. This support, however, was more than women (mostly) just blindly supporting their husbands. It was based on an understanding of the economic issues raised by the union, and a commitment to making those issues public. The women moved very quickly from passive support to public protest: "We went out to banner the plant on payday because it was going to be the guys' first check that had the wages cut and we wanted to show them that we were there to support them."[16]

Very early, the Support Group became a critical institution for the dissemination of information to P–9 families. Both union and Support Group leadership recognized the importance of a communications network to help maintain their group solidarity.

The Support Group was an information center. Jim [Guyette] came to speak at our meetings a lot. Because the union had been so weak in the past, a lot of the men didn't even go to union meetings. Because in the past it didn't matter what they said—they were always told they were out of order. So they quit going. But the women would go home after the Support Group meetings, and say, "well, this is going on, and that is going on"— and pretty soon a lot of the men started coming to our meetings, too.[17]

Information sharing allowed the women to participate more fully in the unfolding political events.

Thank God for the Support Group—because, if we women had stayed home and not known what was going on! A lot of our husbands don't talk, and my husband was one of them. He would probably bottle up a lot. But this way, I knew what was going on and we could talk about it.[18]

The Support Group quickly became the main emotional support network for the women, as they turned to one another for affirmation and nurturing. Outside of the Support Group, there was no place for people to take their pain and frustration.

The Support Group kept the thing together. It was the core thing—the emotional support it offered. We only had one person commit suicide during the strike. If the Support Group hadn't been there, I think there would have been more victims. The alcohol abuse was very high; I know that there were a lot of women and children that were battered—but that went on on both sides, not just our side. But I think the statistics would have been much higher without the Support Group.[19]

The Support Group also met deep human needs for belonging and social interactions: "It was my social contact. I didn't feel comfortable in the outside world; it was like being in an alien country and not speaking the language and being ostracized. So the Support Group was like a lifeline for me.''[20] As the strikers became more alienated from their community, as their economic stability was undermined, and as interpersonal tensions escalated, the stress and emotional fallout was tremendous. For some people, the Support Group served as a substitute family and as a well to draw upon for strength: ''I got all of my strength and resolve and my determination, my stick-to-it-iveness. It gave me the backbone to keep going on and putting up with the sacrifices you had to put up with.''[21]

The women also recognized the emotional needs of the men, who were less likely to discuss their feelings or ask for support: ''I think I got involved because of the stress that my husband was going through. Our husbands were so torn by what was happening to them that wives entered in to try and help them through those stresses.''[22] The men were under tremendous pressure; and the woman felt that, the more they were involved, the better support they could provide. The women's involvement in the strike also defused some of their anxiety and reduced the level of potential conflict between husbands and wives as the family economic situation worsened. Vickie Guyette recalled how the Support Group served to build solidarity internal to the family.

We played a big part in holding our husbands together. Our husbands didn't have to come home and listen to us bitch about not having any money and not having a job. Instead, it was like, okay, this was going on, and you're doing the right thing and it's hard but we'll get through it. It was a lot different. They weren't getting the pressures from both sides.

Although the Support Group started out as a personal support system, it was soon transformed and expanded into the broader political arena. Throughout the fall of 1984, the Support Group and P–9 hoped their educational outreach efforts would put enough public pressure on Hormel that it would reconsider the cutbacks. Early flyers highlighted the unfair treatment and the real deprivation families were experiencing. In the beginning, the women were confident that the company would reverse itself; but as relationships with the company and the community deteriorated and as the certainty of a strike loomed, the women turned more and more to each other to meet the needs of the struggling families.

The need to reach out to the community pushed many of the women into taking a more active role. Not everyone was happy with the change in direction: women were concerned about the move in a more political direction and about the ''loss of personalness.''[23] According to Cindi Bellrichard, the Support Group evolved into a broad-based financial support system, and ''later on, it got into all kinds of movements (which I didn't really care about)—the Indian Movement, Women Against Military Madness. To me it got into things that weren't relevant to what was happening here in Austin.'' Cindi and other women felt the closeness and personal support were the most important aspects of the Support Group.

When it took on issues that were too global or too distant from the immediate needs of their families, or became too political, some of the women withdrew.

GOAL: A MORAL ECONOMY

Once the strike began, the goals of the Support Group changed dramatically. The need for public relations activities, political education, and fundraising thrust the small group into the national and international arenas. Focus shifted from the immediate issues of mutual support and solidarity, to action on a broad-based political agenda addressing the economic survival of 1,500 families. As Vickie Guyette recalled, the women quickly translated the strike issues into their personal and family issues.

We felt that we had a purpose, that we could do something. This wage cut was going to affect us—not just our husbands—and we were angry. And a lot of us could see what was happening, and I think we just wanted to do something. We wanted to be heard. For me, it was telling the company that they were not only going to be fighting with our husbands or wives, but the families, too.

The workplace issues of economic justice and human dignity that the union raised were incorporated into the Support Group goals from the very beginning: rejection of the wage cuts and benefit cuts, concern about the high injury rates of 202 per 100 workers, and the issues of dignity and respect were intertwined with concerns over loss of control of the production floor and the proposed dismantling of the incentive system. In the new highly automated plant where the temperature was kept at 40 degrees Fahrenheit, the working conditions were unpleasant and even unhealthy or dangerous: "Hormel kept speeding up the chain on those different lines; and when they hired new people, they didn't slow the line down." Under the rigid automated process, the workers experienced other indignities: "They had a policy where you had to ask permission to leave the line for anything. So if you had to go to the bathroom, you had to get permission—and you weren't always given permission. The men were particularly devastated by that."[24]

The cut in wages and benefits meant that families were experiencing major economic crises even before the strike started. Rietta Pontius recalled that the company policies hit her family especially hard. Her husband was a new hire at the plant, and they had just bought a new house in August 1984. She felt that the Hormel Credit Union had manipulated them into buying the house.

Right after we signed the papers, the guy said, "You do understand you're taking a 23 percent pay cut?" He thought that my husband would make enough money to make the payments. I said I didn't think that was fair that they sold us that house. The credit union knew about the cut. And then, no sooner did we take the pay cut than they started in on the medical, and Carl sometimes brought home ten dollars a week. We couldn't even use our medical card at the time to buy my insulin. My folks were sending us money enough to buy my insulin. It was bad. We couldn't even buy groceries.

Everything happening in Austin was now cast in a larger context: the struggle of one local union became the struggle for all workers' rights; the survival of individual families became the right of all families to survive; the greedy local corporation (symbolized as a pig by the Support Group) was seen in its national and international political contexts. The women found themselves making history as they stepped into their new roles as activists. Their activities built on a long tradition of women taking strong leadership roles in the labor movement.[25] Historians documenting the involvement of women in labor issues have highlighted the unique perspective that women bring to union activism. Alice Kessler-Harris, for example, argued that women bring to the labor movement their own agenda with its strong sense of justice and fairness, appealing to a morality grounded in the economic needs of their families. By concentrating on family survival issues, women are able to broaden the appeal of the union cause beyond the individual worker. To sway public opinion and resolve strikes in their favor, they count on community outrage over the injustices suffered by families.[26]

Moreover, working-class women have often carried their agenda forward through their own organizations. In her study of women's involvement in the Cripple Creek, Colorado, Mineworkers' Strikes at the turn of the century, Elizabeth Jameson found that women's auxiliaries provided a center around which women could articulate and act on their own unique perspective on economic issues.

Women suffered indirectly when the men's incomes were insecure and when unions could not effectively counter the power of mine owners. The pain which derived from economic and emotional ties to working-class men could be alleviated in part by class ideologies which provided social explanations for the plight of working-class families. Sharing the community and vision of organized labor, women's auxiliaries expressed their own blend of love and militance.[27]

This strong political-moral perspective on economic issues has even earlier roots in what E. P. Thompson called a "moral economy of the crowd." In his study of the demonstrators involved in eighteenth-century food "riots," Thompson found that—rather than being actual riots—these public demonstrations were quite conscious protests against economic injustices. Dominated by women, these collective, community-based economic actions demanded the right to family survival. The crowds did not steal the grain they so desperately needed. Instead, they protested the outrageous prices being charged and demanded a fair and equitable price for all. This collective belief that the community had a "right" to a fair price was the legacy of a medieval social morality that prevailed into the eighteenth century, before the new individualistic ethics of industrial capitalism had triumphed. Medieval tradition had demanded that the needs of the poor be taken into account—and so strongly held was this social ethic that "in many actions . . . the crowd claimed that since the authorities refused to enforce 'the laws' they must enforce them for themselves."[28] The principle that economic justice for all stood over against the individual rights of the owners of the food led the crowds to act on "a deeply-felt conviction that prices *ought*, in times of dearth, to be regulated, and that the profiteer put himself outside of society."[29] These community-based economic actions were not riots so much as organized and disciplined attempts to control the family economics.

This sense of collective right and its political demand for economic justice represented a community-based fusion between family survival needs in the reproductive economy and the market of exchange economy. It was a holistic analysis of economic organization. It touched on basic issues of human survival, of a deep moral sense of justice. According to Thompson, this collective activity represented a nascent class consciousness. It was a consciousness grounded in the economy of the community and was organized around community standards of economic justice. Contemporary Marxist class consciousness, on the other hand, is organized around issues of the workplace and the industrial process, and concentrates on the needs of individual workers. The economic unit is the individual worker, not the family or the community.

The historical accounts of women's activities in labor struggles forces us to look in a new way at both women's traditional political roles and labor movement tactics. According to Martha Ackelsberg in her study of women's political roles in the Spanish Civil War, "Women's traditional household roles may lead them into activities that challenge the very assumption of a dichotomy between public and private, community and workplace."[30] This special focus and intensity that women bring to their political activism is tied to their awareness of family and community. This sense of community is characterized by a deep sense of connection. It is not necessarily political, but can intrude, on occasion, deeply into the political realm. Elizabeth Faue made a similar observation in her study of the Minneapolis labor scene. Women's involvement is an example of what she calls "communal unionism."

For working women, the boundaries between home and work, community and polity were not formidable obstacles to action in the public sphere. . . . The public character of communal unionism created its own logic of solidarity, parallel to the public notion of a class for itself. More important, one of the preconditions for women's participation in social movements historically has been an understanding of the connection between women's wage labor and their family labor and of the permeability of these aspects of their lives.[31]

Factors unique to Austin, and to company towns in general, also contributed to a heightened commitment to community-based economics. The fact that Austin is a rural community with a fairly self-contained economy may have intensified the women's collective efforts and contributed to their highly personal commitment to protest. First, because Hormel was the primary source of economic survival in Austin, any reduction in jobs or wages was a major threat to everyone's way of life and well-being. Second, the women lived in close proximity to one another, making it easier to get together and to spend time together. In her study of the organizing of the working-class community during the Minneapolis Teamsters' Strike of 1934, Elizabeth Faue observed that "the physical proximity of workers to the factory had aided and abetted protest."[32] Unlike in the 1930s when cities still were made up of closely knit neighborhood-based communities, today it is much more difficult to maintain a connection between the community and the workplace in urban areas. This is not the case in rural communities like Austin, however, where community ties and geographic proximity contribute to greater involvement. Third, despite the fact that the Austin community as a whole did not recognize its economic stake in this strike, the strong sense of community in general accounted for some of the women's militancy. It was just such a blend of family, work, and community politics that characterized the activism of the Support Group. The close relationship of factory–work–survival heightens the expectation for the "right" to survival. This close relationship further serves, according to Adrian Randall, as the basis of community identity.

The character of work and work organization give rise to social values and expectations which in turn impinge upon the development of economic relations. It is a reciprocal and symbiotic process, even if it is the economic imperatives which provide the dynamic for change. Where those economic structures had been established and stable for over a century . . . social systems developed in which habituation and practice became ossified and reified as custom and in which a powerful sense of community identity burgeoned.[33]

The lack of economic opportunities for women in rural communities, especially in one-company industrial towns, may also have contributed to the militancy of the women in Austin. The stakes are higher when the only jobs in town become the focus of a strike. In her study of the strikes in the Kansas coal fields in the 1920s, for example, Ann Schofield felt that political tensions were heightened because of the lack of opportunity for the women to become economically independent: "a limited occupational structure and the physical isolation of the mining areas offered little opportunity for women to engage in wage labor of any kind."[34] The more dependent on the company they perceived themselves to be, the more likely they were to become active when their family's economic stability was threatened.

Historically, women's political and economic agendas have often taken on moral overtones in defense of their families. In their study of Arizona mining women in the Morenci Copper Mine Strike of 1983–86, Judy Aulette and Trudy Mills recorded the perspective of one of the more militant women protesters.

As one member put it: "Women are more aggressive when they see something harming their kids. . . . When the strikebreaker or scab, he's taking her husband's job away, taking the food away from your kids, taking the shoes off their feet, I think women are the first to respond to that. . . . They're seeing the destruction of the family, and they are going to come out with tooth and claw."[35]

Inspired by a similar desire to protect their families and their community, the women of the Support Group articulated their moral agenda in a variety of ways: a sense of justice they extended to include the whole community; a belief that their activities would have an impact on the future of the town of Austin; a strong sense of caring for others; and their defense of a way of life or a standard of living. Furthermore, the women knew that at the heart of the strike was an economic justice issue, and they *named* it as an economic justice issue. A widely circulated history of the Support Group concluded with this statement: "We will do everything we can until justice is won for the striking members of Local P–9 . . . [and] we will not quit until everyone is back to work under a fair contract and safe working conditions. We firmly believe that an injustice somewhere, is an injustice everywhere."[36]

Care for the whole community was expressed by individual women in the Support Group in a variety of ways. But most often, it was identified as a link between the well-being of the Hormel workers and the well-being of the community as a whole.

I would like to think that the Support Group's message was that we cared about the families, we cared about the children, we cared about the men and women who were jobless, and we cared about our community to the point that we were willing to fight for its survival. In the beginning, I really believed it was survival of our community.[37]

The Support Group's analysis of the moral structure of the economy challenged Hormel's role in the community. The interests of the company and the community were seen as being in opposition, and the threats to the community were often cast in language that talked about the future: "I became involved because I saw so many unjust and unfair things happening. I could not consciously sit back and watch without trying to help not only the strikers, but for the future of our children."[38]

The women defined the family's standard of living as a moral issue in much the same sense as the eighteenth-century crowds "set the price" below which they could not survive. For the women in Austin, there was a bottom line—a wage below which people could not live. They did not see their demands as radical or outrageous.

I just think that anybody that works forty hours a week should be able to have a place to live, buy clothes for their family, have a car, go on a vacation, and buy groceries and be able to go to the doctor or the hospital if they need to. You don't have to have the luxuries, or a new car—just something so that if you want to go to Minneapolis or take a little vacation, you can. I don't know. Is that political? (Anon.)

The women stood their ground. The company's demand that the workers take a cut in pay and go backward—resulting in a lowering of the family standard of living—was the last straw. There would be no more concessions, no lowering of their standard of living: "I didn't like what the Hormel Company was doing and I thought that, if there was a way to change that, I'd like to be a part of it. It really had to do with our whole life."[39]

Underlying and motivating this agenda of family and community survival was a strong sense of the rightness and justness of the P–9 perspective. First of all, justice meant economic justice: the right to a job and a "fair and just contract."[40] It also meant decent wages and a safe working environment. The demand for justice was based on an expectation of corporate responsibility to the workers and their families. Hormel "owed" the workers a decent income—not out of a paternalistic sense of noblesse oblige, but because a decent income was a right that emerged out of the workers' stake in the work they performed with the company. As one woman put it,

I thought I was doing right. I was trying to hold my husband's job. I can't believe that anybody can stand there and make a million dollars profit and turn around and tell my husband he's got to take a $3-an-hour cut in pay. I don't think it's right. My views got shot down many times. I told a dozen people, "Don't sit there and give advice until you stand in their shoes. I worked nine years over there myself, and I know what they do to earn that money. Don't tell me my husband is making too much money!"[41]

The cooperative relationship that had developed between P–9 and Hormel over many decades, and the Foundation's economic ties to the community of Austin, all contributed to this expectation that Hormel had a responsibility to its workers and, by extension, to the community of Austin as a whole.

Finally, the women's sense of justice included a criticism of the company's manipulation and control of the community overall.

I was so tired of that company harassing us—never knowing if you were going to have a job or not. They always kept you wondering; they were always threatening to leave town, and cut your wages. I think everybody had just had it. It's time to fight back. Everybody was angry. You just did it. You believed in it. You knew that you had to do it right now.[42]

For the many working-class women in Austin who chose to get involved—whether short or long term, full-time or part-time, and at varying levels of activism—the Support Group became the central focus of their lives for several years. It became their family, their circle of friends, their community. Through the long and bitter strike, the lives of these women were profoundly changed. In the simple act of stepping forward, they moved into history.

It has been many decades since the American labor movement has taken up the banner of economic justice for communities. As our society has moved its focus to individual rights over against collective social needs, so too has the labor movement narrowed the focus of its demands to individual worker's rights and such personal issues as seniority, cost-of-living raises, and pension benefits. The voices of labor that used to ring out with demands for a just wage, or the right to a job, or "bread and roses, too," have fallen silent. Unions no longer address the relationship between work and justice. For the women in Austin, however—with the survival of their families and their community at issue—individual and collective justice were inseparable.

NOTES

1. Hardy Green, *On Strike at Hormel: The Struggle for a Democratic Labor Movement* (Philadelphia, 1990), 15.
2. Vickie Guyette.
3. Green, *On Strike at Hormel*, 15.
4. Carol King.
5. Cindi Bellrichard.
6. Donna Simon.
7. Barbara Collette.
8. Judy Himle.
9. Dave Hage and Paul Klauda, *No Retreat, No Surrender: Labor's War at Hormel* (New York, 1989), 236.
10. Ibid., 66–67.
11. Cheryl Remington.
12. Jean (Vietor) Schiesser.
13. Barbara Collette.
14. Susan Benson.
15. Cheryl Remington.
16. Jeannie Bambrick.
17. Vickie Guyette.
18. Dixie Lenz.
19. Patricia Higgins.
20. Barbara Collette.
21. Madeline Krueger.
22. Carol King.
23. Mary Machacek.
24. Patricia Higgins.
25. Items of special interest on women's involvement in auxiliaries in particular and the labor movement in general include the following: Judy Aulette and Trudy Mills, "Something Old, Something New: Auxiliary Work in the 1983–1986 Copper Strike," *Feminist Studies* 14, 2 (Summer 1988): 251–68; Charles J. Bayard, "The 1927–1928 Colorado Coal Strike," *Pacific Historical Review* 32, 3 (August 1962): 235–50; Neil Betten, "Riot, Revolution, Repression in the Iron Range Strike of 1916," *Minnesota History* 41, 2 (Summer 1968): 82–93; Ardis Cameron, "Bread and Roses Revisited: Women's Culture and Working-class Activism in the Lawrence Strike of 1912," in *Women, Work, and Protest: A Century of U.S. Women's Labor History*, ed. Ruth Milkman (New York and London, 1987), 42–61; Elizabeth Faue, *Community of Suffering and Struggle: Women, Men, and the Labor Movement in Minneapolis, 1915–1945* (Chapel

Hill, N.C., and London, 1991); Jacquelyn Dowd Hall, "Disorderly Women: Gender and
Labor Militancy in the Appalachian South," *Journal of American History* 73, 2 (Sep-
tember 1986): 354–82; Elizabeth Jameson, "Imperfect Unions: Class and Gender in
Cripple Creek, 1894–1904," *Frontiers* 1, 2 (Spring 1976): 89–117; Mary Harris Jones,
Autobiography of Mother Jones, ed. Mary Field Parton (Chicago, 1925); Alice Kessler-
Harris, "Problems of Coalition-building: Women and Trade Unions in the 1920s," in
Women, Work, and Protest, ed. Milkman, 110–38; Barbara Kingsolver, *Holding the
Line: Women in the Great Arizona Mine Strike of 1983* (Ithaca, N.Y., 1989); Marjorie
Penn Lasky, " 'Where I Was a Person': The Ladies' Auxiliary in the 1934 Minneapolis
Teamsters' Strike," in *Women, Work, & Protest*, ed. Milkman, 181–205; Priscilla Long,
"The Women of the Colorado Fuel and Iron Strike, 1913–14," in *Women, Work, and
Protest*, ed. Milkman, 62–86; Sally Ward Maggard, "Gender Contested: Women's Par-
ticipation in the Brookside Coal Strike," in *Women and Social Protest*, ed. Guida West
and Rhoda Blumberg (New York and Oxford, 1990), 75–98; Ann Schofield, "Rebel
Girls and Union Maids: The Woman Question in the Journals of the AFL and IWW,"
Feminist Studies 9, 2 (Summer 1983): 335–58; Ann Schofield, "The Women's March:
Miners, Family and Community in Pittsburg, Kansas, 1921–22," *Kansas History* 7, 2
(Summer 1984): 159–68; Sharon Hartman Strom, "Challenging 'Woman's Place': Fem-
inism, the Left, and Industrial Unionism in the 1930s," *Feminist Studies* 9, 2 (Summer
1983): 360–86; Michael Wilson and Deborah Silverton Rosenfelt, *The Salt of the Earth*
(Old Westbury, N.Y., 1978); among others.

26. See Kessler-Harris, "Problems of Coalition-building," 114–15.
27. Jameson, "Imperfect Unions," 96.
28. E. P. Thompson, "The Moral Economy of the English Crowd in the Eighteenth
Century," *Past and Present* 50 (November 1971): 110. Other articles of interest con-
centrated on women's roles: Martha Ackelsberg, "*Mujeres Libres*: Community and In-
dividuality: Organizing Women in the Spanish Civil War," *Radical America* 18, 4 (July/
August, 1984), 7–19; Martha Ackelsberg, "Communities, Resistance, and Women's
Activism: Some Implications for a Democratic Polity," in *Women and the Politics of
Empowerment*, ed. Ann Bookman and Sandra Morgan (Philadelphia, 1988), 297–313;
Dana Frank, "Housewives, Socialists, and the Politics of Food: The 1917 New York
Cost-of-living Protests," *Feminist Studies* 11, 2 (Summer 1985): 255–86; Paula Hyman,
"Immigrant Women and Consumer Protest: The New York City Kosher Meat Boycott
of 1902," *American Jewish History* 70 (Summer 1980): 91–105; Temma Kaplan, "Female
Consciousness and Collective Action: The Case of Barcelona, 1910–1918," *Signs: Jour-
nal of Women and Culture in Society* 7, 3 (Spring 1982): 545–66; Louise A. Tilly, "The
Food Riot as a Form of Political Conflict in France," *Journal of Interdisciplinary History*
2, 1 (Summer 1971): 23–58; Louise A. Tilly, "Paths of Proletarianization: Organization
of Production, Sexual Division of Labor, and Women's Collective Action," *Signs: Journal of Women and Culture in Society* 7, 2 (Winter 1981): 400–417; among others.

29. Thompson, "The Moral Economy," 112.
30. Ackelsberg, "Communities, Resistance, and Women's Activism," 302.
31. Faue, *Community of Suffering and Struggle*, 16.
32. Ibid., 8.
33. Adrian Randall, *Before the Luddites: Custom, Community, and Machinery in the
English Woollen Industry, 1776–1809* (Cambridge, England: 1991), 285.
34. Schofield, "Women's March," 160.
35. Aulette and Mills, "Something Old, Something New," 257.

36. "The Austin United Support Group," Anonymous, mimeo.
37. Barbara Collette.
38. Marie Loverink.
39. Cheryl Remington.
40. Barbara Collette.
41. LaVonne Ferguson.
42. Mary Arens.

CHAPTER 6

"The Heartbeat of
the Strike"

To get involved in the Support Group was to move into a new world. For the women who joined, it was a conscious choice to break with the ordinary. They left the small closed world of their families and the indifferent and hostile world of Austin. They walked away from a lifetime of expectations—concerning the Hormel Company, gender prescriptions, and the loyalties of friends, neighbors, and family. They stepped out of a world of powerlessness into activism, out of their living rooms and kitchens onto the world's stage. They moved to embrace the new challenge before them: constructing a new world, a new reality, an alternative culture.

Creating a new world in Austin required great commitments of energy, an openness to new people and new ideas, and new ways of doing things. As radical feminist Meridel Le Sueur wrote long ago, the impulse that drives change and political transformation has its roots in the desire to create, to move forward.

There is some kind of extremity and willingness to walk blind that comes in any creation of a new and unseen thing, some kind of final last step that has to be taken with full intellectual understanding and with the artist, a step beyond that too, a creation of a future "image," a future action. . . . It is a hard road to leave your own class and you cannot leave it by pieces or parts; it is a birth and you have to be born whole out of it. In a completely new body.[1]

Le Sueur went on to point out that perspective is especially critical to social change: "It makes a big difference whether you see the world from 'inside' or 'outside.' It affects how you see history, how you see time, how you see politics and how you see people."[2] The shift in perspective for the women in the Support Group was from the world view of the Austin community, to that of the Support

Group. Outside was Austin; inside was now the community of the Support Group, P–9, and their supporters.

In his study of the radical culture of the Industrial Workers of the World (IWW), Sal Salerno captured the spirit of the lived experience of a revolutionary workers' union that, in many ways, parallels the P–9 strike culture in Austin. According to Salerno, through their collective efforts, the IWW created a culture characterized by a special "sensibility"—a sensibility they grounded in social networks, in the culture of work, and in the life of political and economic community. It was a culture that surpassed in depth and meaning the camaraderie of a labor union or a class consciousness. At the heart of the IWW sensibility was a belonging together—a solidarity that integrated self, family, friends, politics, and economics. It was a solidarity that took the ordinary lives of people and drew them together into an identifiable group that persisted over time. Something like this sensibility lay at the heart of the Austin United Support Group.[3] According to Susan Benson,

the Support Group was the mother figure. She was the heartbeat of the strike. The men were the force—and the women workers, too—but the women who put that Support Group together directed what was happening on that strike. We looked there to find out what was going on, how it was going on, and how to get together and eat and socialize. I don't think that the strike force could have hung together without the Support Group. It was a network, the fabric of being able to connect with other people and lean on them and have them lean back on you.

The human impulse is always to create wholes, and the strikers did not remain alienated and isolated for long. Like a stone dropped into a still pond, the strike sent ripples of change throughout the P–9 community. What began as an organization, quickly came to encompass a whole culture—one that held the striking families of Austin together, and around which they could organize their lives. The challenge of the Support Group was to nourish both continuity and transition between a past world view dominated by the Hormel Company and the community of Austin, and a future centered around the social, economic, and political life of the strike community.

The Support Group shaped and created itself anew as a viable community, inventing symbols, setting up institutions, building a collective memory of shared perceptions and events, and, in general, meeting the many needs of its members. It was a consciously constructed culture. At its heart was a political and economic analysis. With the inception of the strike, the Support Group set a new agenda for Austin and for itself. For those involved with the Support Group, there was a sense that "normal" activities and the community of Austin were left behind, put on hold, and in some cases openly rejected. The task was to recreate an entire world anew—a just community of commitment and support.

The need for human community is strong, and any breaks or ruptures in business as usual—such as those created by the strike in Austin—provide an opportunity for new social forms to emerge. An intensely political community like the Support Group is characterized by several qualities: it is a highly self-conscious community—people are aware that what they do and how they do it has important significance, and they feel that they are part of a larger endeavor; it is a highly motivated community, deeply committed; it is a community with clarity of purpose; and finally, it is a community that understands it is creating a new world. This chapter will explore the many facets of that new world view and how it organized the internal world of the striking families. The first part of the chapter will examine the boundaries of this distinctive subculture: who was inside, who was outside, and why. The second section will explore the meaning and expression of solidarity as the members of the Support Group framed it; and the third section will examine the outward manifestations of that subculture as the members sought to communicate its essence to one another and the "outside" world.

ESTABLISHING BOUNDARIES

The building of positive community takes place on many levels. Chapter 5 explored the beliefs and commitments that motivated the members of the Support Group. Identification with the group's goals and a commitment to become involved were the first steps that people took as they began shaping the Support Group identity. Bound to one another through these commitments, the members of the Support Group turned next to solidifying the internal cohesion of the group.

One of the first challenges in creating any new cultural entity is how people decide who belongs and who doesn't. People often define their community by establishing borders. Sometimes these borders are physical; but more often, political and interpersonal borders define and determine membership. One of the simplest ways that the Support Group initially defined itself was by its alienation from the larger Austin community. This isolation resulted in something akin to a siege mentality. As Judy Himle put it, "we felt like strangers without a city." She went on to describe how this sense of isolation and alienation contributed to a growing sense of solidarity within the group.

It was the only place they could go where they felt they belonged. They were isolated from the rest of the town. I think a lot of people felt they were looked down on and at the Support Group you had the strength of numbers that said, "We're okay—it's the rest of the world that's nuts." You came out of there feeling good and feeling like you were part of something that was doing something good.

Borders can also be maintained through collective agreement on an enemy. The principal enemy of the Support Group was, of course, the Hormel Company and, secondarily, members of the community identified as nonsupportive. Community institutions such as many businesses and churches, and family members

and friends who didn't support the issues of the strike, and the "scabs"—all joined
the category of enemy over time. Later, the UFCW would become another enemy.
Once those enemies were defined, an important task of the new culture was to keep
them visible. This served three purposes: to help maintain internal cohesion, to remind people that the mission of the community was necessary and just, and to reassure people that their perspective was indeed true. Much of that discussion was
carried out in a dialogue between "us" and "them."

The most obvious us/them split was between the striking workers and the
Hormel Company. The issues of workers versus bosses—traditional class issues—were articulated in such strike rhetoric as pointing out the discrepancy in
wages between Hormel's CEO, who was making $1.5 million a year, and the
23 percent cut in workers' wages. While these and other class issues were not
central to the Support Group self-consciousness, occasionally class distinctions
were the source of personal pain and discomfort. Carole Apold recalled,

One of the best times I had was the bus trip down to Atlanta for the Hormel stockholders'
meeting. It had been in Austin for ninety-eight years; but they heard there was going to
be a conflict, so they moved it. Forty-eight of us went down. Here's all those women
dressed in their furs and these beautiful dresses and jewelry, and I walk in with my
"Cram Your Spam" sweatshirt on. I can remember Chuck Nyberg—one of the senior
vice-presidents—picking me out of the crowd and coming up to me and saying, "Well,
I don't like what your sweatshirt says, but you do look nice in it."

This was one of the first times I did anything that I thought really counted. It didn't
bother me one bit to walk into that room. It bothered some of the [Support Group] people
very badly, because there were tears all over the place afterward. They felt belittled by
them, but it didn't bother me.

Rather than class, the women in the Support Group based their self-conscious
unity as a group and as a subculture more on what Temma Kaplan called a
"shared outrage . . . some violation of the norms they uphold," which were
based, in turn, on the values grounded in their experiences as women and the
issues of community and family survival.[4] The Support Group expanded the
union's agenda to incorporate family and community survival needs. The "us"
were women fighting to save their families. The "them" were those institutions
and individuals who stood in the way of that end.

Speculation about the presence of enemies within the community is another
way of defining borders. The Support Group often debated whether spies were
in attendance at its meetings, or were trying to sabotage activities. This wariness
of betrayal or sabotage by spies is a normal feature of many groups—particularly
those with a political orientation—and it helps maintain boundaries and solidarity
within the group. This was not a case of individuals being paranoid: there was
good cause for believing that spies were actually among them. By definition,
spies have to be close to the action; and from the very beginning, there were
people in P–9 who did not want to strike. These naysayers came to be known
as "P–10," and some of the women felt that P–10ers were informers and spies

for the company. Many P–10ers also crossed the picket lines.[5] Even after the strike was finally "settled," the *Support Report* would carry exposés of spies and agitators. One article, for example, accused an individual of being a spy for the government, and it concluded, "He attended many of our rallies, spoke at some of our meetings and traveled on the caravan to Washington, D.C. to protest the antiunion tactics of the UFCW. He made friends with many of us, and stayed in our homes. . . . An honest to goodness TRAITOR!!"[6] Several women raised related concerns: whether they were being followed; whether the meetings in the Support Group were being picked up on directional microphones; whether phones were tapped.[7] Others identified specific individuals they suspected of being spies. No evidence was ever found, but even the fear of betrayal served to strengthen group resolve.

The biggest concern was what the Hormel Company did and didn't know about the strikers' strategy and the situation of the striking workers. One of the women recalled, "We did a lot of telephoning of people because we didn't want anything down in writing. We thought we were hiding it from Hormels, but we weren't. They knew every move we made."[8] Another woman was convinced that Hormel even knew how much money the Support Group was raising.

They knew. They knew exactly what they [the Support Group] raised. The UFCW knows—the UFCW held out a lot of funds. The one time we met with them they had everything down. You'd be surprised what they knew. You'd be surprised at what the FBI knew, knows. We had two FBI agents sitting in on all our meetings and nobody knew it for months. There was a man and a lady that always sat over in the one corner. She always wore a scarf. Every single meeting. They got a profile on all of us. (Anon.)

Suspicions that the FBI was monitoring individual behavior only served to heighten feelings of alienation, and to sharpen the separation between the Support Group and the larger community. It also served to make the group highly self-conscious, placing tremendous pressure on everyone's thoughts, behaviors, and actions. In a sense, the women were made to feel like criminals—outsiders to their own larger cultural reality.

Another obvious way that group identity can be solidified is through a shared physical and psychological space. The fact that Austin was already fairly homogeneous was reinforced with the transference of old collective habits to the new environment. The geographical closeness of the families also contributed both to a high degree of involvement and to group identity. Early on, the Support Group understood the importance and the necessity for having a space of its own; and when the strikers were forced out of the Labor Center, they immediately set up a new space. In many ways, the Support Group functioned as an enlarged family space, taking on many of the responsibilities of the family—providing an intimate personal space and meeting members' economic needs for food and shelter. The Support Group also created a familylike political space—a space celebrating internal mutual support and an internal ethical structure.

The one-story building that housed the Support Group was located—symbolically—midway between the Labor Center and the Hormel plant. The building had a large open space in the center of the first floor, and a few small offices and storerooms at the front and back. On any given day, a variety of activities was under way throughout the building. People might be sorting food for the "Food Shelf," and the kitchen crew could be found in the basement preparing a huge pot of soup for the daily free lunch. Upstairs, people clustered around five or six tables—some just drinking coffee and visiting or playing cards; others stuffing envelopes or busy with other paperwork. Phones rang constantly, and people talked and laughed as they went about their work.

The walls were alive with posters, photographs, banners, T-shirts, caps, featuring P–9 messages and all manner of strike-related memorabilia—some items advertised for sale, and others just there for decoration. A huge banner hung along one wall, and a photo collection was featured on another. Off to one side was a "store" where supporters could purchase strike-related knickknacks, buttons, tapes, posters, postcards, sweat shirts, T-shirts. There was music playing on a radio somewhere, and a TV sat in a corner where it was visible to the large community space. The atmosphere was busy and upbeat. Everyone seemed to be about some important business.

When people came down to the Support Group building, they came to a social and psychic space as well as to a physical space. They came to community, to camaraderie, to other people who cared about them. Most of the women described the Support Group as a "safe" space—space where they were accepted for themselves, where they were understood and trusted: "I think people stayed together mostly for moral support. It's like we were all in the same situation and nobody else stuck up for us. All we had was each other."[9] This sense of connection with other people was a critical part of the experience of the Support Group, according to Vickie Guyette.

The good days are when we'd all get together. Actually, all the good things were just being down at the union hall. It was like our other home. If you didn't go down there for a day, you felt like you'd missed out on so much and you were away from the people you loved and it was awful.

The Support Group was a very personal space. It was not just a social or a political association; it was intimate in a familylike way.[10] Its intimate character made it a supportive space where people could feel free to share their innermost feelings and their personal problems.[11]

The Support Group also went a long way toward meeting the social needs of its members, and it still serves this purpose today. It became an important place to be—to keep up with things, to socialize and have fun, and to reaffirm one's connection with others, according to Cindi Bellrichard.

You couldn't stand to be at home and not know what was going on. So, every day you made the trek down there. Once you got there, you were there for several hours. It got to be almost like a club. Instead of going down to the bar and having a few drinks every night. I mean, it was addictive.

SOLIDARITY

Perhaps the most critical factor in cultural cohesiveness is what the labor movement has always called "solidarity." Religious communities call it "brotherhood" and "sisterhood"; the military calls it "esprit de corps." Whatever its name, it is a set of beliefs, codes, conventions, perspectives that tie people to one another. A high level of trust was at the core of the Support Group's solidarity, and it served to reinforce and reaffirm the group's sense of separateness and uniqueness. Trust was understood and expressed through unwritten codes of ethical behavior, both personal and political. Members had to feel that their colleagues were politically committed to the same issues and that they could feel free to share the most intimate details of their personal lives.

The principal measurement of trust had to do with whether or not someone was crossing the picket line.[12] For the strikers, the "scab" was the lowest form of human being. Crossing the picket line was not a matter of the individual's right to act on his or her own beliefs; it was a collective betrayal. Another measure of trust and commitment was the willingness to stand side by side in a picket line or some other collective action. Trust meant being there if your striking brothers or sisters needed you. Trust was also a matter of knowing when to keep your mouth shut, and was especially important in those situations where legal consequences could result: "Because people were being arrested so much—what you saw you kept your mouth shut about, so that somebody else didn't get hauled into jail because you blabbed."[13]

Even though there was often disagreement over political strategies and other strike issues, the unwritten code of Support Group behavior called for closing ranks and mutually supporting one another despite those differences. As one woman put it, "I expected loyalty—not necessarily to me, but to what we as a group were trying to accomplish."[14] Carol King understood it this way:

It's just an unwritten code of loyalty that, if someone did something that displeased you, you might talk about it in the union hall or in your own group of friends that were union people, but you never ever would have gone to an outsider. My resentments, for example, about feeling that a clique of women who were friends prior to the strike were really running the Support Group—that, I would never have discussed outside the Support Group. We really closed ranks to that degree.

Politically, people learned to tolerate one another's differences and support each other even though they didn't agree: "Even the outspoken ones! You kind of look at them, and turn your head a little bit when they start going off on their rampages—but you know you still care for them and like them a lot."[15] When anyone in the group was threatened, the others quickly came to her defense, putting aside personal differences: "If push came to shove, you could have been arguing with somebody down at the Support Group, and the next minute the call would go out to go out on the line, and you'd be standing right next to that person, ready to fight tooth and nail for that person."[16]

Solidarity was further reflected in a general sensitivity to reexamining long-held ideas and opinions and changing them to reflect the new union awareness. For example, people's attitudes about the Hormel Company were telling: "We certainly would avoid talking anything good about the Hormel Company! And you certainly didn't say too much good about the community either!"[17] According to Susan Benson, the women were constantly attentive to the political implications of everything in their lives. Her observations suggest that, in a time of cultural and perceptual transformation, people are highly self-conscious of all their actions as they seek to weigh past behaviors and beliefs in order to reassess and conform to the new reality.

You dared not make Spam at your house! If it was in the cupboard for the last five years, just throw the sucker away! You went along with the majority—you didn't want to speak out if your opinions were a little different at that time. It wasn't the time or place to have individual opinions. Or to talk about anything else about life, either. It was all centered on the strike. For instance, I entertained a lot of people that came for rallies. I put them up and took care of them and listened to their problems. They were here for our reasons, they were guests in our homes—so I tolerated a lot of things I wouldn't have tolerated had they been my guests without the strike. Even when I had disagreements, I didn't want to dispute them or make them feel uncomfortable. We did build some real strong bonds with people that we never would have met except for the strike.

In a politically charged climate where there was a fear that secrets were being told and telephones were being tapped, many of the women mentioned that confidentiality was critical to building a place where people felt safe: "If you told someone something in confidence, you knew that it wasn't going to go any further."[18] Without this level of trust, the Support Group could not have maintained itself.

Commonly held beliefs and ideals can be instrumental in bringing people together and providing the critical basis for a strong sense of mutual support. When a strike occurs, latent political feelings of solidarity and bonding are renewed as the strikers move into their own alternative political culture and risk sharing their true thoughts and political views with one another. This was true for the women in the Support Group; they explored a whole range of political ideologies and behaviors in their struggle to shape their own perspective. The process of shaping a shared political agenda brings people together. That process, in turn, is shaped by mutual respect and special care for what each of the members is thinking, as the group works toward a new shared consciousness. In the Support Group, this bonding was an important expression of a collective vision, and it was colored by the particular political environment out of which it grew: "I can't really call them friendships, because I don't see or hear from any of those people now. We talked together constantly and we were together a lot—but it's like we don't want to exist anymore. But at the time, it was very important."[19] Sometimes this political bonding was stronger than friendship. In other cases, people didn't even like each other, but they still supported one another: "There is still a strong bond today between the Support Group women. I care very, very much what happens to each of these people that I learned to know and like—not necessarily even like, but learned to work with and learned to be sympathetic to."[20]

Throughout history, the role of the martyr—the person who dies for a cause—has played a strong role in maintaining political solidarity. The sacrifice of a human life in the service of political ends almost necessitates that the group reassure itself about the justness of its cause. Otherwise, the death of that beloved colleague has been in vain. A sense of martyrdom serves to strengthen the group's resolve and to provide a rationale for continued struggle.[21] Even though no P–9 members died as a direct result of strike-related violence in Austin, the deaths of several members who died from heart attacks and suicide during the prolonged conflict touched the striking families deeply. When Floyd Lenoch died on February 21, 1987, the whole community mourned. Lenoch had been president of P–9 and served as a member of the executive board. In 1987, he was one of the P–9ers on the recall list; but the day before his death, he had been fired for endorsing the boycott.[22] According to Julie Wilson, "He was very active in the union throughout his life, and he had a heart attack and died. The funeral at St. Augustine's—there were so many people there, you couldn't get in the church. It was very emotional. He was like a father figure for the men—and the women, too. That was a real loss." For many of the strikers, Floyd Lenoch became a symbol of the moral rightness of the strike. In a poem of eulogy, Eide Cardel likened Lenoch to an oak tree, and described his contributions to the community and the cause of the strike:

. . . Protective boughs for kith and kin.
Teaching kids, how to Fairly win.
    There was Guidance.
From lofty views of what is right;
always keeping the prize in sight.
    There was Commitment.
Engendered with a facile tact;
giving purpose, to those who lacked.
    There was Friendship.
A forthright soul of integrity,
who championed a Worker's dignity.[23]

The deaths of several Twin Cities media people in a helicopter crash en route to Austin to cover the strike so moved the P–9ers that a permanent memorial was built in their honor. They too were martyred as victims of the strike. Carole Apold recalled that day and her response to the tragedy.

Later on that day, Vickie and Dan Allen and I went out driving around the countryside
when we ran across the flatbed truck that had the helicopter remains on it. They told us
there were no survivors. I was all right coming home and everything. But I got home
and my dad called me, and he said, "I heard what happened." That's all it took—I heard
my dad's voice and I broke into tears. That day was one of the worst times I spent.

Solidarity is sometimes a matter of physically standing side by side and being
together with people of like mind. To be with other Support Group members
and P–9ers was special, as Barb Frandle recalled: "The Support Group was
almost like a Star-spangled Banner or something. It just gave you this kind of
feeling. So many people together were marching down back to the union hall,
and stuff. It was really upbeat to me." It was empowering to look around and
see that others supported your beliefs and were willing to be seen and make
their support public. The large meetings and rallies played an important role in
maintaining confidence and commitment. The physical presence of supporters
in large numbers acted like a tonic to the beleaguered families. Cindi Bellrichard
remembered one of those meetings.

The first thing that sticks out in my mind is our first meeting with Ray Rogers. There
must have been 5,000 people in that auditorium. It was just one of those moments where
you're so filled with pride that it brought tears to your eyes. There were people sitting
there that were crying. I get choked up just thinking back on it. There were many nights
it was just like that at small Support Group meetings. The feelings of pride and patriotism—
the whole thing all rolled up into one just allowed all of your emotions to come out.

The collective memory is strong. According to Madeline Krueger, it was the
intensity of that collective feeling and the shared commitment to political ideals
that kept the group together at the time. For Madeline, those memories will
remain forever.

I'll never forget the comradeship. I think about that all the time—and in fact, now I'm
about to cry. I just feel so strongly about the people that we went through this with. I'll
probably never ever take a stand in my life again, but I think of these people and I feel
this bond. It's like family.

The energies driving the strike culture were not only political. A significant
element of the solidarity stemmed from physically caring for one another and
working on behalf of one another. Since such activism was based on reciprocal
interpersonal commitments, it served to keep and maintain each person's sense
of connection both with the other people and with the issues. The "doing" itself
was critical to maintaining the internal community, as well as to empowering
individuals.

With the Support Group out there and everything working and evolving, you were working
toward something. It wasn't just sitting and waiting for negotiations to happen, and not

knowing. You had a place for your energies to go, a place for your anger. By the time you got done—instead of feeling broken, you felt capable. You didn't feel down. You didn't feel on the ground. You could pick yourself up.[24]

This sense of reciprocity, or mutual activity on behalf of each other, was the impetus behind the massive fundraising and economic support system that the Support Group established. The reciprocity was not just a function of economic exchanges, however. It operated and was primarily maintained at the social and interpersonal levels. For Judy Himle, solidarity was a daily rededication to one another: "The labor saying—'United we stand; divided we fall'—was repeated at each Support Group meeting. The bonds came through working together, hurting together, sacrificing for strong beliefs."

The importance of reciprocity to building a collective consciousness is well documented in both the labor and organizational behavior literature. According to Elizabeth Jameson in her analysis of the women's auxiliary during the Cripple Creek Strike, reciprocity among the women had a special connotation: "mutual assistance was given larger meaning by recognition of shared loss, anger, and oppression, all of which lent coherence to working-class experience and gave it social, rather than individual, meaning."[25] The individual was able to connect personal feelings with the group and with other individuals—and further, to feel that her contribution was critical to the others. One woman in the Support Group echoed a similar sentiment.

Everybody was working for the same goal, and everybody—no matter how little—had something to contribute. That was the biggest thing: you weren't there as a taker; you were there to support, to be giving something. You didn't just come to take. You needed to be involved in working toward the final goal for the entire group. I mean, if one got, they all got. It was just basically everybody working together. (Anon.)

Reciprocity can only operate in an environment where people are empowered to act, to do something, to reach out. This is probably the core of solidarity, more than just supporting each other and presenting a united front. At its heart, solidarity is not blind obedience, but rather this feeling of giving/getting—the self-confidence of giving and the confidence in knowing that it will be reciprocated.

They gave me back as much as I gave them. They gave me back the support I needed. They gave me the shoulder to cry on, and I'm an easy crier. I always knew there'd be somebody down there that would love me and cry with me. I gotta say that the United Support Group and the P–9ers—they're the bond. I can't even find the words—and I've tried—that really do justice to the bond that was formed. It is a family. I know that, if I'm hurting or if I have a need, all I have to do is cry out, "Hey, P–9ers and Support Group, I need you." And I know they would be right there. When one of them hurts, we all hurt. So I got as much from the Support Group as what I ever gave them.[26]

Solidarity on the interpersonal level was characterized among the women in the Support Group by an openness and a vulnerability to one another. It had two requirements: the confidence that your perspective would be respected by the other person; and your own ability to risk opening yourself up to another person, on the most intimate of topics. Carmel Taylor described her experiences of sharing with other women.

This is where a lot of the bonding took place, too. You sit down and you talk with someone who can listen, who's not going to force you to make a decision but is going to help you think. Mainly, if you can spit out how you're feeling to somebody without them saying, "Well, you asshole, how dare you feel that way!" Here I am sitting here doing the best I can to do what I feel needs to be done, and so on. But still, you needed somebody there that could listen and could listen their way—listen to you through your things where you just basically needed to get things off your chest—without condemning you at the end.

On the personal level, being able to "tell" about yourself—and to trust that this personal opening up would go no further—was often mentioned by the women. The telling and keeping of secrets has long been a quality that has reinforced the dynamics of women's friendship, and the Support Group was no exception. The more intense a friendship the women shared, the more secrets they disclosed to one another, knowing that those secrets would stay within the group: "Whether it was problems over money or with the rest of their families, or if someone was angry about something, I think most of the women felt free to talk about it. There was an unwritten law that you didn't run out and tell anybody else about that."[27]

Sometimes the Support Group became an important "reality check" when women grew uncertain about their own feelings. Mary Machacek recalled how important her group contacts were in keeping her on course.

I would sneak down there when I could, just to try and talk to somebody else to see if I was crazy yet, or if I was still hanging together. I think some of us got out some of our innermost thoughts—really, that we thought we'd never share with anybody. Just the closeness—not with the whole group, but with certain people—that's the whole of it. I remember most, people coming together and just being able to flow together when times were tough—which is a lost art.

For many of the women, the freedom to share their emotions with one another was another way of experiencing trust and solidarity. As one woman put it, "When you cry with somebody, you'll always stick by them."[28] Trust within the group also had to do with saving face and with risking: "You could get up in front of a whole group and show your feelings—and the trust was there that nobody was going to make fun of you or spread it to the Austin *Daily Herald*."[29]

Sharing her feelings was an act of personal courage for Vickie Guyette, and it was made easier because the environment was shaped by a woman's perspective. Guyette also came to see emotional sharing as a political act that she deeply respected.

We could sit and cry together and we could sit and laugh together, and I don't think we would have felt as free, as open, to do that if we had been men. We just wouldn't. I know because Jim—whenever I would cry or anything—he would say I was weak. But I don't think so. When a bunch of us would get together and discuss what was going on, and our feelings, and we would cry—we got strength from that. We didn't feel we were weak at all.

However, it was not just the women who felt comfortable sharing their emotions in the Support Group. For many of the men, this was their only opportunity to express their feelings.

The Support Group filled a void. It held a lot of families together and a lot of people together—especially the men. If nothing else, the Support Group helped the men get through this strike. One of the questions in a women's discussion group I belong to was the differences between men and women's attitudes toward problems. My feeling is that women can discuss their problems with someone they don't know very well, but men can only discuss their problems with someone that's experiencing the same problem. So the Support Group really filled that need. It gave them something to hang onto, and I think that's the most important thing the Support Group did.[30]

Several of the women commented on how the Support Group served to strengthen and intensify long-standing friendships and renew old acquaintance-ships. Women who had attended the same high school, or had simply known about each other, found that new friendships grew and blossomed when the strike happened. As one woman put it, "Boy, we're friends now!"[31] These friendships were an important means of maintaining solidarity. Another woman noted, "Nobody can take the bonding from us. Hormels did us a favor in that respect. I can't find words to state how I feel about the fellow P–9ers, I really can't. It was such a fantastic time. The laughter, the fellowship, was just absolutely unbelievable."[32]

MAKING CULTURE

Artifacts, as well as relationships, characterize culture. And indeed, the vitality and viability of a culture can be assessed and validated through an understanding of its symbolic expressions. Symbols, art forms, rituals "make" that culture come alive through manifest representations. Culture is made, created. It is not static; it is not a thing. It is a way of being—a constant making and remaking of the world around us. Part of the way we recognize culture is by its institutions, its values, its art. As an alternative culture, the Support Group created and maintained a wide variety of expressive forms and artifacts that articulated its members' special world view.

The Support Group was always highly conscious of itself as a unique entity, and of the necessity to develop and project a public image. Several of the interviewed women commented on how important Ray Rogers had been in helping them develop good informative brochures, for example. Partly because the Support Group did not have a distinct identity in the media, its images and symbols are difficult to separate from P–9 iconography. Some images, however, did clearly reflect the Support Group. Most of the symbols that emerged were created primarily for internal consumption and cultural maintenance. Others were designed to convey to the wider community the political agenda of the Support Group.

What is highly significant is that the Support Group created these images and symbols in the first place. Generally, only the most highly integrated cultural experiences ever achieve symbolic expression. In the Support Group, the richness of the stories and images that were distilled into the collective statement of the symbols must have reflected the intensity of the strike experience and the degree to which the meaning of that experience was shared collectively. In turn, symbols—by their very nature—have great power to shape and strengthen and deepen the collective experience.

Images can tell us much about cultural ideology. Because the Support Group was primarily a women's group, how gender was portrayed in the group's symbols is of special interest. In labor movement history, iconography has taken on different gendered characteristics at different times. Symbolizing the ideas of plenty and moral uprightness, the iconography of the nineteenth-century labor and socialist movements was dominated by female imagery suggesting the idea of productivity and plenty.[33] By the 1930s, however, labor iconography was dominated by symbols of solidarity grounded in images of masculinity and male bonding. According to Elizabeth Faue, this symbolic shift reflected women's virtual disappearance from the agenda of the labor movement; in turn, the "gendering of solidarity as a masculine trait had serious implications for women in the labor movement."[34] When images of women *were* present, they were of women in mothering or supportive roles, and sometimes as militant mothers. But even there, the iconography served to deny women's active role in collective labor struggles. In fact, according to Faue, "the image of women as solitary warriors contrasted starkly with the public solidarity of men. For while there was ample evidence of women's militancy in labor's history, the silence of union culture in relaying this history suppressed this evidence."[35] Most often, women were portrayed as either nurturers or victims—never in their own right—and, "when women did appear, they often served as witnesses to the drama of male action."[36]

In Austin in 1986, a new icon of labor—one that incorporated the symbol of woman as worker—emerged. The strikers commissioned the painting of the wall of the Labor Center with a large 16×80-foot-long mural designed by Mike Denny, a P–9er. The dominant image in the mural is that of a strong muscular worker in a butcher's apron, her long hair flowing in an unseen breeze. She is

P–9, the union, and she stands proudly and defiantly above the events portrayed in the mural. With both hands, she grasps a bloody cleaver imprinted with "P–9," and she is shown in the act of beheading a serpent—the Hormel Company. She is clearly not a mother, but a packinghouse worker. With its look of determination and its muscular arms, her image is in the tradition of the strong workers that predominate in the Social Realism of the 1930s. Certainly, she is the most active figure in the mural, being the slayer of the serpent. Below her is a male figure carrying a sign that reads: "Families Fight Back." Across the whole length of the mural is a ribbon of words adapted from a Rudyard Kipling poem written in 1914. In the Austin version, the line reads: "But if blood be the price of your cursed wealth, good God we have paid in full."

The mural portrays the Hormel Company as a massive serpent, mechanistically swallowing up long lines of workers and holding the dominant male figure in the mural—a P–9 worker—in its grasp. The male figure holds a torch aloft, with red, white, and blue flames jutting out above the wall. Images of related political events of the time are also incorporated in the mural. Dedicated to Nelson Mandela, it includes multicultural references to abolishing apartheid, to the farm struggles, and to international labor solidarity.

After P–9 was placed in receivership, the UFCW had the highly symbolic mural sandblasted off the wall. With its destruction, the mural took on even greater symbolic importance. The Support Group tried unsuccessfully to get an injunction preventing its destruction, but lost. The strikers argued that the destruction of the mural would deny them their First Amendment rights of free expression. The day the mural was destroyed, Support Group members gathered to watch. Vickie Guyette described her reactions.

I was really angry. I had helped paint it, and it meant a lot. They had a barricade around the parking lot—you couldn't even get in. I went over the barricade and I started going after one of them trustees. If Carol hadn't pulled me off, I probably would have hit him.

Brenda Martel reproduced the mural on a quilt. A photo of the quilt appeared in the June 3, 1988, issue of the *Support Report* along with a statement in which Martel hoped that the quilt might be preserved in a museum someday.

Another symbol often present at public demonstrations in the Hormel/P–9 Strike was a tar-paper shack. The shack was intended to represent the class issues latent in the strike, as well as to be a statement about the importance of home and family to the struggle. Another visual presence around town every day was a gaily decorated pickup truck, adorned with patriotic and P–9 imagery. The truck was driven up and down the streets of Austin for years, and would be found parked at lunchtime outside the corporate offices and other sites around the community. Figures of Uncle Sam and images of the American flag were prominently displayed on the truckbed—all appropriately done up in red, white, and blue. Banners on the sides of the truck read: "850 Workers Still Out" and "Cram Your Spam, Damn Your Ham, and Stuff Your Weiners, Too."

The Support Group was also symbolized in two commemorative plates that were sold to raise funds. Designed by P–9er Ron Yocum, one plate—entitled "Our Struggle"—featured the Support Group activities. In the center of the design was the Labor Center sign, surrounded by images reflecting Support Group activities: a car, to represent the road travel to raise funds; a grocery bag, for the Food Shelf; a small snow-covered house, for Santa's Workshop; and other symbols, including the serpent from the mural and a bullhorn. The second plate—entitled "Memories"—focused on P-9 issues. It highlighted an image of the monument to those killed in the helicopter crash, a protest button, and a meat cleaver. The cleaver symbol, both here and on the mural, was closely identified with P–9—and it seems almost anachronistic to find a tool being used as a primary symbol in our modern, highly automated worklife (such as at Hormel). As the strike activities wore down, the strikers bought small cleaver pins to wear on their hats to honor all those workers who didn't cross the picket line.[37]

Significant symbolic expression can also be found in the lyrics of music composed during the strike. In collaboration with Support Group members and local musicians and songwriters like P–9er Larry Schmidt, the Minnesota singer-songwriter Larry Long came to Austin during the strike and worked with the P–9ers and Support Group women on the picket line to write the theme song of the strike: "Cram Your Spam, Damn Your Ham, and Stuff Your Weiners, Too." An audiotape called "Boycott Hormel: Live from Austin" was produced and distributed nationally, raising about $5,000.[38] The tape featured the "Picket Trilogy"—with new words to the "Hokey Pokey," "Union Maids," and the "Oscar Mayer Weiner" ditty—and new verses to the labor classic "Which Side Are You On."

This use of music as a symbol was especially important. Shirley Heegard recalled, "Our concert with John McCutcheon and Arlo Guthrie and others up in St. Paul was really something super. I think the one thing that will get anybody anytime is when they stand and sing and hold hands with your fellow strikers and supporters. It really means a lot." Celebrating the P–9 strike culture, folksinger-songwriter John McCutcheon memorialized Lefty's Bar in a song he first sang at that concert.

LEFTY'S BAR TONIGHT
Words and Music by John McCutcheon

Mister, this here is a good town, I've lived here all my life
'Cept the two years up in St. Paul, but I moved back with a wife
Well, I got a family, I got a factory, I got a future in this town
Never much for fighting, but we won't be pushed around
Well, sit down here and I'll tell you just what's happened to this place
It's neighbors crossing picket lines, can't look neighbors in the face
But's it's the same the country over, folks with backs against the wall
Needing pride and needing paychecks, it's the toughest fight of all

CHORUS:
Well, it's another round of Millers at Lefty's Bar tonight

Another game of Eight Ball, center pocket on the right
One more quarter for the juke box, while my spirit's on the mend
And another round of Millers at Lefty's Bar again

These Minnesota winters, Lord, they'll chill you to the bone
And the days drag on forever trying to pass the time at home
So I work at the hall when I am able, work at an odd job when I can
(It) keeps the food out on the table, keeps me feeling like a man

CHORUS
So don't you play me no more sad songs, I've squeezed out my last tear
Just give me food to fuel the fight, that's all I want to hear
No sugar-coated love songs just to turn my eyes away
'Cause it's the future and this fire helps me make it through my day (to . . .)[39]

Rituals operate on many levels in people's lives: from the small ceremonies of greeting and exchange between individuals; to social events and experiences that serve to celebrate community; and to more abstract rituals of storytelling and representations of collective experience through such art forms as music and theater. From the very beginning, the Support Group created within its structure a number of small intimate rituals that served to bring the women together. Vickie Guyette recalled that there was a conscious effort to get to know one another: "We would take the first ten minutes of the meeting and we'd go around and just sit by somebody we didn't know, and introduce ourselves and talk to them—so that, the next time, we'd know their names. You just felt so close to everybody." That ritual was special to the women; but according to Vickie Guyette, it "stopped when the men joined the Support Group." Other rituals became a regular part of meetings: "We'd always start with a prayer or something to get us all united. During the strike, that kind of got lost a little bit in the shuffle. We also made sure that, if anyone didn't agree with it, they didn't have to pray with us."[40]

On the social level, the Support Group created many special celebrations— what Meridel Le Sueur called the "rituals of food and feeding" so common to women. For example, one woman remembered, "I always enjoyed to bring food down where there were people coming from out of town for the meetings. I always made a batch of cookies or whatever" (Anon.). The Support Group held many regular social activities: potluck suppers every Wednesday night, sockhops, and many special activities for the children, some of which grew out of larger cultural traditions such as Christmas. These events were important to the group: "One of the highlights for me was the dances, the get-togethers. How so many people could be suffering so much and still not forget to have a good time! I think the women knew that it was really important to keep the morale up. The Halloween party was just the best."[41]

These alternative social events were crucial to maintaining a sense of community and belonging: "We all felt isolated from the community, from our other friends. We couldn't go out eating and drinking with them, couldn't afford it.

So you went out with poor people like yourself and did poor things together."[42] According to Carmel Taylor, this was also a family time: "The Wednesday night dinners. It was a time when you could take your family down there and your kids could be with other kids, and you could sit and talk to other people."

Rituals in many cultures take on a representational role—creating the image of communal life and reflecting it back for people to experience their wholeness with one another. According to Christopher Caudwell, an aesthetician who emerged from the alternative culture of the 1930s, poetry presented as theater in celebration of work is perhaps one of the truest expressions of collective ritual. Through dramatized forms of word and action, the lived history of people is reinterpreted and transformed.[43] As part of a broad contemporary cultural-democracy movement, alternative theater concentrates on the specific expression of people's collective political experiences.[44] In this tradition, we come to understand the power of theater as mythic statement of people's struggles. In 1988, playwright Rob Sullivan and director Susan Franklin Tanner came to Austin to write and produce *Voices from the Killing Floor*. The play grew out of a series of interviews with P–9ers. The Austin *Daily Herald* reported:

[In the play], five former George A. Hormel and Co. employees and one of their wives describe what it was like to work at Hormel, why they went on strike in 1985, and how their lives have since been affected. . . . Music was provided by Greg Hormel, the great-grandson of Hormel founder George A. Hormel. . . . So far, *Voices* has been performed in about a dozen cities, including Chicago and Duluth.[45]

From the very beginning the play was controversial. According to Patricia Higgins, there was even a problem getting a space in Austin to present it. The churches felt that it was "dangerous," and didn't want to rent out their space for a public performance of it. P–9 people were unhappy with the way the play came about: they felt that their stories had just been used by the writers, for the writers' own ends. As a result, local support for the play was very limited. Madeline Krueger, for one, felt that this was a big mistake.

I have not been able, to this day, to understand why the Support Group didn't support the play. The people from Los Angeles came, and anyone who had been involved could talk into a tape recorder. It was our emotions, what we felt. All the lines for the play were just things that came out of our mouths. It went to Chicago, Minneapolis. The response was just tremendous—a standing ovation. I can't figure out why the Support Group didn't support it; it was just like it didn't exist.

One of the most significant ways that communities build and maintain themselves is through the telling of common stories. In the retelling, these stories then enter the realm of symbolic importance. In the gathering of the oral histories for this book, many of the same stories appeared again and again. Sometimes it was the power of emotion that made particular incidents stand out. Many of the women, for example, could recall clearly the day the National Guard came, or the experience of going to jail. Other stories became part of the developing culture—many of these stories having to do with collective struggle. Sometimes the stories were just plain funny; and in fact, humor became an important means of developing and maintaining community. As Mary Machacek recalled, "The stories—I know we had to look for things to laugh about—we laughed about things that weren't particularly funny, but we had to find what humor we could, wherever we could." Carmel Taylor recalled a particularly funny story involving a supporter from out of town.

When Peggy stayed with us we lived on 5th Avenue Northwest. All the houses down there are exactly alike—my husband would get in the wrong driveway occasionally. Well, Peggy came home one night and got in the wrong house! She walked upstairs and thought, "Oh, Carmel must have gotten a new table and put it here in the corner. And gee, she painted." Well, she walked into the bathroom and finally realized she was in the wrong house—she was two doors away from us. The people that lived there didn't hear her. They had teen-aged kids, so comings and goings at night didn't affect them. Peggy was thoroughly embarrassed. I just giggled!

Sometimes, fun was a spur-of-the-moment thing. Carole Apold shared the story of her parody of the National Guard: "I took a gallon ice cream bucket and cut a hole through it for the eyes and used the lid for a shield and put on P–9 riot gear and had my picture taken out in front of the union hall!" The *Support Report* often carried cartoons making fun of the Hormel Company and scabs. One cartoon pictured Abraham Lincoln saying, "Boycott Hormel Products."

One of the most significant of all the cultural activities developed by the Support Group was the continuing publication of the *Support Report*. The importance of media in cultural communication and transmission was not lost on the women, and the *Support Report* provided a window into the activities of the strike for people from around the world, as well as serving internally to maintain community. Patricia Higgins was founder and editor of the newsletter throughout its long life. In the beginning it was published weekly and distributed in grocery sacks through the Food Shelf. In its second year, the staff began selling subscriptions. And it was distributed biweekly to a national and international audience until February 1990.

The *Support Report* included a lively collection of news, photos, cartoons, gossip, and calendar of events. It also served as a major source of background information about the strike, gave an account of related labor activities around the world, and made connections with other political movements. At one point, the newsletter had more than 2,000 subscribers. Although some of the women felt that toward the end it had lost its personal touch and become too national and international in its perspective, most people liked and supported the newsletter: "It was our link to the outside world. We heard from other unions around the country and their issues. It was a really good tool for spreading the word."[46] Credit for the transition to a more expanded—and more political—vision must go to Patricia Higgins as editor. Her shift in focus allowed the striking workers to understand how their struggle fit into the larger economic and political context. Several women commented on how important the *Support Report* was for them after they had left the day-to-day environment of the Support Group. People that had to leave town to find jobs, or those women who had to quit the Support Group to go to work, were able to stay in touch with what was happening.

The Support Group was, as Susan Benson said, the heartbeat of the strike. The secret of the group's success was the ability of the women to create and sustain a vital subculture that incorporated and then went beyond economic concerns. The sharing of work with other people—just the physical doing of things together, being together, accomplishing, succeeding—is central to all community building. Running the Support Group programs that maintained the economic base of the strike culture was work. Solidarity was not just a function of thinking alike or believing. It was a function of doing. When the town of Austin turned its back on the striking families, they drew together and created the culture of the strike, bringing together P–9 and the Austin United Support Group into one unified collective community to celebrate their ideas, their work, one another. Caught up in a passionate struggle for their very survival, they took the time from moments filled with need to find creative ways of making concrete their deep vision of how the world should be—at the personal level, at the political level, and at the economic level.

It is important to study their experience, because it allows us to move beyond the traditional models for labor movement strikes and other political actions. Setting up and maintaining a food distribution system is not as glamorous as having pitched battles in the streets—but it is more important in the long run, because it provides the stability and base for more sustained efforts. The alternative culture the Support Group created was more than a union culture, more than a class culture. It was a holistic culture of community; and it bore the unique imprint of women's understanding of culture, based on a broader consciousness of the intimate relationship between the personal, the political, and the economic. The task the women of the Support Group set for themselves was to create an environment that supported all their activities: protesting and demonstrating, dancing and laughing, distributing food and making Christmas happen for hundreds of children. They achieved their objectives through a shared political agenda, shared work, and shared lives. In the following chapters, the contours of this rich culture will be explored.

NOTES

1. Meridel Le Sueur, "The Fetish of Being Outside," *New Masses* (February 26, 1935): 22.
2. Ibid.
3. Salvatore Salerno, *Red November Black November: Culture and Community in the Industrial Workers of the World* (Albany, 1989).

4. Temma Kaplan, "Female Consciousness and Collective Action: The Case of Barcelona, 1910–1918," *Signs: Journal of Women and Culture in Society* 7, 3 (Spring 1982): 551.

5. Vickie Guyette.

6. "Kassing Is a Spy!!" *Support Report* 2, 19 (June 3, 1988): 1.

7. Barbara Collette.

8. LaVonne Ferguson.

9. Barb Frandle.

10. Cheryl Remington.

11. Carmel Taylor.

12. Cheryl Remington.

13. Patricia Higgins.

14. Barbara Collette.

15. Carmel Taylor.

16. Billie Goodeu.

17. Julie Wilson.

18. Jeannie Bambrick.

19. Jan Kennedy.

20. Barbara Collette.

21. Elizabeth Faue, *Community of Suffering and Struggle: Women, Men, and the Labor Movement in Minneapolis, 1915–1945* (Chapel Hill, N.C., and London, 1991).

22. Hardy Green, *On Strike At Hormel: The Struggle for a Democratic Labor Movement* (Philadelphia, 1990), 279.

23. Eide Cardel, "In Memory of Floyd Lenoch," *Support Report* 3, 6 (March 3, 1989): 9. In a letter written to the author dated March 3, 1993, Mr. Cardel noted that Floyd Lenoch was a "good example of a union man." Cardel went on to share some of his own history: "My dad, Soren Cardel, was one of the 3 men who chartered P–9's beginning. Along with Frank Ellis and Harold Harlan in July of '33." He continued, "Though P–9 could not get a good grasp on a well grea$ed bra$$ [*sic*] ring, the substantial efforts of the Support Group should be recognized and acknowledged. I'm sure that in this age of corporate indifference and timidity inherent in job insecurity; that knowing you are *not alone* will be a very important future factor to labor."

24. Susan Benson.

25. Elizabeth Jameson, "Imperfect Unions: Class and Gender in Cripple Creek, 1894–1904," *Frontiers* 1, 2 (Spring 1976): 96.

26. Billie Goodeu.

27. Shirley Heegard.

28. Susan Benson.

29. Billie Goodeu.

30. Carol King.

31. Joyce Ball.

32. Billie Goodeu.

33. Eric Hobsbawm, "Man and Woman in Socialist Iconography," *History Workshop Journal*, no. 6 (Autumn 1978): 121–38.

34. Faue, *Community of Suffering and Struggle*, 70.

35. Ibid., 89.

36. Ibid., 96.

37. I am indebted to Patricia Higgins for this explanation of the symbols on the plates.

38. Telephone conversation with Larry Long, Winter 1990–91.

39. John McCutcheon, "Lefty's Bar Tonight," published by Appalsongs (ASCAP); copyright 1986 by John McCutcheon. Used by permission of John McCutcheon.

40. Jeannie Bambrick.

41. Cheryl Remington.

42. Jan Kennedy.

43. Christopher Caudwell, *Illusion and Reality* (New York, 1977).

44. *We Are Strong: A Guide to the Work of Popular Theatres across the Americas* (Mankato, Minn., 1983).

45. Austin *Daily Herald*, March 6, 1988.

46. Judy Himle.

CHAPTER 7

"I Felt Like I Had a Little Bit of Power"

Central to all cultures are the deep structures of economic and political organization. In fact, they determine culture to a large extent, because they encompass the important human activities of material survival and social stability. The manner in which people organize themselves to meet their collective needs determines how effectively that culture maintains continuity. In the case of the Support Group, economic and political activism became the primary means by which people took control of and shaped their lives. Their economic activities were directed toward meeting basic survival needs. Political activities operated on two levels: internal processes to organize and maintain the objectives of the strike culture; and external processes that focused on active confrontation. This chapter will examine women's role in strategizing and implementing the economic support system for the families on strike, and in carrying out the strike's political agenda, primarily through the politics of confrontation.

Women have always had a stake in the deep cultural structures of economics and politics, but have not always had the opportunity for leadership in these areas. In the nineteenth century, the general cultural climate dictated separate spheres for women and men. Men were to assume public leadership roles; women had the care of the private world—the world of family and home economics. As a result, most women either self-selected out of public roles, or were consciously excluded by men. This was true in labor movement as well. Despite the growing numbers of women in the workforce from the nineteenth century onward, the labor movement—by and large—used a variety of means to keep women out of the workforce in general and the labor union movement in particular. Unions, for example, supported protective legislation, consciously refused to organize women workers, and maintained male union leadership, even in all women unions such as the International Ladies Garment Workers Union (ILGWU).[1]

As a result, women had to find other ways to articulate and act on their economic views. Sometimes they formed their own unions; or when strikes were called by the largely male unions, they organized in supportive associations, or auxiliaries. Through these auxiliaries, women were able to influence the working-class agenda of the American labor movement, and play central roles in meeting the basic needs of families and confronting the powers opposing the workers. In general, the women's auxiliary activities centered on more traditional "women's roles": cooking in community kitchens; setting up clothing exchanges; running their individual households on less money; providing moral support for their husbands. In these auxiliaries, the family space was made larger, more collective, and women's activities concentrated on meeting family needs.

As the labor movement grew, there was a corresponding increase in women's activism, and auxiliaries went beyond their traditional support activities to take part in more militant actions. We can attribute this increased political activity on the part of women to many environmental factors: legislation limiting the activities of strikers; the changing roles of women generally, which allowed them more independence and freedom of action; and families becoming more dependent on the income from wages. Their own increasing participation in the wage-based economy in significant numbers contributed to a greater awareness of labor issues and activism, as well.[2] Further, labor historian Elizabeth Faue has argued that during the 1930s women became more active in the labor movement, when unions turned toward organizing around community issues.[3] Union movements more broadly organized around community rather than workplace issues tended to attract a greater involvement on the part of women, Faue believed. Women may also tend to take more active roles in their own particular subculture or organization in times when the cultural climate is supportive of social change generally, or a change in women's status in particular. The increased level of working-class women's activism may also reflect women's growing interest in developing and promoting their own economic and political agendas. The introduction of gender-based issues into traditional labor activism has sometimes resulted in tensions between women's concerns and traditional union issues— partly because both men and women experience conflicts over women's "proper" roles and how to integrate the two parallel agendas.

Whatever the specific influences or motivations, the result has been an increase in women's participation in strikes and other economic struggles at all levels. In some cases, female labor activists only took a few steps away from traditional women's roles. They placed traditional women's skills in the service of activism, for example, by babysitting for one another so that everyone could march on picket lines, or by cooking food for strikers, or by pushing baby carriages in parades. In other instances, however, women labor activists became active protesters, stepping into more aggressive—traditionally male—labor activist roles: women on the Iron Range carrying picket signs, sabotaging company equipment and attacking scabs;[4] women in Kansas marching 3,000 strong to shut down the coal mines;[5] and the Support Group civil disobedience in Austin. It is as a part of this tradition of growing working-class female militancy that we can best understand the economic and political activities of the members of the Support Group.

ECONOMIC SUPPORT PROGRAMS

Out of necessity, once the strike began, the activities of the Support Group were quickly channeled into developing a system to ensure economic support for the striking families. The first order of business was survival. The decision to go out on strike put 1,500 families in economic jeopardy. They were used to comfortable wages; but during the strike, their only income was $40 a week in strike benefits from the UFCW. When P–9 was disenfranchised, even those meager dollars dried up. In addition, the striking families were not eligible for food stamps or welfare; and as we saw in Chapter 2, other charitable organizations stayed at a distance. Something had to be done to stabilize the families' economic situations.

In response to these immediate economic needs, the Support Group initiated a wide array of programs: a Food Shelf was one of the first programs to be established, and an Emergency and Hardship Fund was set up to cover minor emergencies. In cooperation with Corporate Campaign and P–9, the Support Group was active in direct fundraising to run these and other programs. The Adopt-a-Family program, for example, was designed to provide funds for on-going basic needs such as mortgage payments and rent, car payments, and other larger debts. Santa's Workshop was a program that met many needs: the immediate one of providing the children of strikers with gifts at Christmas, and an opportunity for people in the larger Austin community to make a contribution and express support for the strike.

Direct Fundraising

While women's auxiliaries historically have been quite involved in fundraising, the Austin United Support Group, P–9, and Ray Rogers's Corporate Campaign raised political contribution solicitation to a high art form. Before the strike began, the Support Group raised small amounts of money in traditional "women's" ways: "craft sales and bake sales; a couple of dances."[6] They also solicited small amounts of money from one another: "We got money from donations. The guys all went to work and said the women are trying to form a Support Group and they'd pass envelopes in their departments."[7] Once the strike loomed, however, it quickly became clear that these efforts could not generate the tremendous income that the union would need to sustain its members. It was then that Corporate Campaign entered the picture. Hired by P–9 for its organizational and public relations skills and its ability to fundraise nationally, Corporate Campaign was something of a "giant killer" in the union business, especially after having successfully defeated the J. P. Stevens Company in a long and bitter strike and boycott. The Campaign's talents were quickly implemented in Austin: mass mailings of up to 50,000 pieces were organized, and teams of women and men criss-crossed the country giving speeches and passing the hat.[8]

Corporate Campaign also put together a public relations/fundraising program marketing souvenir items: T-shirts, bumper stickers, sweatshirts, seed caps, commemorative plates, handmade wooden pig keychains—and even P–9 "scab clippers"—all carrying the striking workers' messages. "P–9 Proud" and "Boycott Hormel" stickers appeared everywhere, and buttons adorned every jacket and sweater. Supporters could wear "Cram Your Spam" T-shirts, or send messages to friends on postcards picturing civil disobedience or the barn on the outskirts of Austin emblazoned with the words *Austin: Scab City, USA*.

Support for P–9 was widespread and is well documented in other sources. Other than some small local fundraising efforts, the bulk of economic and political support came from outside the community of Austin. Fundraising support groups were set up in several cities across the country, including the Twin Cities; and contributions of money and food started flowing into Austin. But as Shirley Heegard recalled, "the big money came when people went out on the road," and most of that support came from other unions. Susan Benson received an especially warm reception from women coal miners in Appalachia, for example.

Because of my husband's efforts there, we had coal miners from Kentucky, Tennessee, Virginia, West Virginia, Pennsylvania come to our rallies. I was invited to go speak woman to woman, instead of him, but he accompanied me. I don't know how many hundreds and hundreds and thousands of dollars we collected. He would get pretty excited sometimes—he said, "That old milk pail really got a lot of bucks in it this time." So he was out actively raising money, and I was feeding the people he would send to town and then we'd both go out on trips.

It was not always easy raising money, especially after the UFCW/P–9 split. The UFCW mounted a national campaign to discredit P–9's fundraising efforts. According to Carol Kough, "they sent telegrams all over the country telling people not to support us. You wouldn't believe the stories they told us why we couldn't speak to their unions." Carol talked to one representative from a teacher's union who sent a personal check in response to their requests for contributions: "He said, 'You would not believe the mail, the telegrams—there are stacks of them, page after page—from the UFCW, telling us not to give you any money.' " Sometimes the unions would not even allow P–9 to make a presentation; and according to Carol, it took a lot of convincing to get audiences to listen.

In one place we persisted and they did give us five minutes during their lunch hour. We didn't lose a single person. When we got done, they asked us to join them for lunch—

and not only lunch. They asked us to stay for about two hours that afternoon, and we gathered up close to $1,000.

Carol didn't find it easy to beg for money from strangers. But like many of the women in the Support Group, she found courage from her commitment to the strike and pushed herself into new experiences, using her newly discovered talents.

You're not accustomed to public speaking, or ever thinking that you were going to have to be a public speaker. Let's face it—you're begging. You're trying to tunnel into their pocketbook and send it back home. I guess I acquired that skill.

Surprisingly—or maybe not so surprisingly—the striking families raised money from one another. Internal contributions took a variety of forms: jars were left sitting out on the tables at the Support Group, for example, where people could throw in their loose change.[9] There were in-kind contributions as well: people made toys to be given away for Santa's Workshop and, early on, P-9 set up a mutual aid program called the "Tool Box": "People helped each other. If somebody needed something done to their house or their car needed repair or a kid needed a haircut there was somebody to do it" (Anon). The strike brought people in intimate contact with one another's lives. This caring for one another's economic needs at an interpersonal level served to build solidarity in meaningful ways. People knew they could count on each other to help out with a variety of problems—no matter how unusual!

Our cows got out early one morning, and I went down the Support Group at 3:30 in the morning and got people to help me rustle cattle. Once, I had a skunk and someone came out to shoot it. A lot of different people you'd never met would come and help you. It was wonderful.[10]

Another successful fundraiser was the silent auction, organized by Judy Himle. During our interviews, she recalled how much fun they were.

I came up with the idea of the silent auction. We'd get people from the Support Group to donate handmade items—crocheted, [and] all sorts of things. And we'd set up tables at some of the meetings and we'd raised $500–$600. The bidding was silly on some of those things—ridiculous! But people did it to support us.

Another important source of support was contributions from retired P-9ers. Many of them contributed time and money both, often ignoring their own immediate needs in order to support the strike. They were active on the picket line and in the mass demonstrations. There were many—like Judy Himle and her husband—who stood solidly behind the strikers.

When the strike first started, I talked my husband into retiring; and the money that he received for a pension, we used in every way we could to help people—to pay rent; to buy Christmas presents for people; pay utility bills; pay back taxes. We donated almost all of that money to keep the people that were out.

The striking families expected retirees to support them without question, so the women were both dismayed and disgusted when they didn't get that support from all the retired Hormel workers. Like many people in Austin, some of the retirees supported Hormel. As one woman in the Support Group noted, "They supported Hormel because they had worked there, they got the good retirement, and "Hey, why knock them [Hormel]?!" I don't want to have anything to do with some of these people anymore. Their attitude was, they got theirs—and not caring about their kids" (Anon.). Another woman commented bitterly, "It wasn't the plant that was good to them; it was the union. The union got them all their benefits—and all they get, to this day" (Anon.).

Despite the success of its many fundraising efforts, the Support Group was clearly "outgunned" from the start. According to LaVonne Ferguson, "Rumors have it that the Hormel Company spent $90 million, and the UFCW is rumored to have spent $30 million. And we raised about $2 million. That's kind of what the odds were."[11] Nevertheless, the fundraising succeeded in providing some measure of economic support to the hard-pressed families.

Food Shelf

The Food Shelf was one of the longest running and most successful of all the economic support systems the Support Group set up. Once a week for several years, two bags of groceries went to each of more than 800 families. Several of the women pointed out that the Food Shelf touched more families than any of the other Support Group programs, and was one of the most meaningful.

Nobody had any money and it was the one thing that everybody had to have was food. I think the other unions and people that supported us could see that when they brought down a truckload of food it was appreciated. It made them feel good to give it, and it made us feel like, "Gosh, we're not going to starve to death."[12]

The Food Shelf was in operation from the fall of 1985 until the summer of 1988—nearly three years. Much of the food came from a large and sympathetic segment of the Twin Cities labor community. Starting in 1985, the Twin Cities Support Group—headed up by labor historian Peter Rachleff—was critical to the Food Shelf's success. According to journalists David Hage and Paul Klauda,

One of the group's members was Jake Cooper, a former truck driver and veteran of a famous Teamsters strike in Minneapolis in 1934, who now owned a suburban supermarket. With Cooper's semitrailer and access to wholesale grocery purchasing, the group recognized that it could make enormous contributions to the P–9 food shelf. During the Labor Day weekend the committee organized a 125-car caravan that delivered two hundred tons of food to Austin, enough for more than two hundred pounds of food for each striking family.[13]

Brother Paul's Mission in Minneapolis was another contributor to the Food Shelf. The Support Group had the opportunity to repay Brother Paul's generosity by helping him prepare food for general distribution through his programs in the Twin Cities.

About three times a year—Thanksgiving, Christmas and Easter—Pastor Paul would help us. A lot of the group went up there about once a month to help fill the bags for the poor. He'd get government sacks of food, flour, and different commodities, then we'd go up a day and we'd work on dividing up the commodities. We would freeze—in a boxcar with a Nipco heater! It was very dusty. Nobody would do it. But we did it to get food for the P–9 people. We came home with a busload of sacks and a lot of food. (Anon.)

By contributing their work in exchange for food, the Support Group was also able to retain some sense of dignity and pride. As one grateful recipient recalled, "You always knew you were going to get something to eat. I had enough beans to last me the rest of my life!"[14]

The Food Shelf was very popular and heavily used, and it met real needs in an immediate way. Not all individual preferences could be met; but overall, every effort was made to match up resources and needs and to be fair to everyone. There were a few people who were not happy with the gifts—a problem anytime that a program is unable to respond to individual needs or desires.

I remember the potatoes and the onions—a whole batch of dirty, filthy, wet onions. Nobody would take them because they were so messy. So I took them and spread them out all over the floor to dry. I was there 'til ten o'clock that night. Next week, everybody took some. We also had stuff sitting around here that people wouldn't take, and I got upset with people.[15]

Even when attempts were made to meet special needs, sometimes mistakes were made.

Some people would come in and dump their groceries out and say, "I want more than this." Or, "How come I only got this much and that person gets that much?" One time, just before Thanksgiving, we got all these chickens. We didn't have a cooler, so we had them out in the truck to keep them cold. So they were distributed from there. The person doing that didn't know that the bigger families got more—so there was this poor woman with seven kids who got only one chicken![16]

Despite these minor inconveniences, the Food Shelf was mentioned by all of the women as an extremely effective program, and one that was deeply appreciated.

Adopt-a-Family Program

One of the most successful, and the most controversial, of the support efforts was the Adopt-a-Family program. It began in 1985 with a mass mailing that asked supporters to send monthly contributions to help an individual family.[17] People all across the country contributed to the program. From November 1985 to December 1986, the Support Group raised approximately $375,000 and helped about fifty families per month, with an average amount of $500 per family. From December 1986 to December 1988, they raised another $173,000 and helped approximately ten to fifteen families per month—approximately $600 per family. The program ran until December 1, 1988.[18]

Striking families had to apply each month, outlining their need and their current financial situation. A six-member anonymous committee made the decisions about who would receive support, and the amount. Julie Wilson was the go-between.

The committee met once a week, if not more often. They would look over the applications. And they knew most of these people. They knew a lot of things about them outside of what was on the application. And based on the amount of money that came in, and what the requests were, they decided who received how much. They would tell the office, and the office would contact those people to come and get their checks. There was a general rule that no one got more than $600 a month. It was really difficult being the go-between.

In general, most of the women thought the Adopt-a-Family program was effective. Barbara Collette summed up her overall impressions: "It was absolutely, without a doubt, one of the most ingenious things I ever saw work. I do believe, 90 percent of the time people that needed it got it. There were flaws; but it was the best thought out and the best planned, and worked the best." The success of the Adopt-a-Family program meant that pressures to cross the picket line were eased. Toward the end of the program, the guidelines were changed somewhat to reflect political realities. According to Julie Wilson, "when the money got short, some people who really needed it quit putting in for it so that the people who were still doing things as activists could get more money. They did it because they felt they weren't as active as they should be."

More than any other program, however, controversy and bitterness surrounded Adopt-a-Family. Establishing need was an extremely complex and largely subjective process, and the committee depended on information submitted by the individual family. No matter what the committee did, there were bound to be differences of opinion. Vickie Guyette admitted, "I'm glad I wasn't on that committee, because trying to decide who was more needy—it's a terrible decision." Familiarity, the old adage goes, breeds contempt; and when it came to disbursement of these funds, sometimes hard feelings surfaced because people had different lifestyles resulting in different needs, and because a few people just plain cheated. People were upset about a variety of real or perceived inequities: perceptions of favoritism; criticisms of people who had a lot of personal possessions such as campers and snowmobiles and were too deeply in debt; concerns that families with a spouse working were being treated the same as a family with no income; the perception that the same families were always getting the money; or indecision about whether families should spend down to nothing before they applied.[19] However, discussions of these matters were a necessary part of shaping the economic guidelines for the program—despite the fact that conflicts over distribution of the funds created divisiveness and threatened solidarity. It was the first time that people found themselves in the position of having to evaluate the individual economic behavior of their friends and neighbors, and the stress was tremendous. The question of fairness motivated much of the criticism.

Our daughter and son-in-law spent every penny they had before they came for help. Other people did not. My brother cashed in his IRA, [and] his kids' insurance policies. He had nothing before he came for help. The money part really has bugged me. I think those that hung around most and cried the most got the money, and the other people who were proud enough to live on their own suffered for it. I think there was some real unfairness in that area. But that's my feeling. I have no proof of it.[20]

Other critics felt that the money should have been divided up equally somehow, or different priorities should have been used.

It should have been divided between the members who stayed out on strike. Maybe people wouldn't have crossed the picket line. I think money should have gone to the older workers. These young people with the families—they lost their houses anyway, but they can go on to make something of themselves. Some of them could have gotten a part-time job. I saw a lot of people who just didn't even try to work, because the money was down there for handouts.[21]

There were accusations that people hid assets so they could qualify,[22] and some of the women were especially incensed with incidents of open cheating and lying.

We were paying certain people's house payments and their bills when they [Support Group members] found out they [recipients] had money in the bank. I don't know how the Support Group could have gotten that information. We trusted that people were telling the truth; and it was hard to know, because their names weren't on the application forms. I turned two people in, anonymously.[23]

People who cheated even bragged publicly about how they were taking advantage of a variety of economic support programs in the community.

I know of one person who admitted to getting welfare and also coming down to the Support Group, getting money. They had a brand-new car they were paying on. We had to sell our car, but they bragged about how they had to make a $400–$500-a-month payment. He was also getting helped by the church.[24]

Billie Goodeu suggested that more people would have benefited had the Support Group implemented the program a bit differently. In hindsight, she felt it should not have dispensed the money so freely, given the length of time the strikers were out: "If we could have seen into the future, perhaps we would have spent or divided the money a little more wisely." She also thought the committee should have paid special attention to commitment to the strike as a major criterion for receiving funds.

They should have screened people more, maybe. Because if they were going to scab, they didn't deserve a darn thing. Maybe each and every one of us that received money should have signed an agreement that stated, once you went back to work—Hormels or wherever—that you would start to pay that money back. I'll bet there wouldn't have been so many greedies coming in with their hand out. I think that's where we made our biggest mistake. I don't think people would have taken money like they did, and I don't think the scabs would have been so ready to use the Support Group like they did.

Despite all the difficulties, the Adopt-a-Family program (along with the Food Shelf) helped meet some of the basic survival needs of more than 1,000 striking families.[25] For a time, it allowed people to keep even with their car payments and avoid losing their homes. Toward the end, it allowed the work of the strike to continue. In addition, its longevity and its success speak volumes about the support that the strike had across the country.

Santa's Workshop

Although it was not one of the largest support programs, Santa's Workshop was one of the most visible and most successful (and also controversial) programs. Christmas is a central holiday in American culture, and the Support Group wanted families with children to have a good Christmas. Santa's Workshop was set up to make that happen. It was coordinated by Jan Butts, president of the Support Group; and through the efforts of hundreds of volunteers, it captured the spirit of the strike culture more than any other program. Even though the major focus of the Support Group was concerned with meeting survival needs— providing "bread"—the women also worked hard to bring joy and pleasure, too—the "roses"—to their community.

One of the women attributed the success of Santa's Workshop to its narrow but appealing focus on Christmas and kids.

The first year, when we had the room to work out of the Labor Center, we had people working as carpenters, women sewing—you'd have fifty to a hundred people down there any given day, just all working together. That's what you needed—programs to bring the people together. The first year we gave out 2,000 bags. We generated $20,000 to fund it. The second year was about 1,500 bags. We advertised for support on all the news media, and raised money through mailings, too. (Anon.)

Many gifts were handmade, providing an outlet for creative energies. The women sewed teddy bears, "pound puppies," and "cabbage patch dolls." Donna Simon and her sister Lois made a major commitment of time and energy to training people.

My sister and I had the patterns to make these cloth bears, so one night we took some samples down to the Support Group and told them we could teach them to make them if they wanted to—to make dolls or bears. We said we'd be happy to donate our time. I worked from nine to four, and Lois worked from four to nine in the evening. We had a very good turnout and we had an awful lot of support.

Santa's Workshop also provided adults in the Austin community who were reluctant to become involved in other aspects of the strike an opportunity to support the striking families. Because the program concentrated on children's needs, it was seen as outside of the political arena, and people felt more comfortable making contributions.

K-Mart—they let us buy toys at discount prices. I know one woman—her husband wouldn't let her do anything, but she brought down two presents and she said, "Don't you ever tell him I was down here with these." Even women who couldn't come down helped. I know of two women who took material home with them and made beautiful dolls' clothes.[26]

Santa's Workshop contributed to a sense of self-esteem and pride, according to Jan Kennedy: "It helped everyone's self-esteem, because we made things. We weren't just sitting back. It wasn't just handed to us. Whoever was behind giving all the presents to kids—it was an excellent idea." At the very deepest level, Santa's Workshop distilled the essence of community spirit and contributed immensely to community well-being. As Susan Benson recalled,

Santa's Workshop was significant. Because it brought a comfort and spirit back into the holidays. Made them happen. But more importantly, it touched the lives of children instead of always focusing on adult needs. I remember that time being really special. It wasn't that our kids didn't get presents—we wound up getting them presents, too. But the Support presents were a little extra. We couldn't give them what we normally did, but it didn't matter. And whatever they got, they felt really comfortable. The handmade items were appreciated tremendously. My children are grown and they can remember that Christmas. They remember that people cared, and these strikers were important people. They didn't just walk all over you and ask for things and not give back, but they were willing to share everything.

Santa's Workshop was unique among all the Support Group programs, because it met a variety of emotional and social needs at a critical and sensitive time. It brought people together to do meaningful, creative work; it allowed them to set aside their own pressing needs and concentrate on the children's needs; it brought traditional "women's work" into high relief and integrated it into the culture of the strike; and it brought home for many the true spirit of Christmas. The strikers' efforts to retain their dignity and their jobs were, after all, for the future, for the children.

Miscellaneous Programs

Several smaller economic support programs are worth mentioning. A Clothing Exchange was set up at the Support Group offices, as well as a Soup Kitchen where hot lunch was served on a daily basis. The Emergency and Hardship Fund met immediate needs—money to pay utility bills, to replace broken hot-water heaters, and a myriad of other small one-time-only needs. The fund often covered necessary medical expenses, for example: "People that had to have medical insurance because they had heart conditions and stuff. We set up a fund at a local drug store so they could get their prescriptions and pay their medical insurance."[27]

Together these programs represented a comprehensive effort to respond to family economic needs at all levels: food, housing, services, small gifts to cheer the heart. This attention to the intimate details of living and surviving brought the striking families together in a broad system of mutual aid. Their efforts seem, at this distance, somehow heroic. Keeping 1,500 families fed and housed and clothed is a major undertaking for any organization, let alone one called into action during a tense labor crisis. As the Support Group women concentrated their efforts on establishing and maintaining these various economic lifelines, their alienation from the larger community became all the more acute as they saw the town of Austin proceeding with business as usual.

Despite their significant efforts, however, the women still fell short of sustaining basic economic needs. As the strike wore on, economic pressures and heightened levels of frustration forced them to seek more assertive methods to pressure Hormel to negotiate an end to the strike. One option was to adopt more direct-action strategies grounded in collective political activity.

ACTIVISM—DIRECT ACTION

On the political front, from the very beginning the women took a visible and active role in protesting. This commitment to activism was in response to several factors: the limits placed on P–9 activism by the union contract and labor legislation; the development and articulation of the women's own political agenda on behalf of family and community needs; and a growing awareness that the strike would not be settled quickly. In response to these various agendas, the women took on activist projects on many fronts: civil disobedience leading to arrest; verbal taunting and harassment; boycotting; demonstrating.

Initially, in the fall of 1984, public political activism by the women in the Support Group was limited to bannering and educational outreach efforts. These early activities concentrated on providing moral support for the workers.

The first time we went out to banner, we stood in front of the Hormel plant. To show you how it can boost the workers' morale, the word passed inside the plant that we were out there, and the guys on their breaks (or what have you)—they'd be up on the roof and they'd be shouting at us just as loud as they could. It meant so much to them. When they'd get out, they'd come by and they'd honk and wave at us. It was really a morale-lifting experience for those guys.[28]

Gradually and somewhat reluctantly, the women increased their activism by reaching out to educate the community. They were not accustomed to approaching strangers and discussing labor politics, but they overcame their hesitancy because they needed the support of the community. Up until the strike started, P–9 and Support Group members went door to door in Austin with leaflets explaining their position on the strike issues. This was an especially empowering experience for one woman: "I learned about going out and leafletting. I didn't think I could ever do that. It was a little more aggressive. But because I believed in it, then you do a little more" (Anon.). For many women, this was their first venture into the public arena, and they weren't always comfortable: "I did some bannering when the strike first started. It was really pretty nice because people would go by and honk and wave. It would have been difficult when people went by and gave you the finger. I'm just not a political-type person, but I'd do it again because I still think we were right."[29]

Later on during the strike, and especially after the plant was reopened with replacement workers, the women participated in more militant public protests and demonstrations. They joined P–9ers on the picket line; and when the union was limited to only a few pickets at each gate, they took up the task of mass picketing in place of the men. According to Vickie Guyette, the strike would have been difficult to sustain without the women.

The company said the union members couldn't do this, the employees couldn't do that. But the women could. We could get away with a lot that our husbands couldn't. They tried to limit our activities. I think it prolonged the strike and made things a lot harder for them because the families were involved. I think we were very effective.

In addition to raising public awareness, these large public events served to reinforce the Support Group's collective sense of solidarity: "The rallies were a necessary thing. Not just because they pumped people up, but it was a time when people could get together and feel good about themselves and could hear from speakers who told us we weren't dumb and that it was good what we were doing."[30] Another woman recalled nostalgically, "I can remember lots of highs—like when we had parades. We had 5,000 or 6,000 people here. It was wonderful to know that that many people in the country supported us. They came from all over the United States'' (Anon.). Although the support of strangers was important, the daily acts of standing side by side and protesting or going to jail together brought the women closer and strengthened their commitments to one another and the strike. They took deep comfort in these small acts of rebellion and protest.

I remember some of those early, early mornings of picketing. In order to get to the plant, we would drive by the hospital and from there we could kind of look down across the river at the plant. The whole thing had good high fences around it, and the lights—it was just like looking at a prison, or a war zone. Then, when the Guard came, you could see how they were lined up in a formation around it. It was like you were going to war at four A.M. in the morning. I hated going out there, but I always went, because it was something I felt I had to do. Once you got out there, and once you got on the line and things started happening, you always felt good about it. And you came back to the Support Group and had your coffee at eight, nine, in the morning when it was all over. You always felt like what you'd done was the right thing, even though you hated getting up, you hated bundling up—it was cold and everything.[31]

There is a lively history of women union activists engaging in civil disobedience. Once the predominantly male leadership in the labor movement discovered that women were willing and able to become directly involved in labor struggles, their activism was encouraged. Their militancy in the Lawrence, Massachusetts Strike of 1912, the Minnesota Mesabi Iron Range Strikes of 1907 and 1916, the many strikes in the coal-mining regions, all contributed to reassessing the role of women in labor activism. One of the most active women was Mary "Mother" Jones, who organized and led demonstrations of thousands of women in mining communities across the country.[32] In another example, during the Colorado Coal Strike of 1927–28 women were actively engaged in civil disobedience on the picket line and in demonstrations. According to historian Charles Bayard, under the leadership of women like Milka Sablich,

women marchers and leaders became so prominent and successful that by the end of the first week, fifteen were jailed in Walsenburg. . . . Ten other women led pickets in a demonstration . . . and threw rocks at the twelve mounted and armed guards and dared them to start a fight. . . . The new technique of using women strikers was soon extended into the Trinidad region.[33]

In another famous strike in the coal fields of southeastern Kansas in 1921, women took the situation into their own hands. In some ways, their story parallels what happened in Austin. During the fall of 1921, the local union president called for a work stoppage. He was taken to court and found guilty of breaking a state law requiring the use of an industrial court to mediate labor disputes. When he was jailed for breaking the law, the members of his local union protested by going out on strike. The local union's decision to strike was overruled by the international union—in this case, the United Mine Workers of America:

"John L. Lewis, the international president of the UMWA, condemned this action as a violation of contract and ordered the miners back to work. . . . The miners stayed out on strike without benefits from the national union."[34] On December 11 the women took action: 500 of them met in a church and issued a statement that supported their husbands, condemned the industrial court legislation, and addressed issues in support of democracy and justice.

According to historian Ann Schofield, the women "considered their cause one of conserving values, rather than one of revolt"—a militant defense of their basic rights to economic justice for their families. The next morning, December 12, between 2,000 and 3,000 women took to the streets to close down the mines throughout the region. A newspaper sympathetic to the strikers reported that the women's actions were peaceful; but other papers reported that strikebreakers' lunch buckets were smashed, and there were reports of men being attacked and badly beaten by some of the women. Forty-nine women were arrested as a result of the day's activities, and the Kansas National Guard was called in to keep the peace for the next two months.[35]

Women could get away with actions the men couldn't. The authorities were reluctant to attack the women, fearing a backlash from a public still protective of "fragile" womanhood. These advantages were quickly put into practice by labor activists. Elizabeth Jameson noted how women involved in the Cripple Creek Mining Strike used cultural taboos very effectively, by appealing to latent moral outrage over the treatment of women activists.

Notions of feminine weakness and gentility were used as class weapons in publicizing the excessive force used against labor. When the Women's Auxiliary was invaded by soldiers, women and children beaten by mine owners' gunmen, and women separated from their husbands, the employers and the state were attacked for violating womanhood and destroying the home. Women, however, could sometimes do things which men could not. . . . They crossed military lines without being imprisoned or shot; they and their children taunted scabs and soldiers, and otherwise harassed them. The militia tried to stop the women, but did not jail them.[36]

Very quickly the unions—and the women activists—learned to use women's gender to political advantage. According to Sally Maggard, in the 1973 Brookside, Kentucky, Coal Strike "no one seemed to know what to do with these disorderly women. It was a situation with no rules or norms."[37]

Gender was also a factor in Austin. For example, the training in civil disobedience tactics conducted by the Twin Cities chapter of Women Against Military Madness (WAMM) included gender-specific strategies.

We learned how to relax so it would force the police to use four officers to put you in the van. We also learned that if they touched you, you were to say, "Rape! You can't touch me there, you're a man!" We also were told that we had the right to have a matron, that they couldn't search us. We had them real baffled for a while. They didn't have a female matron. The sheriff's wife had to take on that role for a while. It was an experience for the police department to deal with women.[38]

Gender clearly was a factor in how police responded to and handled the protesters in some situations.

The day all the women went to the corporate office to shut that down—I was part of that, and I felt that, [we] being women, they were going to be more lenient. And I felt that they were. When the men got involved, the police got really crazy. They were a lot more tolerant of a bunch of women; they're a lot less threatening than a mixed crowd.[39]

The women in the Support Group had no trouble reconciling the contradictions between their newfound empowerment as women activists and their use of their gender to achieve their political objectives. As Patricia Higgins concluded, "The police were a lot more intimidated by a woman. They're not used to handling women. So, I really felt at times a sense of power. Being a woman was a plus more than a negative."

As the mood of the strike grew more embittered and the confrontations increased through the fall and winter of 1985–86, the women were not content with just bannering and passive picketing. After the plant was reopened in January, they took more direct action—including mass civil disobedience—that put them into direct confrontation with the company, with local law enforcement, and ultimately with the National Guard. Like the women in earlier strikes, the women in the Support Group were involved in a wide range of civil disobedience tactics such as blocking highway access to the plant, closing down the corporate headquarters by blocking the entrance, sit-ins on the streets, blocking the plant gates, and verbally harassing strikebreakers who crossed the line. In further defiance of the company, they actively organized local and national boycotts of Hormel products.

Participating in civil disobedience was an empowering and transformative experience for many of the women. Many were radicalized by standing up against the authorities and putting themselves personally at risk for what they believed. It brought the women together in a new way, changing them individually and as a group; and they were energized by the experience.

You got so caught up in what was going on, you didn't really think or worry about anything—being arrested or going to jail. I mean, you just got in the swing of it. When you stop to think, we stood out there—what was it? Seventy-two below zero? Froze our tushes off. You were scared to death, in a way—especially when the police started coming after you and shoving you around. You have all these people coming in from other places—all different cross sections of people. It was just the excitement. Your adrenaline was flowing. It was great. (Anon.)

Most of the women felt that the strategy of civil disobedience had a positive impact. These highly visible activities brought in the national media to report on the strike and expose the brutality of the police, thereby shifting public opinion behind the workers.[40] The women's training in nonviolent resistance served them especially well as they assumed a passive role, which was intended to make the police appear even more aggressive. Judy Himle recalled her experience as a protester.

The only civil disobedience I was part of was the closing of the north gate to scabs. We gathered at 4:30 in the morning. It was very dark and very cold. We were given a briefing on what would happen and what people should do. I remember the march the several blocks from the Support hall to the gate. Someone had a boombox playing "Which Side Are You On." In the darkness, with the numbers of people marching, it seemed a very sad and scary time. We grouped together and I didn't see anything there other than people holding hands and chanting and singing solidarity songs. The police came with their guns, dogs, gas masks, and tear gas and billy clubs. We were all standing there with no weapons—and ended up with such a bad image! What did they think we were going to do with no weapons? It was a nonviolent protest. And we always seemed to get bad PR.

For many of the women, the civil disobedience during the strike was their first experience with taking charge of and acting on their own beliefs. For Cindi Bellrichard, it was an empowering experience: "I felt strong. I just felt like I knew what was going to happen to me and I couldn't wait for it. I felt stronger than I've ever felt in my whole life." Many of the women talked about their fear and how they had to work hard to overcome it.

I didn't want to be arrested. I was scared. I was scared somebody would get hurt. The police came so close so many times to losing it. They saw civil disobedience as a war, as a defiance, and wanted to punish someone. There was also a sense of power, a sense of control. Civil disobedience wasn't over winning or losing. There was just a sense of control. In that situation, I controlled my own body. There was no anger involved in just sitting tough. It was just a big feeling that, by sitting in front of the gate, we had the power to shut down the Hormel Company—even for fifteen minutes or an hour or whatever.[41]

An important part of feeling empowered was sharing the experience with others and recognizing solidarity with others: "It just felt good as a group for me. I was very impressed with the unity of everybody. I felt like I had a little bit of power for a few minutes."[42] These collective activities made Rietta Pontius feel stronger and more powerful: "It was exhilarating. One time I thought we should just push it a bit more. You felt like you had some power behind you. There was numbers—and how could they pick out just you?" Another woman found herself taking risks with her physical safety.

Your adrenaline gets flowing when you're out on that line and you're going to stop those cars. I mean, you're just going to stop those cars. You think you can go and stand in front of these cars and they are going to stop. This one day, had not my girlfriends pulled me back, a scab would have run over me![43]

Most of the women who were involved in one or more direct-action activities felt strongly that these were important actions—even when they had to leave early, to get to work: "I had to be at work at seven. I worried that I would get arrested. I could never get arrested. I have claustrophobia very bad. When they gave the second call—'if you don't break it up, you're going to be arrested'— I was long gone under the viaduct!"[44] Not everyone was active or supportive, however. Some of the women were fearful of being involved, and others chose to sit on the sidelines.[45] A few women were very critical of the strategy of civil disobedience, feeling that the money spent posting bail was wasted and that the arrests only gave people criminal records.[46] Most, however, felt that civil disobedience was an extremely effective tactic. "Doing something" was extremely important to these women; and more than anything else the Support Group did together, the direct-action activities served to strengthen their resolve, to cement their unity, and to empower them.[47]

For many of the women who participated in civil disobedience, getting arrested and going to jail was another powerful radicalizing experience as they came into direct contact with the power of the police, the military, and the courts. Despite their fears and uncertainty, most of the women were quite willing to break the law nonviolently—and pay the penalties—to advance their cause. Going to jail clearly traumatized them but, at the same time, reaffirmed their commitments to the strike agenda and one another. It was their first experience with a jail environment: ordinary, law-abiding women seldom find themselves locked up in overcrowded and filthy cells. The women seemed to be particularly appalled by the dehumanizing conditions they found in the jail. The situation was exacerbated by the fact that Mower County was neither prepared for the massive numbers of protesters nor ready for the fact that they were women. Cindi Bellrichard's experience was representative.

I was one of the last ones arrested that day. They started at 7:30 in the morning, and it was about 12:00 or 12:30. They put us in the drunk tank. I think there were 115 of us that day; so by the time everybody had shuffled through there with their dirty snowboots, the place was filthy. There was just a couple of benches to sit on, so people were on the floors and all over the place where there was room. Then we got put into this cell. There was just uncovered mattresses on the cots. I think we had six bunks and there were thirteen of us. We had five toothbrushes to share. The toilet was filthy, the shower was filthy, and you felt like you didn't want to touch anything—you didn't want to lay on the mattress because you just knew there were bugs in it. It was very unpleasant.

Mary Arens was especially upset by the indifference to basic human needs for privacy, cleanliness, and medical care.

My whole body was broke out after I left that place. There were bugs, the place was filthy, paint was peeling off the walls. There was no privacy for the bathroom, we had to hold up blankets—the stool just sat right out in the middle of the room. Barb was sick, and she asked for a doctor and it took them hours to get her out of that cell.

Jeannie Bambrick was one of the woman who spent the night in the jail: "We were thrown little ratty blankets that had big holes in them. I mean, pathetic blankets. We didn't have enough cots for everyone, so they threw us some mattresses. And I mean literally *threw* us mattresses. It was just awful. We were treated like dirt." Despite the deplorable conditions, Marie Loverink looked back on her jail experience with a sense of humor: "I was supposed to be at work the next morning. My mother-in-law called my job and told them I was in jail. My boss thought it was funny and excused me. I guess the only real big problem I had was the Hormel chili they fed us in jail!"

For the women in the Support Group, putting their bodies on the line in a nonviolent way was an extremely effective way to argue their moral position. It was not just a technique to lower the level of violence or potential violence, but a way of taking the moral high ground. As Joel Kovel pointed out in *History and Spirit*, "Nonviolence is not an absence of violence . . . and it is certainly not passivity or inertia. . . . To be a nonviolent activist, rather, is to make oneself a kind of spiritual warrior."[48] According to Kovel, the task of the spiritual warrior is, first of all, to raise political consciousness in a given situation and, second, to undergo suffering in order to reduce the level of violence.

In a word, the nonviolent person accepts suffering. . . . It has to be picked up and shouldered before it can be thrown aside. By suffering and acting according to *ahimsa* [doing no harm], the nonviolent person is breaking the cycle of revenge by means of which violence reproduces itself. At the same time he or she is establishing a bond with the oppressed.[49]

This bond with others, this awareness of the collective nature of suffering in a specific political context, drives the moral imperative of nonviolent civil disobedience and gives it its sense of justice, its moral rightness. Nonviolent direct action strengthened and deepened the ties within the Support Group. Several women made reference to the feeling that what they were doing was right and how empowering it was to stand up for right.[50] As Barbara Collette recalled,

I don't think you can really "learn" civil disobedience. I think you have to do it to know what it is. The secret was believing that what I was doing was right. I'm not sure it accomplished anything, but I'd do it again, because you have to do something. I don't know if it was good or not. It was necessary.

Overall, the policy of nonviolent civil disobedience was extremely successful. Everyone kept their cool; people followed the rules and did not overly antagonize the police. Therefore, it was surprising that, given hindsight, many of the women felt more violence at the beginning of the strike might have shortened it. As their comments below attest, the women's candor and open advocacy of violence is not only surprising, but extraordinary, given that their actual behavior was nonviolent. And the advocacy of violence makes it seem all the more remarkable that more violence did not occur. The potential was certainly there: the lack of support and isolation from the community; the refusal of Hormel to negotiate; the loss of the strikers' livelihoods to replacement workers; the anger the strikers held toward the international union. In many ways, they had nothing to lose, and violence seemed an appropriate response.

Although legislation now outlaws the sit-down strike, one woman insisted that P–9 should have taken control of the plant in the very beginning.

When they first went out, and they showed the Spam line going on TV that night, I said to my husband, "You know, if it was me, I'd be on the phone and I'd have all 1,500 of you over there, and those foremen would not be running that line." I said, "You should have shut it down Day One." That's how I felt about it. They should have fought it from the inside [even] if they had to stay there a week. They could have done much more damage inside that plant than they ever did outside.[51]

The day the plant reopened was a turning point in many ways. One woman felt they compromised their position by not being more violent.

Maybe if we had been a little more violent, things would have been different. I know my husband feels that the very first car that went across should have been turned over and set on fire. If you're going to take a stand for something you believe in as strongly as we believed, you've got to go all the way. (Anon.)

Sally Ward Maggard noted a similar reference to violence in her study of the Brookside strike, where the women believed they should have used "ball bats" more.[52]

Historically, strikebreakers in particular seem to have elicited a violent response in women. Many political protests—and incidents of violence—involving women have been directed at strikebreakers. Perhaps this was because the strikebreaker was the most obvious threat to their survival, or perhaps because the strikebreaker represented an easily identifiable target for confrontation on the personal level. At the turn of the century on the Iron Range in Minnesota, for example, women smashed lunch buckets and threw "ancient hen fruit" at strikebreakers.[53] Many of the women in the Support Group expressed similar deep frustrations with strikebreakers—frustrations that almost pushed them to the point of interpersonal violence: "It's like you'd like to take them and shake them or hit them or kick them or something, just because you have nothing else that you can do about it and they had the upper hand. You felt like picking up a rock and throwing it" (Anon.). Several other women echoed this call for violence against the strikebreakers in particular, rather than against the police, the company, or other symbols of power: "The first person that walked across that picket line should have had their knees broken" (Anon.). Another woman put it this way: "We should have become mean, plain and simple. We should have put the fear of God into those scabs and they never would have crossed the line (Anon.).

This seeming advocacy of violence might be indicative of the level of frustration over the failure of their tactics to win the strike. It might be that women become more provoked when they believe their very survival is at stake. For women to be active at all requires, first of all, abandoning their traditionally passive role. Once women step out of that role, there are few rules to guide their behavior. The women's hindsight call for more drastic action, with its all-or-nothing edge, certainly spoke to the intensity of their commitment and the desperation they must have felt.

The potential for violence in labor struggles is always high, and the situation in Austin was no exception. Despite the length and bitterness of the strike, and the threat of state violence created by the presence of the National Guard, there was, overall, remarkably little overt violence. This was probably due, in part, to the early commitment by the Support Group to nonviolent tactics.

For the women of the Austin United Support Group, direct action took two separate but complementary tracks. These actions were critical to maintaining the strike culture. Economic direct action was organized around establishing and maintaining internal support systems to meet the striking community's survival needs. Political direct action focused on confrontations with external power structures to bring public opinion to bear on the company and the state. Both forms of direct action served the purpose of enhancing solidarity behind the strike objectives and of giving those involved a sense of power and control over their lives. As one woman put it, "I felt like I had a little bit of power" (Anon.). It was the power of solidarity through collective action—a power that drew its energy from caring for and mutually supporting one another, and from a commitment to economic democracy.

NOTES

1. There are innumerable resources on women's participation in the labor movement. Selected items of interest include: Diane Balser, *Sisterhood and Solidarity: Feminism and Labor in Modern Times* (Boston, 1987); Ava Baron, ed., *Work Engendered: Toward a New History of American Labor* (Ithaca, N.Y., and London, 1991); Rosalyn Fraad Baxandall, *Words on Fire: The Life and Writing of Elizabeth Gurley Flynn* (New Brunswick, N.J., and London, 1987); Lynn Beaton, *Shifting Horizons* (London, 1985); Dorothy Sue Cobble, *Dishing It Out: Waitresses and Their Unions in the Twentieth Century* (Urbana and Chicago, 1991); Carole Conde and Karl Beveridge, *First Contract: Women and the Fight to Unionize* (Toronto, 1986); Cynthia B. Costello, " 'WEA're Worth It!' Work Culture and Conflict at the Wisconsin Education Association Insurance Trust," *Feminist Studies* 11, 3 (Fall 1985): 497–518; Nancy Schrom Dye, "Feminism or Unionism? The New York Women's Trade Union League and the Labor Movement," *Feminist Studies* 3, 1/2 (Fall 1975): 111–25; Herman Erickson, "WPA Strike and Trials of 1939," *Minnesota History* 42, 6 (Summer 1971): 202–14; Elizabeth Faue, *Community of Suffering and Struggle: Women, Men, and the Labor Movement in Minneapolis, 1915–1945* (Chapel Hill, N.C., and London, 1991); Elizabeth Gurley Flynn, *The Rebel Girl: An Autobiography* (New York, 1973); Jim Green, "Culture, Politics, and Workers' Response to

Industrialization in the U.S." *Radical America* 16, 1–2 (January/February, March/April 1982): 101–28; Maurine Weiner Greenwald, "Working-class Feminism and the Family Wage Ideal: The Seattle Debate on Married Women's Right to Work, 1914–1920," *Journal of American History* 76, 1 (June 1989): 118–49; Mary Harris Jones, *Autobiography of Mother Jones*, ed. Mary Field Parton (Chicago, 1925); Alice Kessler-Harris, *Out to Work: A History of Wage-earning Women in the United States* (New York, 1982); Molly Ladd-Taylor, "Women Workers and the Yale Strike," *Feminist Studies* 11, 3 (Fall 1985): 465–89; Ellen Lewin, "Feminist Ideology and the Meaning of Work: The Case of Nursing," *Catalyst* 10–11 (Summer 1977): 78–103; Ruth Milkman, ed., *Women, Work, & Protest: A Century of U.S. Women's Labor History* (New York and London, 1987); Hanna Papanek, "Family Status Production: The 'Work' and 'Non-work' of Women," *Signs: Journal of Women in Culture and Society* 4, 4 (Summer 1979): 775–81; Greta Foff Paules, *Dishing It Out: Power and Resistance among Waitresses in a New Jersey Restaurant* (Philadelphia, 1991); Vicki Seddon, ed., *The Cutting Edge: Women and the Pit Strike* (London, 1986); Sharon Hartman Strom, "Challenging 'Woman's Place': Feminism, the Left, and Industrial Unionism in the 1930s," *Feminist Studies* 9, 2 (Summer 1983): 360–86; and Guida West and Rhoda Lois Blumberg, eds., *Women and Social Protest* (New York and Oxford, England, 1990).

2. Louise A. Tilly, "Paths of Proletarianization: Organization of Production, Sexual Division of Labor, and Women's Collective Action," *Signs: Journal of Women in Culture and Society* 7, 2 (Winter 1981): 400–17.

3. Faue, *Community of Suffering and Struggle*.

4. Neil Betten, "Riot, Revolution, Repression in the Iron Range Strike of 1916," *Minnesota History* 41, 2 (Summer 1968): 82–93.

5. Ann Schofield, "The Women's March: Miners, Family, and Community in Pittsburg, Kansas, 1921–22," *Kansas History* 7, 2 (Summer 1984): 159–68.

6. Cindi Bellrichard.

7. Jeannie Bambrick.

8. Carol King.

9. LaVonne Ferguson.

10. Linda Novak.

11. Hormel increased its advertising expenditures 50 percent from 1984 to 1985, for example, to an amount of $70 million. Profits in 1985 were up 30.9 percent over 1984. Doniver Adolph Lund and V. Allan Krejci, *The Hormel Legacy: 100 Years of Quality* (Austin, Minn., 1991), 188.

12. Cindi Bellrichard.

13. Dave Hage and Paul Klauda, *No Retreat, No Surrender: Labor's War at Hormel* (New York, 1989), 204.

14. Susan Benson.

15. Carol Kough.

16. Mary Arens.

17. Hage and Klauda, *No Retreat, No Surrender*, 201.

18. Patricia Higgins.

19. Vickie Guyette; Jan Kennedy; Cheryl Remington.

20. Mary Machacek.

21. Cheryl Remington.

22. Carol King.

23. LaVonne Ferguson.

24. Carol Kough.

25. Hage and Klauda, *No Retreat, No Surrender*, 201.

26. Donna Simon.

27. Carole Apold.

28. Billie Goodeu.

29. Julie Wilson.

30. Judy Himle.

31. Cindi Bellrichard.

32. Jones, *Autobiography of Mother Jones*.

33. Charles J. Bayard, "The 1927–1928 Colorado Coal Strike," *Pacific Historical Review* 32, 3 (August 1963): 240.

34. Schofield, "The Women's March," 164.

35. Ibid., 164–67.

36. Elizabeth Jameson, "Imperfect Unions: Class and Gender in Cripple Creek, 1894–1904," *Frontiers* 1, 2 (Spring 1976): 105.

37. Sally Ward Maggard, "Gender Contested: Women's Participation in the Brookside Coal Strike," in *Women and Social Protest*, ed. West and Blumberg, 85–86.

38. Patricia Higgins.

39. Cheryl Remington.

40. Donna Simon.

41. Barbara Collette.

42. Michelle Hendrickson.

43. Billie Goodeu.

44. LaVonne Ferguson.

45. Carmel Taylor.

46. Carole Apold; Cheryl Remington.

47. Judy Himle.

48. Joel Kovel, *History and Spirit: An Inquiry into the Philosophy of Liberation* (Boston, 1991), 150.

49. Ibid., 151.

50. Carmel Taylor, Susan Benson.

51. All of the comments in this section where the women talk about violence are cited as being "anonymous," whether or not the women asked for that designation.

52. Sally Ward Maggard, "Women's Participation in the Brookside Coal Strike: Militancy, Class, and Gender in Appalachia," *Frontiers* 9, 3 (1987): 19.

53. Betten, "Riot, Revolution, Repression."

CHAPTER 8

"Everybody Just Pitched In"

While most of the public attention on the Hormel/P–9 Strike was focused on the highly visible protests, rallies, and demonstrations, the real work of the strike went on behind the scenes. The logistics involved in creating and maintaining an economic and political organization that could sustain the striking families for more than three years were staggering. To the casual observer, the Support Group did not seem a likely vehicle for raising millions of dollars, maintaining an international public relations outreach effort, planning and implementing strike strategy, and caring for the day-to-day needs of from 800 to 1,500 families. So how did the members do it? How did they organize themselves to get the work done? This chapter will explore the critical questions of organizational structure and maintenance, the relationship between the Support Group and P–9, and issues surrounding leadership, conflict, and gender expectations.

The organizational structure of the Support Group was, from the very beginning, a fairly haphazard affair. The women who organized the early meetings were not terribly concerned with establishing a formal institution. Vickie Guyette reported, for example, that a few women "just kind of did the meetings until we had an election." Although the Support Group eventually did elect a formal slate of officers and for a while functioned in fairly traditional ways, it was probably best characterized as a highly effective informal and participatory democratic organization.

This informal structure emerged in part from a conscious commitment to democratic principles, and partly in response to the disestablishment of P–9. In June 1986, the UFCW trustees—armed with court orders covering everything from banning boycotts to taking control of checking accounts—moved to replace the now outlawed P–9.[1] All semblance of official organization and structure among the strikers quickly disappeared as the precarious legal situation forced both P–9 and the Support Group into a new combined informal organization: "for legal reasons we were absolutely structureless. If you had walked in and said, 'Who's in charge here?' everybody would have looked at each other and said, 'I don't know.' "[2]

The new structureless turned out to be a godsend, according to Vickie Guyette: "I remember Jim telling me that one of the beauties of it was that we were so loose knit, so the lawyers couldn't get at us, the company couldn't get at us. We weren't incorporated or anything. We were just a bunch of people getting together." The fear of potential financial and criminal liability meant that many individuals were reluctant to shoulder formal leadership responsibility, as well. The less anybody knew, the less they could tell if they were ever called into court, and the less likely it would be that individuals could be held personally responsible.

INFORMAL STRUCTURE: GETTING THE WORK DONE

Despite its informality, the Support Group was not without order and direction. According to Vickie Guyette, business was conducted without benefit of officers, constitution, or bylaws: "Before all the fighting started, I think the structure was informal. Probably just groups of women just talking and saying, 'Hey, that would be a good idea.' We'd always bring it up at a meeting and discuss it." In a now classic article on informal women's organizations—entitled "The Tyranny of Structurelessness"—Jo Freeman identified some of the characteristics of such successful, informal working groups: they are task oriented, small and homogeneous, and committed to a high level of communication—qualities emphasizing intimacy and a high degree of interaction.[3] Like traditional volunteer associations, radical political collectives, and modern feminist organizations, the Support Group shared these same organizational characteristics. It was a very personal organization, the foundations of which were a deep respect for the personal lives of members, an attentiveness to maintaining strong interpersonal ties, and an appreciation of individual contributions. Information was widely shared; there was open communication and a high degree of personal interaction.

In addition, the members of the Support Group placed a high value on participation. They were consciously committed from the very beginning to democratic principles: decision-making was nonhierarchical and structurally decentralized; and in the large open meetings, the majority ruled and everyone had a right to speak. According to Jo Freeman, such democratic processes are vital if an organization seeks to enhance members' participation. Structural criteria that ensure democratic process include the decentralization of authority and information, the self-directed leader, a close relationship between doing work and exercising power, and democratic decision-making.[4]

Although informal organizations enhance participation, according to Freeman, they can create other problems. There must be some structure—some organizing principle—and "the structure must be explicit, not implicit," she concluded, because in the absence of formal structure a power vacuum occurs, and it is more likely either that power will be abused or that none of the work will get done.[5] Several women felt that this was a problem in the Support Group. The organization was chaotic and ineffective because it lacked explicit structure: "It was entirely too informal. It was terribly disorganized. But we just didn't have the time to prepare. We were all thrown into it. There was no organization whatsoever."[6] Without knowing who was in charge of doing what, resources of time, money, and people were wasted.

Nevertheless, the majority of the women felt the informal structure worked very well, and that by and large the Support Group had accomplished its goals. Some of the women felt that the organization worked even better *because* the structure was informal. Two qualities of the informal structure that were most appreciated were the Support Group's decentralized decision-making and its record of timely task completion. The decentralized, loose-knit structure was open to everyone interested, and served as a mechanism for involving many people and giving them a personal stake in Support Group activities. It also created an environment for appreciating diversity and difference. Because communication and action involved many people and did not just come from the top down, people learned to interact with one another in a collaborative manner. This, in turn, facilitated getting the work done in a timely manner.

Most of the work was done in committees formed by women stepping forward and volunteering to work on a given task or program.

The committees came about afterwards as they were needed. You just kind of rose to the occasion. The informal power structure was basically within the committees. Sometimes there was a crossover about who's responsibility something was, and it caused some hard feelings. But basically, people got together and got things done.[7]

Each committee operated relatively independently, with its own checking account and internally selected leaders.[8] The committees reported their decisions back to the larger group on a regular basis; "and if anybody had a problem with it, they could speak up then."[9] The heads of the committees also met together; and occasionally, decisions were made at this level: "We had a steering committee. That worked pretty good. Actually, the steering committee was just everybody who did anything."[10] The committees were very task-oriented work groups. And although each committee functioned fairly autonomously, the women quickly realized that it was important that the committees work together cooperatively.

The only way anyone had any power was if everyone worked together. You had to raise funds, for example. You had to go out and do whatever had to be done. That's the only way individuals had any power. Then you have to give power to someone to stay in the office and do whatever had to be done there. It took everybody working at different things.[11]

Within the committees, the organization of the work itself was based on individual volunteerism. In fact, in describing what they did in the Support Group, many of the women characterized themselves as "volunteers." The essence of such volunteer work—in Mary Arens's eyes, for example—was that it was driven by personal motivation and allowed freedom and independence of action.

I don't remember electing anybody. The way I ended up in the Food Shelf was, one day I went down to fold leaflets and the tables were all full. And Lorraine said, "Well, why don't you go down and see if they need some help with the Food Shelf?" And I never left.

Several of the women commented that their volunteer status gave them a feeling of independence and power: "Everybody was a volunteer, and you couldn't tell a volunteer what to do and how to do it."[12] Furthermore, volunteers were free to express their own ideas: "It doesn't matter whether it's the church or Scouts or wherever, but when you get volunteers, they're gonna get in their little niche and express their opinions. I don't think it's because they're women; I think it's because they're volunteers."[13] Because they were all volunteers, the women found common ground for mutual respect. The willingness of the volunteer to work hard was deeply appreciated, as was the commitment to the cause of the strike. This mutual respect for each others' contributions was important in the exercise of leadership, as well: "A lot of it got started with somebody just volunteering. Pretty soon, well, they're doing such a good job, we'll just put them at the head of this. I'm sure I wouldn't do something that was delegated! People just started in and pretty soon they involved other people."[14] Sometimes this spirit of independence and the refusal to control or direct others took on a humorous note: "Somebody—that was the word, 'somebody'—needs to do this. We all laughed about that—'Well, who is somebody?!!' "[15]

Overall, the work of the Support Group was suffused with this volunteering and cooperative spirit. In times of community crisis or natural disaster, people are especially motivated to help one another, and the strike created just such an occasion for mutual aid in Austin. According to Joyce Rothschild-Whitt in her study of 1960s counterculture institutions, informal volunteer efforts are often initiated in response to situations of great economic need or when an organization is short of funds. Economic need, in turn, helps build community because work then becomes a "labor of love," bringing people together to support and sustain one another.[16]

Volunteer efforts in the Support Group contributed to an appreciation of others and helped build a climate of inclusiveness and tolerance. Because it was a volunteer effort, the organization was open enough that differences were overlooked and the contribution of everyone was appreciated and respected.

There was a lot of flexibility in it, I believe. I think no matter how you felt you could probably find someone else who felt the same way. It wasn't like all those people just had one opinion. If it had been that way, I don't think it would have lasted so long.[17]

The very nature of volunteer work meant that one couldn't choose one's help-mates. This contributed, in general, to an atmosphere of tolerance. Differences had to be overlooked in order to get the work done.

More or less everyone seemed to be able to work together. I think that anybody that rubs elbows, that spent that much time together, it's gonna be like a family. You love one another, but you're also not always gonna get along. You're always going to see some abuse. Everybody comes from a different perspective.[18]

By empowering a wide range of people to become involved, informal structures encourage diversity and difference as leadership becomes decentralized and as individuals find that their viewpoints are welcome. But like "family," informal structures can also mean conflict and other tensions, leading in some instances to open challenges to power or refusal to cooperate. For example, people could just pick up and leave whenever they felt unappreciated. It was important to the group's solidarity, therefore, that people learn to get along and accommodate their sometimes vast differences.

In this atmosphere of freedom and independence, democratic decision-making processes were consciously set in place. There was always a strong commitment to the democratic principle of one woman, one vote—with the majority determining the outcome. Both within the committees and in the large open meetings that the group held for many years, open discussions sometimes went on for hours and were followed by a vote of those present.

We never did do a fluffy formal stage where you had to second motions and things like that. I don't think any of us cared too much about whether we were formal or not. If somebody had something to say, they could just raise their hand, be called on, and then stand up and talk. If a decision had to be made, the president would just say, "Let's take a vote"—and there would be a show of hands. I don't think we ever took written secret ballots.[19]

There was a keen sense of the power of the group, according to Donna Simon, and the desire to respect it as a collective decision-making body: "I think decisions were made democratically. It's the whole people that are the Support Group. The majority of decisions were group decisions." Judy Himle, too, felt that everyone had a voice in making decisions.

People were made to feel welcome and asked to participate. I think the people were the power in the Support Group. Those people that were in power, or that were some of the leaders in the Support Group, never made final decisions on what got said and done. It was always the vote of the people.

For the most part, the Support Group was perceived to be open and democratic. This was due in part to the freedom that people felt in expressing their viewpoints and criticizing decisions being made. Many of the women commented on the openness of the discussions: "It was always a free forum. Anyone could be there and state their opinion. It didn't necessarily end up with everyone agreeing, but at least people got to come and state their side of the issue."[20] This openness was a major factor in maintaining the group's solidarity, because people felt they could participate.

When the need for secrecy developed after the UFCW takeover, these open forums were seriously compromised, and group solidarity was weakened. Democracy is, by its nature, intensely personal and requires face-to-face interaction and communication. We often overlook this expressive aspect of democracy and the need for debate, dialogue, and even dissension. In an environment where people feel free to be themselves and to express their opinions, open communication enhances a participatory and democratic style. The climate of secrecy hampered this communication, and was the source of much conflict and tension in the group. One woman noted its impact on the decision-making process: "To start with, they used to vote on things—if there was something to be changed; or, 'Shall we do this?' But after a while, that process just wasn't there anymore. The decisions were just made. And that's not good. Decisions should have been voted on."[21] When the open forum was shut down, decision-making was redirected into the committees and work groups, each with its own agenda. The climate of secrecy also led to an increase in contentious individual and personal politics.

It was supposed to be a democratic organization—you should have the right to agree or disagree. Many times I did disagree, and I didn't tell it to someone else—I told it to the mass of people. I have a lot of bad feelings about what went on. I'll name names and tell it to people's faces. That's what was lacking. People were being talked about behind their backs. It was all this little secret group here, and little group there. It was never brought to the mass of people to decide on democratically. I mean, heavens, before we had the first bake sale, everybody voted on it! Then down the line, nobody knew what was going on. You got bits and pieces. Nobody was allowed to vote. (Anon.)

LEADERSHIP ISSUES

Leadership is an issue in all organizations, formal or informal. In formal structures, everyone "knows" that an individual is the leader of the group merely by virtue of that person's holding the office and title of "leader." The absence of a clearly defined leadership structure in informal organizations, however, enhances the potential for confusion or conflict over who does, or should, lead. Despite the fact that there was an elected leadership, most of the women in the Support Group agreed that an informal leadership network really ran things. As Barbara Collette recalled, President Jan Butts's leadership was superseded by a group the women called the "inner circle" or the "network": "Jan was in charge of holding meetings and helping to organize some of the demonstrations, but I never believed for a minute that she was the person with the power. The president's job was basically a figurehead job. There never was a real chain of command."

Theoretically, then, in the absence of an agreed-on leadership, anyone could be in charge of the Support Group. When one woman was asked who ran things, for example, her response was quite pragmatic: "Who we went to to get the money to buy the groceries."[22] Reflecting this general confusion over who was doing the leading, Jan Kennedy recalled, "I felt like everyone was just saying and doing what someone told them to say and do. I guess the stardust just kind of blew right away. I think somebody else was directing it." In addition to the working committees, there were other informal power relations that operated in the Support Group. For example, the group's founders had a strong influence; and the women who worked in the office—Carole Apold, Barbara Collette, Vickie Guyette, Patricia Higgins, and Cindy Rud—functioned fairly effectively as a work group and were perceived as having major leadership roles. There were also external groups that had varying degrees of input into both the operations and the decision-making process: fundraising work groups; the executive committee of P–9; Ray Rogers and the Corporate Campaign; the UFCW. Several women felt that P–9 and Jim Guyette—and to some extent, the Corporate Campaign—really controlled things. However, while these "outsiders" did have some influence, according to Patricia Higgins, they never actually took control of Support Group activities. One of the women also mentioned that the Socialist Workers Party (SWP) had a leadership role. The SWP had done some organizing nationally around the strike issues, and had provided other assistance; but by and large, the Support Group was free of external ideologies.[23] And anyway, despite their acknowledgment of these competing influences, everyone in the group believed that the inner circle was the real leadership.

One major problem with informal leadership like the inner circle, according to J. Freeman, is its relationship to the group as a whole. Without some kind of public group affirmation of the leadership, there is no way to control what informal leaders do. In the case of the Support Group inner circle, the failure of the group to recognize its power formally, and the lack of a formal means of accountability for its decisions, raised questions about the legitimacy of its power. Others in the group then tended to become anxious about decisions made by this ad hoc group. Freeman comments that, in the case of such leaders, because "their power was not given to them; it cannot be taken away."[24] According to Freeman, informal leadership like the inner circle is often based on close personal friendships; and in fact, several of the women who were perceived as leaders in the Support Group had been close friends for some time.[25] This can be problematic, in Freeman's eyes, because "the informal structure of decision-making will be much like a sorority—one in which people listen to others because they like them and not because they say significant things."[26]

In the absence of a process for legitimizing the Support Group's informal leadership, problems determining the locus of decision-making emerged, and power struggles erupted on several fronts. Several of the women resented the inner circle because they felt those women purposely clouded the issues and kept information from the group as a whole: "Sometimes decisions were handled by the group, but often the group was not given the information to be able to make a decision. A lot of information was withheld, I think, and decisions were made by the network."[27] The critics were especially uncomfortable with what they perceived to be an ad hoc class structure in the Support Group. It was dominated by the inner circle, with everyone else at the bottom.

No one really knew what their duties were. The only time we knew what work was done was when they didn't want to do it themselves—then they'd give it out to the rest of us. They didn't delegate the responsibility; they delegated the work. I don't think the inner group ever trusted the drones, the workers, the people that did the work. I felt I was just as good and equal to those that were in the inner circle, but they wouldn't allow me to be equal. I wasn't jealous exactly, but I felt I would be able to step in and do whatever they were doing, too.[28]

In the absence of formal lines of power, there was a perception that individual contributions lost credibility as the inner circle became the decision-making body: "I remember one time I spoke up and said what I thought, and Jim Guyette put it down; but when it was brought up later by Vickie, it became a good idea. Until it became the inner circle's idea, it meant nothing."[29] The inner circle could also wield a subtle power on the interpersonal level. Linda Novak felt some of these pressures.

If you were supposed to do something—like getting arrested or something—if that was the thing to do according to certain people, you had better be there. Otherwise, they wouldn't talk to you. It was as simple as that. I just overcame it; I just did what I wanted. I know a couple of times I called Vickie and they would say, "We don't need any help." You knew darn well there were fifteen women down there doing something. So I quit calling and just barged right in and started doing something. If you didn't just take charge and not let these women affect you, you probably wouldn't go.

While some of the women saw groups of women—or cliques—in the leadership roles, others identified powerful individuals who led by force of character or personal charisma. Vickie Guyette was most often identified as a strong leader. Although a few women felt that her leadership hinged on the fact that Jim Guyette (president of P–9) was her husband, Vickie was generally perceived as a strong charismatic leader in her own right.

Vickie Guyette was a strong leader. Just imagewise, too. She was there all the time, and she was behind the efforts. She emulated what we all felt. Everyone got to know her fast because of her long hair. If you didn't know her before, you knew her after the first rally. She was a force just by her presence and her motivation. Her attitude—she was energy.[30]

Other individual leaders identified by the interviewees included Carole Apold, Barbara Collette, Michelle Hendrickson, Patricia Higgins, and Carmine Rogers. Shirley Heegard commented on some of the qualities that made these women stand out.

I think Barb had a lot of power. She had one of those personalities that people felt comfortable with following. I think that Carmine was very, very supportive, very, very hard working. I think she probably did a lot of leading, not realizing that some people are just leaders.

In general, however, more of the women defined "leadership" in terms of personal qualities, rather than personality. It was not so much who you were that made you a leader, but what you did, how committed you were, what kind of skills you had, and what kind of person you were. Women who were well spoken and articulate, for example, were often seen as leaders: "I think a lot of it depended on how well you could address the group of people. If you were a good speaker, you could convince people to do almost anything."[31] The relationship between the ability to speak and leadership may be especially important to women, since communication and social skills are perceived to be highly gendered in American culture. Verbal skills were also tied to the ability to articulate the group's vision. Vickie Guyette's strong leadership role hinged, in part, on her communication skills. Her abilities made her stand out, according to Barb Frandle, but did not necessarily give her power: "I can't say who controlled it. It's just that they are far more verbal types of people. Vickie had a way of saying things; she had a lot of emotion—like she's saying a lot of things from her heart."[32]

Leadership was not only a matter of personal characteristics. It was often shaped by general environmental, organizational, or structural qualities. The open informal structure had an additional dividend: it provided a space where women had the freedom and opportunity to develop leadership skills. Further, the supportive climate enhanced the belief that individual women could take on new challenges, and any woman could become a leader. Susan Benson expressed this growing sense of collective self-confidence and empowerment.

For a while, we followed Ray Rogers. But as things progressed, we learned more and more about the tremendous talent and expertise and skills and leadership qualities that others had. When they arose, they weren't objected to. If somebody took a leadership role and banded a group together and took them out on the road, one became the leader and nobody else minded.

The women identified two major organizational characteristics that influenced the locus of power and control in the Support Group: (1) power could be informal and decentralized; and (2) leadership was closely linked to taking responsibility for work. All of the women were in agreement that the formal elected leadership did not have any power, and that power operated instead in many informal ways at many levels. As a result, leadership was fluid and dynamic: it could be found in groups or in individuals, and it could change from time to time or from task to task. Susan Benson described how this informal leadership style worked.

I never experienced any power struggle. When the leaders emerged, they never saw themselves as leaders; they weren't on an ego trip, because there was no title, no paycheck, with it. It was just a job that had to be done. And they got agreement from other people—they confirmed that it was a good idea. The other people were glad they came up with the idea, and worked just as hard as the leader did in developing that idea, to make that idea work. Now that I think about it, it was probably a perfect example of leadership and workers working together, because there wasn't the division of classes. That's how leadership should work. Everybody just pitched in.

Leadership was often defined in a very instrumental and pragmatic way. People who did the work got to be the leaders: "If you could type, or run copies off—that was just your position if you were qualified to do it. It just seemed like everything did fit in place and everything did get done."[33] In the informal environment of the Support Group, leadership was "doing," and not just being up in front running the meetings. There was little respect for people who didn't want to work; and it was clear, from many of the women's comments, that it was the women who did a lot of the strike's work. In general, respect for each other's work was essential; and whenever this mutual respect was absent, there were tensions within the organization. Carol King, among others, felt that the contributions of the "drones"—as she called herself and the other women who did a lot of the work in the Support Group—were not always appreciated.

I was resentful. And I still am, to a certain degree. The thing that makes me the most angry is that—now that it's done and broken up, where is the inner circle? They're gone. It's the drones that are still here. They're the ones that are keeping the unit together.

Leadership was also linked to time spent on the task—a perception common in settings where informal leadership operates. According to Jo Freeman, the amount of time that people can spend with a group is directly proportional to their ability to participate effectively in decision-making or to take a leadership role.[34] Leaders in the Support Group often tended to be individuals who had the time to spend down at the office; and the more time they spent there, the more likely they were to solidify their leadership roles. As one woman noted, she was quite comfortable deferring leadership to her more active colleagues.

I had no problems with how it was handled. The people who had to take those offices worked twenty-four hours a day, and some of us couldn't do that. They gave their whole lives to it, and everyone should be darn thankful. Even though they weren't voted in, if we had not believed in what they were doing we would have pushed for more democracy. But everybody felt it was fine.[35]

Being a leader in the Support Group was not always easy. The people who did the most work also came in for the most criticism—sometimes unfairly: "The ones that had authority, they always got criticized because they weren't doing something right. But the people that were criticizing were sitting there doing nothing" (Anon). Over and over, the women identified "doing something" with having the right to make decisions about it, and they resented it when criticism came from others: "The same with the Food Shelf. People griped, but nobody wanted the job."[36] Carole Apold was one of the women who had been criticized, and she remembered how she felt: "I think some people wanted me off the checking accounts, but nobody wanted to take that job over. Nobody was willing to do what I did. I'd spent twelve hours a day down at that union hall. I was there from morning to night, working."

Work was also seen as a great leveler; and leaders had a special responsibility consciously to reject internal differences and power differentials, and to do their share of the common work. Those leaders who did not carry their weight by performing mundane tasks met with resentment and hostility.

The drones. I was a drone. I'd go down and work eight hours a day mailing out that stuff. It might take us a week to get that done. The inner circle was laughing and drinking coffee, playing Ping-Pong, eating popcorn. And I felt that, if there wasn't work to be done at that time in their office, they should have been helping us fold and stuff envelopes—not just the glory jobs.[37]

Overall, this identification between work and leadership was so strong that some women joked that they would just as soon not be leaders: "It got to the point where you didn't want to suggest anything because you had to do it!"[38]

CONFLICT ISSUES

People are generally reluctant to acknowledge the presence of conflict within their organizations; but according to political theorist Jane Mansbridge in *Beyond Adversary Democracy*, conflict is healthy—and indeed, quite important—in maintaining open democratic organizations.[39] Ironically, the more democratic an organization is, the more conflict there will be. Mansbridge argued that, where principles of direct democracy operate, there is a high level of bickering and arguing: "politics involves conflict. Face-to-face confrontation increases the tension dramatically."[40] A corollary to this premise, however, is the assumption that, in democratic organizations, conflict will eventually come to closure. No organization can sustain continued divisiveness, and the challenge is to maintain a subtle balance between conflict and consensus. Not everyone is comfortable with conflict, Mansbridge pointed out; and an aversion to conflict can lead people to leave the group. So, every effort must be made to resolve differences. People may also be too intimidated to speak in a conflict-filled situation.[41]

As an informal organization committed to highly participatory and democratic principles, the Support Group found that conflict was inevitable. As one women cynically commented, "They fought over the money, the power, who said what or supposedly who said what, who did what, and who went where."[42] In particular, there were power struggles over who should lead. In general, however, these debates seemed not to focus on anyone's desire to *be* the leader or to take control, but rather on limiting the power of others, or at least seeking clarity and affirmation about who was really in charge.

Conflict can take many forms, and can erupt over seemingly petty things. But despite the discomfort that many people experience with it, conflict can be an important way to maintain group solidarity and reestablish the balance of power in the group while keeping the overarching goals and objectives intact and free from conflict. Arguments in informal organizations must be resolved quickly, though. As Billie Goodeu pointed out, unresolved internal tensions within the Support Group tended to drain energy away from the real enemy: "When I would hear there was dissension, I would try to patch up that dissension, because we were bucking a powerful greedy corporation—we didn't need fighting amongst ourselves."

It is especially difficult for women to deal with conflict, because being nice to others is an important part of how women traditionally have defined themselves. As Jeannie Bambrick put it, women learn to play by "Mommies' rules" that teach us to be nice and avoid confrontation: "It's the way you're raised. Men go to work and they play by men's rules. Women learn Mommies' rules— to be polite, to not mouth off to people." Sometimes, as one woman charged, this attitude went too far—as when the women tried to cover up the presence of conflict because they were concerned about maintaining an external image of solidarity.

The Support Group got good publicity because nobody really knew what the inner workings of it were, what was really going on, the turmoil. You could put on a really good show when people would come from out of town and they wanted to know how to form a support group. You never told them anything bad. It was always the good things: how you can form one; what your goals should be. Not what was going on actually. (Anon.)

According to Mansbridge, the more homogeneous an organization is and the more informal the leadership is, the more personalized the conflict within it will be and the "more likely [its members are] to explain conflict in terms of will or personality."[43] This was often the case with the Support Group. In the absence of a formalized and open collective forum in which to resolve their disagreements and resentments, the members of the Support Group tended to personalize their complaints. Sometimes, tensions erupted in verbal attacks on individual women:

"It would be like a personal attack or vendetta if you disagree with them. They'd find some way to get rid of you" (Anon.). There was no collective means of channeling or controlling confrontations between individuals, as Rietta Pontius recalled: "It started that problems were brought out in the group or the committees and talked about. But it got to a point where people were stabbing people in the back, talking behind their backs." According to Carmel Taylor, this fear of being personally attacked sometimes served to stifle dissent.

When I didn't agree with what was going on, I sat back and talked to somebody else about it later. It wasn't worth getting into a shouting match if you didn't agree. It was better than opening your mouth and have somebody sit there and say, "Who does she think she is?" I just wasn't up to the criticism that could have gone on.

Mansbridge also pointed out that conflict can sometimes result from "differing interpretations of the common interest."[44] This premise is especially important in analyzing conflict within the Support Group because of the ideologically charged atmosphere in which the organization operated. There were a variety of ways in which the women evaluated one another's commitment to the common good. Sometimes, tensions over the acceptable level of time commitment would influence a woman's decision to quit, for example. Either she was shamed by others for not coming to the meetings very often, or she would censor herself and drop out: "If you hadn't been around for a while and you came in, you felt kind of guilty and uncomfortable. So, once you left, it was easier to stay away. I don't think people made you feel that way; I think it was just your own discomfort."[45] In other cases, women just weren't about to make the kinds of political or ideological commitments they felt were required of them—either because they didn't fully support the goals of the group, or because they didn't like the way things were done. Jan Kennedy expressed her disappointment over the general direction of the strike.

I guess I wasn't hearing enough answers, enough right answers—why they were doing these things, and what their ultimate plan was. It bothered me that we were supposed to blindly sit there and say, "Yeah, we're winning." I think I saw things that people who were there every day didn't see. It's like, if you watch a movie with bad language in it for the first time, you notice it; but after you watch them over and over, you don't even hear the words anymore. I was home most of the time. And the few times I'd come down, I'd see things. There was no plan, and it was like you were constantly brainwashed into some false hope or something.

The excessive demand for commitment of both time and energy resulted in high levels of stress that soon approached the burnout level. According to Julie Wilson, it was usually at this point that people left the group.

I think everybody had a burnout point. Sometimes it would be a silly thing that would trigger it, and then they'd be done with the Support Group. As people dropped out, they really dropped out. It was like you couldn't come day-to-day and then miss a week and come back. Once you left, it was really hard to come back. I don't know how you overcome that. Also, they usually left angry about something. But it wasn't actually what they were angry about; it was burnout.

It might have been only a minor thing they were angry about. People who couldn't keep up the pace—whether they set it for themselves or whether it was expected of them by other members of the group—soon dropped out. The all-or-nothing environment left people with few options.

Everything was so concentrated—the energy was so concentrated that I think they failed to see that you're going to reach burnout. Maybe what we needed was some kind of oasis for people to go to—maybe even have a nice dinner—where it's off limits to talk about the strike, or Hormel. It maybe would have given them a chance to regroup and come back and fight hard the next day. Some strong leaders burned out. Maybe if they could have come back and worked at a different level—not speaking, but just folding envelopes or something. It would have been nice for people to have worked at different levels and not always at the top and be pushed.[46]

Conflict is further compounded in informal organizations where leadership is not clearly defined. Barbara Collette felt that this was the case with the Support Group, and that it hampered the group's effectiveness: "We were always trying to find out who was the leader, who was it. And I think it switched daily, hourly, minute-by-minute sometimes." Without formal leadership, control of an organization can fall into the hands of "stars," where individual women end up capturing the limelight for any number of reasons—either because they are more articulate, or because they happened to be in a certain place at a certain time—but not because they were chosen by the group to speak for the group.[47] These stars, according to Freeman, are then subject to attacks from their sisters for being power hungry, lacking illegitimacy, being egotistical, or any other reason that will justify hostility about their unendorsed power. LaVonne Ferguson recalled that similar tensions emerged in the Support Group. Many women, for example, voiced dissatisfaction with the group that initially ran the meetings, criticizing it for taking charge without group approval. This was one reason, according to LaVonne, that the Support Group finally held a formal election of officers.

Even within the inner circle, there was conflict. Barbara Collette was accused of wanting too much power. Although she initially ignored those criticisms, they eventually led her to step down from her leadership position.

Some of the rest of us whose feelings were hurt numerous times believed in what we were doing and, so, kind of tolerated some of the things that were going on. I can tell you one experience—it really did hurt and I wanted very badly to walk away, but I just kept telling myself I couldn't do that. There came a point in time where nobody really wanted to lead the meetings. It was something I found that I really did enjoy. Maybe it *was* my power thing; but I could do it, and it was a good experience and it gave me a sense of contributing. Pretty soon, I was doing the meetings every night alone. But I didn't complain because I was enjoying it. People started coming to me about a lot of things, then—and it was perceived by a couple of individuals who felt they were in control, and I stopped doing the meetings. It was like I was no longer needed and there was a real effort to get me out of that role because, obviously, they thought I had too much power or too much something. I gradually quit doing the meetings. I did walk away.

The constant challenges to her leadership within the organization was too much for Barbara. Other women had similar experiences, she recalled; and like her, they too left the Support Group "because they no longer had the energy to fight the Hormel Company and their friends in the Support Group."

According to Patricia Higgins, a lack of leadership experience may also have contributed to some of the power struggles.

Most of these women were very traditional women and had no training in leadership skills. Even though they had the ability to do it, they had no training and they didn't know how to handle conflict resolution, and they couldn't always compromise, and they couldn't work out a consensus. There was this pushing and shoving that went on continuously. I think both the stress and the lack of training contributed to that.

Barbara Collette agreed:

We were doing things that weren't so traditional, and we had never done that before. We had no examples of how it was done, and so—to get along with other women when we were used to being led by men, and now other women were telling us what to do. I think, yeah, there was that kind of conflict going on.

In the absence of clear leadership, the Support Group split roughly into two adversarial camps: the informal leadership and the elected leadership. At one point, this divisiveness threatened to tear the Support Group apart, according to Judy Himle.

There was a lot of conflict—power struggles between some of the main people in control of the Support Group. I think this was really evident partway through the strike when both people left the Support Group and tried pulling people with them to start their own little area—and trying to draw people away from the Support Group. And it became a divided group because some of the people believed in what this person was saying, and some believed in the next group.

Although the women were reluctant to identify specific individuals on the two sides of the power struggle, and often avoided any in-depth discussion of the conflict during the interviews, it was fairly obvious that Vickie Guyette and the inner circle led one contingent; and Jan Butts, the elected president, the other. Vickie recalled the beginnings of the conflict.

How things started between Jan and I was that one night we had a meeting—all the guys met downstairs, and they were going to close the plant down the next day. Some of us women were there, and we said, "Okay, we're going to go banner at the front gate." It was when Judge Nierengarten passed that law that we could only be so many feet from the plant gate—that restraining order. It was to be the next morning, so we didn't have time for a Support Group meeting. Probably ten of us showed up at the gate and then the cops came and took our names and we got called to the police station. Jan was really angry with me because we didn't go through her. That's why informal stuff stopped happening.

The power struggle erupted at one point over the disposition of a small amount of money remaining in the Santa's Workshop account. Jan Butts, who had originally headed up the committee, felt that it should decide what to do with the money. However, as one woman explained, the inner circle had other ideas.

They had $300 left in the account. They had decided not to give gifts the next year. I thought it should have been left and used in some way, like for the Support Group. Well, they ended up buying chickens with it. After the meeting, I went up to Jim Guyette, and I said, "Why are you so concerned about the $300? Hundreds of thousands of dollars have gone through here, and nobody cared about that. And you got $300 in that one little account and you want that out." I thought that was absolutely asinine. (Anon.)

The rancor generated by the power struggle persisted and spilled over into other Support Group activities. Even though she agreed with the final decision about what to do with the $300, Barbara Collette identified the real issue. What was at stake was power.

There was also part of me that really understood that Jan could have been a wonderful, excellent, brilliant person and still had been forced out because they didn't want her anymore, and they wanted to control. But it wasn't over Santa's Workshop; it wasn't over Jan. It was over who had power, and Jan had stopped being controllable. Jan had stopped being so easy about being pushed into leading a certain way. And that's what it was all about.

The administration of money in general was another major source of conflict, reflecting the group's concern with equity and fairness: "I think there were disagreements about the power certain people had over the checkbooks. There was a checkbook for almost every committee; and basically, those people who held the checkbook held power over that committee. I think the power and the money is all tied up together."[48] In addition to conflict over individual fiscal decisions, there was concern over general financial strategy. For example, several women questioned the financial management of the fundraising and public relations efforts.

The way the money was handled—it was really a sloppy affair. So many T-shirts; so many buttons. They went a little bit stir crazy, like somebody was going to buy all this stuff. Sometimes they kind of went overboard. The traveling business, too. People who were on the road—they would fly here and fly there; and they'd sit here at the table and they'd say, "Why don't you go to California this morning." Now who operates like that? They'd buy one-way tickets, and they're twice as expensive as two-way tickets. I'd say that to them, but it would pretty much fall on deaf ears. They had all that money, and they thought they'd just go out and raise more money. (Anon.)

Most of the women, however, agreed with Judy Himle that generally the money was spent wisely: "I would say that 80 percent of the money that came in got spent for what it was meant to be spent for. The other 20 percent, I'm not sure."

A few of the women alluded to alleged fiscal improprieties, and an occasional accusation would surface to the effect that certain individuals were benefiting unfairly: "Some people believed that some of the people and the officers were getting paid a salary. They weren't, but some people were convinced."[49] Several women expressed suspicions about a woman who had bought a new car. During her interview, the woman in question—Carole Apold—commented on those accusations.

I think one of the biggest concerns was the time I got a convertible. People would say, "How'd she get that convertible?" They didn't understand that my husband was getting two paychecks: he was getting his Worker's Comp check, and he was getting his retirement check. I was not taking money out of those accounts like people thought.

Conflict over money escalated in the climate of secrecy after the UFCW put P–9 into trusteeship. All of a sudden, as LaVonne Ferguson put it, "the books just disappeared." Vickie Guyette recalled some of the difficulties that resulted.

Later on, some of the fighting was about information. We were getting involved in lawsuits. The P–10 group—one of them wanted, ordered, us to tell how much we had in our treasury. And we said it wasn't any of his business. We knew that this person was talking to the international union, and we knew—our lawyer said, "If you tell them how much you have, they're going to be able to figure out how long you can go, and how bad off you are." So we kept it a secret. And then people started saying, "Well, what are you doing with the money?" The money started people not trusting each other.

Some of the most bitter confrontations between the women occurred over this need for secrecy.

I remember the big meeting down in the basement at Cindi's. That was awful that night! They were all going to quit, and they took the books and threw them in the middle of the floor. Jan or whoever was accusing them of not spending the money right, or of favoritism.

We did have meetings about why we had to keep the money secret, but they still kept fighting about it. They did have people rebelling; but that night when they threw the books on the floor, nobody moved to pick them up. All they wanted to do is speak. I don't think anybody wanted that responsibility. Absolutely not. But they were so desperate to see them.[50]

According to Carmel Taylor, the secrecy—coupled with the presence of strike-breakers and a consequent feeling of distrust—contributed to a general climate of political paranoia. This, in turn, created even more internal conflict. All of this upheaval led women like Patricia Higgins to believe that some of the conflict may have been instigated.

I always felt that we had people planted in the group—agitators. I can't prove this, but I suspect it was some of our own people. You'd be sitting around having coffee and you'd hear people talking, "Well, I wonder what they're doing with the money?!" Then pretty soon we've got an uproar. It would go for a while; then it would be calm. And then it would all flair up again. I always felt it was either the Hormel Company or the UFCW that was sticking somebody in.

Power struggles also emerged over who had access to information. As Susan Benson pointed out, access to information is critical to exercising power.

I had a supervisor once who didn't want to teach me anything—didn't want anybody knowing as much as she did. And I think that's what was going on in the Support Group. Everybody didn't want anybody to know as much as they did. That's my opinion. They wanted to be in the know.

Some women, for example, felt that Vickie Guyette's power rested partially on her proximity to information from the P–9 leadership. Information was used by the inner circle to maintain control of the Support Group, according to Carol King: "I think they guarded their knowledge, their jobs, very tightly. They did not want anyone from the outside coming in and helping or learning what was going on."

The need for secrecy required that there be limited access to information. It shut people out and denied them a sense of belonging.

I think we could have used a little more openness. I think sometimes there were too many secrets or too many things that were kept quiet. Sometimes people felt like they weren't part of making decisions or that they weren't kept informed about things. So what happened was, things got way out of context; it was blown up into something it really wasn't.[51]

In this environment, hearsay and gossip reigned, rather than truth. This weakened the group considerably.[52] In retrospect, the forced secrecy proved to be a major source of discontent and disruption: "I think part of my unhappiness about how money was spent was not knowing, rather than how it was spent. I was really satisfied with the decisions, but frustrated that the group as a whole wasn't allowed to make the decisions."[53]

In general, however, a spirit of cooperation prevailed. The women worked hard to resolve conflicts and reduce tensions. Carmel Taylor recalled,

The Support Group as a whole would sit down in their meetings and, "We've got this difference in opinion"—and it was discussed and aired. "You've got to get back to the point where you are clear about what we're here for, what we're going to do." Even when there were shouting matches, you always had somebody there with a level head that was able to take them apart and say, "Wait a minute. Sit down and think about it."

Some of the tensions were resolved through the somewhat chaotic democratic process and the mutual commitment to the Support Group agenda. In general, the sense of solidarity between the women was strong enough to overcome some of the power struggles.

THE RELATIONSHIP WITH P–9

One of the most problematic organizational issues for the Support Group was defining its relationship with P–9. That relationship went through several phases. Prior to the strike, the Support Group saw itself in a supportive, almost cheer-leading role. Once the strike was declared, the role of the Support Group changed dramatically as the women took up the strike issues as their own and were caught up in the work of fundraising and other activism. By the time P–9 was outlawed, the situation was entirely reversed. The P–9ers "joined" the Support Group, and the Support Group became the primary vehicle for organizing all the ongoing strike activities. In this later stage, tensions were heightened between the two organizations as the Support Group struggled to maintain its independent role at the same time that it took on a new and broader mission.

Tensions were concentrated around three themes: (1) appropriate gender roles; (2) the Support Group's role as an auxiliary organization to the union; and (3) conflicts over decision-making about strike strategy. According to researchers Judy Aulette and Trudy Mills, historical accounts of labor struggles in general have been silent about any tensions between men and women—perhaps because strikers and their supporters wished to present a united front. Some of the gender conflict that emerged in the Morenci Copper Mine Strike in 1983–86, Aulette and Mills believe, resulted from the changing status of women in contemporary American culture. Due to a heightened feminist awareness in the culture overall, the women involved in the strike redefined "acceptable" women's behavior. As a result, tensions between the genders increased because the men felt threatened.[54]

Gender-based conflict is not necessarily a factor in all labor activism, however. In her study of women's involvement in the Brookside Coal Strike of 1973, Sally Maggard found that the women played an active role in the strike; and even though "research on women and the labor movement has revealed a long history of male resistance to women's active involvement in unions and in organizing efforts," the men at Brookside were receptive to women's involvement. Maggard argued that this was because basic gender roles were never challenged during the strike activity. Even though the women temporarily stepped out of their traditional roles to carry picket signs and to protest, they still maintained their traditional women's roles—taking turns on the picket line so they could continue to keep up with their household and family responsibilities.[55]

While gender was not the primary lens through which the women in the Support Group understood and evaluated their interactions with P–9, it was a factor in exchanges between the organizations. There were complaints that women were too assertive; that they should stay in their own sphere and not get involved in "men's" activities; about who did what work in the Support Group. If women were assertive at all, the men—and even some of the women—saw them as a threat.

You get a bunch of women down there, and there were a lot of them who were very, very outspoken and wanted to go into the union meetings and felt that we should be allowed to go in there because we were supportive of our husbands. It got to the point where some people, I'm sure, viewed it as the women are not here to help—they're here to take over.[56]

According to another woman, some men went so far as to try to deny their wives an opportunity to participate in the strike.

A lot of the husbands didn't want their wives involved—the strike was their thing, it wasn't their wives'. After the strike got going and the P–9ers started coming to meetings and more or less stepping in and kind of taking over, then you had a lot of the men that said, "Well, hey, this is my strike; it's not yours. You stay home and take care of the kids—I'm going to Support Group meeting." (Anon.)

In general, however, the women were not concerned about establishing hard boundaries between P–9 and the Support Group, or between men's and women's tasks. Vickie Guyette noted that the women were involved in the full range of strike activities. In addition to traditional women's jobs such as typing, "we went out and we leafletted, we stood on the line with our husbands, we got arrested, and we did everything. We weren't behind our husbands; we were right beside them all the time. Everything they did, we did." Indeed, the women seemed fairly oblivious to the distinctions between the work of the men and the work of the women—so much so that it is hard at times to sort out the actual differences between the two groups that organized this strike.

Several of the women commented on who actually did the bulk of the work. One woman was annoyed, for example, that she had to stand on the picket line in twenty-below-zero weather while P–9ers drove by in warm pickup trucks to check and see who was on the line. Another women noted that "the women did most of the work, if you're talking men and women. The men would sit in the back room and drink coffee. They'd get yelled at and stuff, but some of them would just look at you and keep drinking coffee."[57]

One criticism the women heard from the men was that it was not the Support Group's place to be actively involved in the strike. According to labor historian Ava Baron, many meanings of gender coexist within a society and within individuals, and these ideas of gender are played out in a variety of ways in shaping our understanding of labor issues.[58] As the women in Austin saw it, the tension between P-9 and the Support Group centered around the belief by some men (and some women) that the strike was part of traditional "male" labor union culture, and that the auxiliaries were "female" organizations supporting the "men's" struggle. The belief that women should be supporters—rather than leaders or active partners—in the strike was debated in a variety of settings. This relationship of wives to the wage laborer and the labor struggle has always been problematic—especially whenever the idea of two distinct and separate spheres for men and women is entrenched and the gender lines are rigid. Elizabeth Faue suggests, for example, that when labor concerns extend beyond the immediate workplace issues and become community concerns—as she argues they did in Minneapolis during the 1930s—then women are more welcome in the struggle.[59] This was probably the case in Austin, as well, where the community context for the labor movement issues was emphasized by the women from the very beginning. Nevertheless, while the Support Group women were relatively welcome and active, there was a certain undercurrent of resistance to their involvement. The boundaries between the genders were shifting, and sometimes the new lines drawn by the women were challenged.

At Hormel, the labor culture was distinctly male, despite the fact that many women worked in the plant. The work was hard and dangerous. It was "men's work" in the eyes of many people; and the women were admonished that only men could really understand the "men's work" in the plant and deal with union issues: "We were told we never worked over there so how do we know what's going on over there?—until we experience it, how can we know what it is to work like a man?" (Anon.). The union culture, including the leadership at both the local and national levels, was also primarily male. In addition, the women had by and large remained outside of the contract negotiations between the union and the Hormel Company. As a result, the men saw the strike as "their" strike, and felt it was only natural to reject the women's intrusion. The Support Group was even excluded from union meetings—a policy that Carol King protested: "I also didn't agree that the wives had to leave the meetings—nonunion people had to leave." Sometimes the women's involvement was openly challenged: "No one criticized *my* activity to my face. But yes, I was aware of one case in particular where a women did not have the right to carry a banner in a peace parade in D.C. before a P-9er did. But—good for her—she did!"[60]

Gender was also a subtle factor in defining the proper missions of the two organizations. The history of the labor movement has traditionally been cast as a struggle between two titanic male forces: the male worker and the male business owner. As a result, the work of women's labor auxiliaries was invisible, according to Aulette and Mills, "partly because the women stood outside the traditional arena of labor disputes—they were neither workers nor management.''[61] Once women did become involved, however, they quickly developed their own agenda with roots in the deeper survival issues affecting the family and the community. The auxiliaries' introduction of a "women's agenda" into the labor movement cast a new light on old relationships, requiring both auxiliaries and unions to reexamine and redefine boundaries and issues.

As long as the two organizations in Austin remained separate, according to one woman, there was little gender tension; but "we got more of that feedback once the strike began, and the massive amount of P–9ers would come down. Then all of a sudden we didn't know anything—I mean, we're a bunch of dummies" (Anon.). On one occasion, male criticism of the women was very vocal and very public. According to Rietta Pontius, the women who went out on speaking tours were challenged when they got up in a union meeting to report on their trips: "I can remember one man who stood up and said 'You women and you kids have no business up there on that podium. This is our strike. You're just in the background.' And it was true—it was really true." She felt the women had crossed some invisible but important boundary: "I felt like we were getting in the way. We were starting to get involved in the strike. We had gone over bounds. We had gone way over bounds."

Defining those boundaries between P–9 and the Support Group was both an organizational and a gender issue that took on greater significance when the union was put into trusteeship: "The men were more or less pushed into the women's organization because there was no place else for them to go."[62] Many of the women commented on how difficult the transition was, for both men and women, as they attempted to define their new relationship.

It was like one big mess. It would have been better if one night it would be the Support Group meeting and the next night the union meeting. As it was, the whole group just came flooding into the union hall, and there were too many opinions at that point. The men didn't want the wives involved in union issues, but yet they felt they were free to stick their noses into Support Group issues.[63]

Not all the women were convinced that the Support Group maintained its integrity and remained independent of P–9. The strike changed the entire focus of the Support Group, according to one woman, and the women were no longer in control: "We were just being manipulated by Jim Guyette and Ray Rogers, is what the feeling of everyone was. We were no longer the Support Group trying to help people. We were a Support Group trying to support their campaign against the Hormel Company" (Anon.). Some of the women disagreed among themselves as well. They felt that the Support Group had no right to be involved in the strike: "We needed to maintain the separation. We were there to support, not run it or criticize it."[64] Another woman expressed her discomfort with the women making union decisions.

I remember occasionally thinking, "Now, I don't really agree with that." But my feeling was that I wasn't a worker at the plant, and my husband was—and he has to make the decision that's right for him. I would feel offended if he started making decisions about my job for me.[65]

It was not always big issues that caused disagreement and tension between P–9 and the Support Group: "I heard all kinds of complaints from the union: they never got the money; we were stealing money from them—you constantly heard stuff like that."[66] Another woman noted simply, "There were millions of power struggles going on."[67] In general, however, the men never did try to take control of the Support Group, and the women continued in leadership positions.

The men never tried to take over. They had a healthy respect—and still do, to this day—for the Support Group. They didn't try to come in and say, "Now, we're going to take over and you guys will have to be out of here." They just went along with whatever the women that were in control decided to do. In all fairness to the men, they were pretty fantastic. They cleaned the bathrooms and worked in the kitchen. There was a lot of mutual sharing of skills that went both ways.[68]

Despite the hesitancy of a few women, it quickly became clear that the Support Group had a crucial role to play in developing and implementing strike strategy. With P–9 leadership in disarray after the trusteeship move, the whole strike probably would have folded had it not been for the continuing efforts of the women in the Support Group. According to Patricia Higgins,

after the union was put in trusteeship and P–9 was dissolved, the whole ball of wax was put on the shoulders of the Support Group. The executive board went separate ways—they were forced to find jobs; and for financial reasons, a lot of them had to bail out. So the Support Group was left kinda holding the bag.

The women's efforts should have been more appreciated, Patricia felt: "They played a huge role, but they've never been given any credit for their participation. The union also failed to acknowledge the Support Group; it [the union] was male dominated, and I think that had something to do with it."

In general, the women felt free to disagree with the men over strike strategies. As we have already seen in Chapter 7, many of the women believed that the strikers should have taken a stronger stand and been more violent. Others disagreed with P–9's decision to hire Ray Rogers: "I'm not the cheerleader type and there were too many that stood there as cheerleaders behind him."[69] It was not always easy for the women to act independently. When the men tried to tell the women what strategies to use in their demonstrations, for example,

it really muddied the waters a lot. It doesn't work too well for somebody who can't do anything to tell the ones that are doing those things just exactly how and what to do. I think the P–9ers wanted to direct everything, but I don't think it worked—simply because the Support Group was doing everything and the Support Group was going to have a say in what was being done.[70]

Overall, the informal organizational culture that the women created in the Support Group was able to surmount all its potential difficulties with organizational structure, conflicts and uncertainties over leadership, and gender-based tensions with the union. When the women assessed the overall effectiveness of the Support Group's organizational structure, most of them felt that the informal environment was a major contributing factor in the success of the Support Group. According to Cheryl Remington,

they got the job done, but it wasn't through organization. If you happened to be standing there and you wanted to do it, no one forced you into anything. I've never been in a group as dedicated. No one looked down on you if you had to go home. There wasn't any organization; but there were so many people around and with the key people to organize, things just got done. And it wasn't like, "Okay, you're in charge of canning now, all the time"—just, if you were there, fine. It was so disorganized. But it really worked.

It was important to the women that their organization be flexible and friendly: "By it being informal, it was a lot more friendly. If you have to go by Robert's Rules of Order, then we never would have accomplished what we did."[71] People worked better in the informal power structure, Carole Apold felt.

I think, if people don't have titles, they work better with one another. I don't think there was any one real power in the Support Group. Everybody had a job to do and they did it. There were people that stood out more than others, but that didn't mean they had more power.

The Support Group was a hardworking, open, friendly, egalitarian organization. It was a "women's space" from the very beginning: women made most of the decisions, did most of the work, and even expanded the traditional gender boundaries into new arenas in the labor movement. However, upon deeper probing, a much more complicated organizational reality emerges. As we will explore in Chapter 9, doing political work with other women was a new experience. At the same time that they were seeking to push gender boundaries outward in new directions, the women found themselves working to reconfigure reality on yet another front: their relationships with one another.

NOTES

1. Hardy Green, *On Strike at Hormel: The Struggle for a Democratic Labor Movement* (Philadelphia, 1990), 246–81.
2. Patricia Higgins.
3. Jo Freeman, "The Tyranny of Structurelessness," *MS* 11, 1 (July 1973): 87.
4. Ibid., 88.

5. Ibid., 77.

6. Cheryl Remington.

7. Carmel Taylor.

8. Vickie Guyette; LaVonne Ferguson.

9. Jeannie Bambrick.

10. Julie Wilson.

11. Carol Kough.

12. Julie Wilson.

13. Susan Benson.

14. Mary Machacek.

15. Patricia Higgins.

16. Joyce Rothschild-Whitt, "Conditions for Democracy: Making Participatory Organizations Work," in *Co-ops, Communes, and Collectives: Experiments in Social Change in the 1960s and 1970s*, ed. John Case and Rosemary C. R. Taylor (New York, 1979), 224.

17. Julie Wilson.

18. Carol Kough.

19. Billie Goodeu.

20. Judy Himle.

21. Mary Arens.

22. Mary Arens.

23. Green, *On Strike at Hormel*, 113, 206–8.

24. Freeman, "Tyranny of Structurelessness," 86.

25. Ibid., 78.

26. Ibid., 86.

27. Barbara Collette.

28. Carol King.

29. Carol King.

30. Susan Benson.

31. Cindi Bellrichard.

32. In an interview about power relations in the radical feminist *Heresies* collective, one of the women made a similar observation: "Even though it wasn't supposed to happen, leaders emerged. Those with big mouths, those who talked fast—they became leaders." *Heresies* Editorial Collective, "True Confessions," *Heresies* 2, 3 (Spring 1979): 96.

33. Judy Kraft.

34. Freeman, "Tyranny of Structurelessness," 86.

35. Cheryl Remington.

36. Mary Arens.

37. Carol King.

38. Julie Wilson.

39. Jane J. Mansbridge, *Beyond Adversary Democracy* (New York, 1980).

40. Ibid., 65.

41. Ibid., 34.

42. Rietta Pontius.

43. Mansbridge, *Beyond Adversary Democracy*, 228.

44. Ibid., 165.

45. Rietta Pontius; Julie Wilson.

46. Susan Benson.

47. Freeman, "Tyranny of Structurelessness," 86.

48. Cindi Bellrichard.

49. Linda Novak.

50. Mary Arens.

51. Judy Himle.

52. Rietta Pontius.

53. Barbara Collette.

54. Judy Aulette and Trudy Mills, "Something Old, Something New: Auxiliary Work in the 1983–1986 Copper Strike," *Feminist Studies* 14, 2 (Summer 1988): 261–62.

55. Sally Ward Maggard, "Women's Participation in the Brookside Coal Strike: Militancy, Class, and Gender in Appalachia," *Frontiers* 9, 3 (1987): 19.

56. Carmel Taylor.

57. Mary Arens.

58. Ava Baron, "Gender and Labor History: Learning from the Past, Looking to the Future," in *Work Engendered: Toward a New History of American Labor*, ed. Ava Baron (Ithaca, N.Y., and London, 1991), 37.

59. Elizabeth Faue, *Community of Suffering and Struggle: Women, Men, and the Labor Movement in Minneapolis, 1915–1945* (Chapel Hill, N.C., and London, 1991).

60. Marie Loverink.

61. Aulette and Mills, "Something Old, Something New," 265.

62. Jeannie Bambrick.

63. Jeannie Bambrick.

64. Carmel Taylor.

65. Susan Benson.

66. Madeline Krueger.

67. Barbara Collette.

68. Patricia Higgins.

69. Carol King.

70. Julie Wilson.

71. Joyce Ball.

CHAPTER 9

"Some Very, Very Strong Women"

Many environmental factors—some organizational, some personal, some political—contributed to the formulation of the strike culture around the Support Group. As we have seen, these factors included such things as identifying a common enemy and challenging the rigidity of that enemy[1]; building an alternative culture and community in response to alienation and isolation from the larger community of Austin; the close geographical proximity that enabled the strikers to work more efficiently together; a high level of ideological commitment and activism; and a strong sense of the justness of the union's cause. There is one additional factor that shaped the strike culture of the Support Group: gender.

To talk about gender is to talk about power. Gender shapes social behavior, and women's activism and their use of political power in general is colored by their participation in socially determined constructs of gender. The lines that divide society by gender are carefully constructed and maintained to the benefit of some and the disadvantage of others; and according to Canadian feminist philosopher Mary O'Brien, any change in the relationship between the genders—especially when women move from the traditionally female private sphere into the public realm—indicates a radical shift in a given society's overall power relations. To challenge society's perceptions of women's proper role is a radical act, according to historians Jill Conway, Susan Bourque, and Joan Scott, because "the production of culturally appropriate forms of male and female behavior is a central function of social authority"—and to challenge social authority is to call into question all relations of power as they operate in culture.[2] Thus, to challenge gender is to challenge the nature of power and authority at all levels, and challenging political authority can also lead to questioning social and moral authorities, including gender prescriptions.

In the ambiguous environment created by the strike, the women in the Support

Group were free to redefine and articulate their own perspective on the political and social life of their community. The strike in Austin—upsetting as it was to the structures of the traditional economic and social order—also upset the traditional gender ordering. As we have seen, the women redefined their gender roles with individual men, with the male-dominated unions, and with Hormel and other institutions of power and authority in their communities. In the process, the women grew more sensitive to the nature of power relations in their lives in general.[3]

According to Guida West and Rhoda Blumberg, women bring a unique gender-based perspective to political activism in three areas: (1) their initial justification for becoming activists; (2) the ways they organize and mobilize themselves and other women; and (3) the methods they use to confront authorities.[4] With regard to confrontation tactics, Chapter 7 explored how the women selectively used gender-inspired tactics in their nonviolent encounters with the police and the National Guard. These tactics were shaped by traditional stereotypes about how men should treat the "gentler sex." The hope was that women could get away with more, since the authorities would treat women more kindly just because they were women. This chapter will explore the first two areas as they pertain to the Hormel/P-9 Strike: the role gender played in motivating women to social-change activism and conversely, how their activism influenced perceptions of gender; and how gender influenced the structure and operation of the Support Group, and women's interactions with one another.

WOMEN'S POLITICAL CULTURE: GENDER AND CHANGE

In the process of becoming a social activist, the individual undergoes a major personal transformation. Often there is a conscious break with traditional habits and practices. This transition is different for men and women, and the difference is often grounded in the traditional social constructs of gender. Men, for example, are acculturated to be generally more assertive. For them, the transition to political activist may be more one of degree, rather than kind. Women have an additional challenge. They must often undertake a major restructuring of gender roles as they make the political shift from woman as private and individual, to woman as collective and public; from woman in the family, to woman in community; from woman as passive and nurturing, to woman as active and demanding. It is in this process of transformation to public political roles that women are forced to confront and transform the gendered nature of their world, for in "the separation of public and private is the material locus of generic struggle," writes Mary O'Brien; and it is here that the personal and the political meet.[5] According to O'Brien, as "women are drawn into overt public conflicts, shaking off their conventional conservative image and startling the public realm with protest, prophesy and profanity," gender roles undergo radical transformations.[6] The act of becoming politically active can—in and of itself—result in a major shift in gender roles. Involvement in social activism has often been the "excuse" and the occasion that women needed to reexamine and adapt the social construction of gender.

Women who become activists encounter two conflicting gender-based political agendas: whether to act from the gendered perspective of a "traditional woman" and articulate a politics motivated by care for others, or whether to challenge or reject traditional gender roles and carve out new political identities.[7] The women in the Austin United Support Group articulated both perspectives, and essentially saw no conflict between the two. When asked directly whether they saw their activities in the Support Group as an extension of women's traditional roles or as a challenge to those roles, all of the women said their new activism challenged their traditional roles as women, forcing them into totally new configurations that represented a sharp break with tradition. Even those women who defined themselves as "traditional" and conservative women—even they still described their experience as one of change. Their activism was regarded as merely an "extension" of their traditional roles. Most of the women took those traditional roles as given, even as they moved to extremely radical positions. At the heart of their new insights into gender was the recognition that they were moving beyond the limitations of traditional female roles, and exploring an "unarticulated acknowledgement of life beyond domesticity."[8] They were changing; and as part of that change they saw, and celebrated, women adopting new roles, expanding beyond traditional expectations. Their experience supports the view that gender role definitions can be extremely flexible. Where the boundaries of gender lie is seen to depend on where women individually and collectively choose to draw them.

The transformation from mothers and wives to political activists took place on many levels in Austin. The women identified several such levels: feeling more independent and empowered; seeing the positive effect of their activism on their families; taking pride in doing the same things that men did; daring to confront authority; and developing a strong sense of the collective power of women. For each woman in the Support Group, the transformation was unique and personal. They each had to overcome external constraints to their actions, as well as what Emma Goldman called the "internal tyrants"—the voices and habits of mind that keep women in their gendered and powerless places. Carol King, for example, described her process of transformation as a gradual one, at the end of which she was a new and different person.

I'm sitting in the middle of the generations. More than my mother's generation that was supposed to stay home and be a wife and a mother, but like my daughter's generation that is more equal with the men. I'm kind of sitting out there in both areas. I always said for a long time that I was "Mrs. David King," and I'm now—"Mrs. David King" is my title—but I'm Carol King. I'm now Carol King. Mrs. David King is who I happen to be. Does that make sense to you? I think that transition started before the Support Group, but I feel I really became my own person—more than just as a wife.

There was not always universal support for the changes the women were undergoing. One of the ways that the women were alerted to how dramatic and threatening their personal transitions were being perceived by others was through criticism of their involvement in the strike's activism. Comments from people in the community and the men in P–9 made it clear what women should or should not do. Although not all of the women experienced criticism—and overall, the amount of criticism the women reported was small—critics were vocal at every level, seeking to maintain the traditional parameters of women's behavior.[9]

Some of the strongest criticism was aimed at how the women's activism impacted their families or how their behavior was unladylike. "Proper" women stayed in their "proper" spheres and exhibited "proper" behavior, and the family was deemed women's proper sphere. Family life inevitably underwent changes as the women's primary caretaking focus shifted from the culture of the family to the culture of the Support Group, but critics felt that women should be home taking care of their husbands and children.[10] Barbara Collette, for example, was taken to task for neglecting her husband.

I took some heat because I was married and on the road. I did some traveling and people thought I should be home with my husband. And people thought that I shouldn't leave him alone, and they wondered how he was eating. That was kind of strange, because he can cook and wash and clean. I never gave it a second thought, but other people were quite concerned about it. They saw my place in the home. And there were certain people within the organization that didn't think it was "right"—whatever that meant.

Jeannie Bambrick, who had a small baby, was criticized for getting arrested. Her children were never far from her thoughts, however, even on the day she went to jail.

One of the very last things I did was, I turned to my husband when they were arresting me and I said, "Get home to the kids." Some people thought that was kind of funny; but being a mother, that was the very first thing that was on my mind. If he gets arrested too, who's going to be there for those kids?

The women's involvement generally had a positive effect on their families, despite the concerns of the critics. Several of the women commented that their families not only survived mother's activism, but even thrived and learned new skills of self-sufficiency.

My husband handled it well. It was harder on the kids. All of a sudden I left home and went down there, and [with] my children and husband [it] was everybody for themselves: "Go home and, if you need something to eat, get it." "I'm getting a bus tomorrow and I'm going to the [Twin] Cities to hand out leaflets!" And you know, they became independent![11]

Julie Wilson felt that her family benefited from her activism: "my being involved with the work of the Support Group was good for the kids—and good for Steve.

It was good for him to babysit with them once in a while. That was the first time he ever really had to do that." Julie was careful to see that her family was not neglected, and she noted that the women often assisted each other with their family responsibilities: "I could work at the Support Group because another P–9 wife, Vicky, ran a day-care center, and she'd watch my child at no charge. It was good for all of us, but I just had this feeling that people thought I should be home."

If the women worked, their economic status in the family was also changed. In a highly gendered world, men were supposed to be the primary breadwinners. The whole gender dynamic in Susan Benson's family changed when she became the sole support of the family.

> Because I had been a single parent—I was head of a household for so long—it wasn't difficult for me to step in and take over. Oddly enough, it was a little relief because I had my position back again, where I had been sharing it for a number of years! It strengthened my relationship with my husband. It also turned things around a little bit because he was a very traditional person. You could work outside the home as long as you got your duties done at home. The children were always my responsibility, and the house was always my responsibility.

The literature on working-class women's political involvement has documented a variety of gender-based motivations to explain their increased activism. The justifications women commonly expressed fell roughly into three categories: women become politically active to ensure the survival of their families;[12] out of a broader concern for the economic security of their communities and their way of life;[13] or to defend their individual rights as wage earners and consumers.[14] While the women in the Support Group were motivated by all three rationales, their primary justifications were the defense of their families and their community as a whole.

By and large, the defense of the reproductive or household economy in general, and family survival in particular, has been underappreciated in contemporary analyses of the economics of the working class. The family—being regarded as woman's sphere—was seen as secondary and subsidiary to the real struggle of the individual worker in his or her workplace. Despite this gendering of the family as women's sphere, the household is nevertheless an important locus of political and economic struggle.[15] In an article exploring women's activism in the Lawrence Strike of 1912, Ardis Cameron uses the term *the radicalization of women's sphere* to describe the process by which women enter the political arena in defense of their families.[16] Temma Kaplan called the women's defense of the reproductive economy in Barcelona, Spain, in the early 1900s, an expression of a "female consciousness." Women were inspired to act from their economic roles within the family as wives and mothers and producers. According to Kaplan, the importance of their work to the survival of the family radicalizes women and empowers them to social activism. Further, the female consciousness is a radical consciousness because it places "human need above other social and political requirements and human life above property, profit, and even individual rights."[17]

As the striking families' economic agenda became politicized and radicalized through the activities of the Support Group, activism was seen as a natural extension of the women's traditional roles as wives and mothers. As one woman put it, "I think women are more survival oriented. Women think of family and children first."[18] Still another woman described how those women who had never worked were especially aggressive in defense of their families. These women—being economically dependent on their husband's paychecks—were more vulnerable than the women who worked outside the home.

As a woman you had a different perspective on it than a man did, because you were always the one that was at home nurturing and taking care of getting the groceries and things like that. Men went to work and brought the paycheck home; and that was the end of that, for a lot of people. And all of a sudden, the rug was pulled out from underneath you. And you know there's no check and, "What's going to happen to my children, my family?" I think that's where a lot of the women—and especially the ones that were not working—had such a different attitude. With the working women, it was a different perspective because they still had a paycheck coming in. But for the ones where there was suddenly nothing, almost panic would set in. I think that got more women involved. It got them more independence. It was an awful big blow. (Anon.)

Clearly, economic survival of the family was one of the strongest motivators to political action; and as Carol King remarked, it went beyond gender: "I think a lot of it was not women's view and men's view, but became a struggle for both men and women for their family unit." Maintaining the unity of the family as a social unit motivated another woman's activism: "The purpose of this Support Group was to keep the circle within the family. In other words, instead of staying home, not knowing what was going on, we were part of it, down at the union hall, husbands and families."[19]

While some of the women acted "as women" in defense of their families, others described their new changing roles as traditional "men's" roles. The women took great pride in being equal to the men and were annoyed when their contributions were not recognized: "We helped just as much as the men. We got involved just as much as they did. I'm sure they'd say the same thing. Without us women, they couldn't have done as much as they did" (Anon.). Women were, after all, "doing the same things the men did" in the strike. They were doing "men's work." To act "as men," however, meant to act as citizens, not to act "like men." To act "as men" meant acting either in solidarity with the union members or on behalf of the larger community of Austin.

Doing "men's things" often meant—when all was said and done—that the sex roles were blurred, the tasks degendered:

The men and the women worked together, so there weren't any definitely "women's things" to do. The kitchen was run by the men. I mean, sure, a woman could step foot in there and maybe help out with something, but the men did it. There weren't any traditional "women things" to do down there. Men and women traveled together and they did their thing together. There were some women that were a lot stronger that were involved in that. But as far as working with the men or working with the women, it wasn't cut-and-dried that way. It was working together. I don't care if I'm a woman or a man, or what it is, you know—whether it's hauling boxes or holding up a piece of plywood so somebody could finish it off or what it was—let's just do it and get it done.[20]

The necessity for teamwork meant that people didn't get hung up on gender, according to Billie Goodeu.

I can remember a group of five of us gals going down to Milwaukee. We slept on floors just like the guys, and we split up into groups—part guys and part women—and we'd go around to the unions to drum up the support. And we took the insults with the guys; we took the compliments with the guys. There was teamwork there, again. It didn't matter if you were a man or woman at that time. The main issue is to get the point across, because being a man or woman didn't enter into it.

This blurring of gender tasks, and the increased involvement of women in the conduct of the strike, were not universally accepted. Criticism often centered on the belief that women did not belong in "men's" areas: "I think sometimes people thought, because we were women, that we should just stay out of it and let the men do it" (Anon.). Vickie Guyette encountered this kind of resistance when she tried to stop the destruction of the mural: "I remember going after a man once when they took down the mural, and they told me I should let the men do that. 'That's not your place.' "

Although tension between the genders was not a serious problem, the Support Group was not as egalitarian as some of the women would have liked: "I don't think it was free of the man/woman issue. I do remember times saying, 'Well, a woman can do that, too.' I do think that there was a certain mentality that some things were women things and some things were men things to do."[21] When asked about how working with men was different from working with women, another woman retorted, "You really want to know? They're a pain in the ass. The men. I think they tend to get chauvinistic. They needed us. They were really lucky. I think they realize that, too."[22]

Being politically active was a new experience for many of the women in the Support Group. As one woman put it, "it was a role I wasn't used to" (Anon.). Before the strike, the women in the Support Group were probably most comfortable focusing on their private lives and being relatively passive politically. It took tremendous motivation to venture into the uncertain political arena of labor activism. Vickie Guyette commented on the changes the women underwent.

A lot of older women went through big transitions because they had been home for years and it was not heard of to be out there bannering and getting arrested. They talked about their experiences to me. It was things like, "I can't believe I'm doing this! Who would have thought?!"

Activism and confrontation were important to the women's feeling empowered; and with that empowerment and the decision to challenge authorities—whether it was male authority, or institutional authority—came radicalization of the women's gender roles. Prior to the strike, power was Hormel, power was the government and the police, the business community, the church, the media. With the strike came the awareness that women could effectively challenge that power and authority. Whether the women defined their activism as an extension of their traditional roles, or as a challenge to these roles, the results were the same: they acted. And their activism forced many of them to reexamine and adapt the role of women in public life generally. For the most part, the women in the Support Group were not only comfortable with their new perceptions, but eager to act on them.

Maybe in my mother's time the women would have stayed home and tried to make ends meet and figure out ways to pay the bills and be kind of behind the scenes. Where [instead] we took a really up-front view of everything. We were right out in the open. Very few of us sat at home.[23]

Patricia Higgins described the conflicting pressures and the internal and cultural resistances that she and the other women had to overcome in becoming activists.

It certainly wasn't a traditional woman's role; and even though this was volunteer work—which I've done tons of—it wasn't in that category at all. My husband was very supportive so it didn't cause a conflict within our family. It was definitely an extension of that. Women just simply are not encouraged to stand up and speak their mind at all. Especially in Austin, Minnesota, which is a very conservative rural community. Women just don't do those types of things. Women don't go out and stand on the picket line. Women don't do civil disobedience.

Despite the contradictions they experienced, the women persisted in their activism. As another woman noted with some amusement, "I never did anything like this before—get up in the morning to get arrested!"[24] An important outcome of their activism was a major shift in everyone's perceptions of women's roles.

It was definitely a challenge to the traditional role of women in Austin, Minnesota. The sexual revolution has happened everywhere but in Austin. I believe that there were very, very large numbers of women who, for the first time, saw themselves very differently because of what they were doing in the Support Group. I think each of us learned that we did have a place; each of us individually as women had a place in the Support Group. I think a lot of men woke up, too. I think a lot of men saw their wives differently because of the things that went on and the things that women did.[25]

It was difficult for the community as a whole to accept women as activists. Among the several factors that contributed to the community's rejection of women's activism were the gendering of labor activism and political activism in general, and also small-town conservatism. Political activism in general is identified as "male" behavior—a notion that probably grows out of the early American tradition of linking property ownership, citizenship, and the vote with the male gender. Also, political activism has always taken place in public places, and was sometimes tinged with violence. Convention long confined women to the private sphere of home and family. Therefore, women's activism was discounted on two scores: it was against a woman's nature to enter the public arena; and the contributions of women were not to be seen as "activism" in its own right, but merely as women's work in support of male political activities.

Small-town life can also inhibit political activism. In small towns, people generally tend to act more conservatively than in urban areas, and homogeneity is highly prized. Any behavior that might make someone stand out from the community is strongly censured. Further, the desire for belonging—especially in an intimate small-town environment where exclusion would be painfully obvious—serves to inhibit challenges to the social order. Fitting-in is a kind of survival, in a small town.

People in Austin who were not comfortable with women taking an active public role would base their criticisms on its being inappropriate behavior for women; they would say the women were stepping out of a woman's traditional sphere. According to Jeannie Bambrick,

a lot of people felt that the women shouldn't have gotten involved. It kinda goes back to what I said before about Austin being the perfect little town. Women never do things like that in Austin. I mean, I'll bet you anything, when people were burning bras, nobody in Austin even considered it. It's just, this town is not a real town. Now it's gotten more so; but up until that point, things just never happened in Austin. The women just were never that outspoken. Actually the men never did, either; but it's harder [for women], for some reason. It's harder for some people to take it when a woman is the one out there verbally getting her feelings across. Women should be seen and not heard—kinda like kids—is the conventional wisdom.

Several other women reported being told that speaking out or acting publicly was not their proper place, and that confrontations and civil disobedience were unseemly behaviors for women. As a result, the women were self-conscious about even small acts of political expression. Billie Goodeu recalled her own transformation from being a "lady" to being an activist.

When we went down to the stockholders meeting in Atlanta—my daughter had made me a "Cram Your Spam" sweatshirt. I used to always want to get across that I was a lady; but since I'd stood up, it had gotten to be quite a joke. So the shirt she made for me didn't just say "Cram Your Spam." It said "Cram Your Spam, Please." The TV people picked up my picture, and people back in Austin saw me. And several of them said it couldn't have been me because I'd never wear anything like that! I guess I've probably never been totally a lady.

If nothing else worked to keep the women in line, their critics tried shaming them by calling into question whether the men in their lives really cared about them. This criticism also implied that male paternalism was threatened by the women's activities: "I took a lot of criticism for my activity from the people I worked with. They said sending the women out front was a cowardly thing to do. Or if they spotted me in a parade, or saw me in the news, they'd always ask, 'Well, where was your husband?' "[26]

WOMEN'S POLITICAL CULTURE: THE GENDERING OF POWER

The traditional structures and modes of power—government, corporate, religious—that the women had known their whole lives failed them in Austin. As those traditional forms of authority were called into question, the women sought to replace them with new, more caring, more egalitarian structures. As a result, they found themselves consciously assessing the nature of power—especially as power was manifested in the dynamics of their interactions with one another. As they underwent the process of personal and political transformation, their perceptions of themselves and other women were often described in ambiguous and contradictory terms. This was especially true as they turned to an examination of the use of power within their own organization. On the one hand, caught up in contradictions over the proper roles of women, they questioned women's abilities to use power effectively. On the other hand, they found themselves serving in strong leadership positions, and they then spoke eloquently about how effective in using power the women were.

As the women worked together, their experiences shaped their own meaning of political power. First of all, they concluded, in an ideal world the power should be shared. Secondly, it should be wielded on behalf of others, and individuals should make every attempt not to act too independently. Competition should be avoided to keep conflict at a minimum, and equity and fairness should be guiding principles.[27] Finally, power should be exercised in an objective, unemotional manner.

Furthermore, the women were committed to making these ideas operational in the Support Group. It was not easy for them, however, to make the transition from an organizational world view based on exploitation, individualism, competition, and self-interest to their new community of sharing and cooperation. As the women talked about the power dynamics in the Support Group, their discussions reflected the ambiguity inherent in any transition. The dialogue was often colored by gendered language and metaphors. Especially troubling and problematic were the negative comments they made about one another, and about women in general. Troubling as they are, however, these kinds of comments are common in many social-change situations—especially in groups where powerlessness has been the dominant politic and has been internalized.

There is another way to interpret these comments that appear, on the surface, to be divisive or counterproductive: they can be understood as a code for discussing the nature of power. In general, the negative comments were not meant to be statements about how women *actually* were or should be, so much as metaphorical glosses to explain or frame the context of the discussion of power and its uses. The careful reader, then, will take notice of this coded language in the excerpts from our interviews, and will read between the lines for a critique of power.

As the women turned to their analysis of power, they often sprinkled their discussions with this gender-coded and weighted language. Woven throughout the interviews was a pattern of critical comments about the nature of "women" and "men" that at first hearing seemed to be nothing more than a verbal trashing of women—or at best, self-deprecating statements about their own gender. These comments were often parenthetical in nature, delivered in an unconscious or offhanded manner, or offered as similies or metaphors to explicate other issues and questions. What was even more confusing, sometimes they were offered in the same breath with positive comments about women.

"Women," the implicit argument underlying these comments went, were not suited to holding power or assuming leadership roles in organizations because, first, they were uncooperative, strong willed, and independent; second, they were competitive with one another; and third, their emotions got in the way of effective work because they were too subjective and tended to personalize everything. As a result, women created dissension and could not be effective leaders and speak for the group as a whole.

This ambiguity about the nature of women's use of power was at the bottom of much of the conflict among the women in the Support Group. Most of the conflict centered around issues of power and control: "who was going to run it, who wanted to be the top one, who wanted to be in control, who wanted to handle money" (Anon.). According to journalist Judy Remington in a series on "Women Working Together," women are suspicious of power and are ambiguous about strong women leaders.[28] The woman who empowers herself creates a dilemma for other women because, Remington writes,

the shared experience of victimization is an essential "glue" that bonds women together in the framework of this philosophy, [and] powerful women threaten the group's identity and existence. Consequently, only a limited degree of empowerment and certain prescribed ways of expressing it can be tolerated.[29]

Women are more likely to be openly critical of women who wield power because to use power is to contradict the traditional image of woman as powerless. To challenge traditional roles on one level destabilizes women's roles on many levels; so, women who step out of traditional roles induce uncertainty and even fear in other women. Assertive women have to be criticized, or the whole gender reality is upset. In her study of small democratic organizations, for example, Jane Mansbridge found that "it was hard for women to visualize any female leadership that was not 'bitchy.' "[30]

Anxiety about women's use of power was manifested in a variety of ways. As the newly empowered women moved to take on leadership roles in the Support Group, other women expressed the concern that the leadership would become too independent. Women who were too strong willed would not be cooperative, one of the arguments went. Men were easier to work with, one woman stated, because they "just kind of go with the flow"; independent women are "more opinionated. They're more strong willed, and don't necessarily like to be told what to do or be influenced in a decision. Once they have their minds set, it's harder to change them" (Anon.). Strong-willed independent women have difficulty working together, according to Billie Goodeu, because such women become too competitive: "They always say, 'No two women can be in the same kitchen at the same time.' That's probably the problem we had with the Support Group. We were together all the time." The situation was described as too many women trying to exercise power at the same time, with the women being perceived as meddlesome and uncooperative. The implication was that, when women get together, there is so much conflict and disagreement that nothing will get done: "Women are naturally, I don't know—PMS. I worked at the hospital in the kitchen; and when you put thirty women in the kitchen, you're going to have the same thing—always conflict."[31] Mary Arens believed that women learned about power and leadership in the isolation of their families, and those individual experiences made women so independent they were unable to cooperate: "Put a group of women together who are married and have raised children, and everybody has their own ideas about how things should be done— and you'll have conflict." It wasn't easy trying to get things done in this tense environment, as Linda Novak lamented: "There were days when we said, 'If you want the keys to the Food Shelf and you can do it better, take them!' You know, you get tired of it."

Remington identified two additional problems that women must resolve vis-à-vis the use of power by strong individual women: (1) women who are already empowered are seen as a threat to women who see themselves as lacking power, because the former are seen as acting like men; and (2) because the women's movement has such a strong emphasis on equality, powerful women are a threat because they introduce the idea that women are not all equal. If she is more, I must be less.[32] The women in the Support Group shared similar concerns. Women were constantly measuring their power against one another, Carol King believed, because they were afraid of losing power: "There is more jealousy between women—so afraid someone is going to step in their role or step on their toes." Jan Kennedy analyzed it this way: "I think women are too competitive. I guess maybe women feel threatened. Men feel so damn superior and we know they are, so it kind of works out good. There's no problem." Jan seemed to imply that, when men are in charge, there are no power struggles between women because the women defer to male power. But when women want to assume a power (read: male) position, they become competitive. This talk of competition was also a screen for discussing the tension the women were experiencing as they struggled to work together cooperatively.

This constant monitoring of levels of power was further reflected in a heightened sensitivity to fairness and justice. Once again, the issue of competitiveness was gender coded. Women are so competitive that they cannot be fair, Carol King concluded: "The distribution would have been more fair if men had done it. It's just the nature of men to be more fair with each other. Women are so afraid they're going to be left out—'Someone's going to get something more than me.' "

Concerns were also raised about how women's emotional nature influenced their use of power. Behaviors such as talking behind people's backs, backbiting, or holding grudges were gender coded as "women's behavior" because "women" personalized things too much. Women were described as being as "catty" or "backstabbing." According to Jeannie Bambrick, "When women get with each other, you might have one that's over here badmouthing someone else behind her back and then the next minute they're over here being that one's friend. Men just don't act like that, and I don't know why." Carmel Taylor felt that women should be more direct.

Men don't pull any punches. They spit it out. I feel some of the women I worked with could get further ahead if they'd just do that: spit it out. If you don't like his tie or his haircut, just tell him. Don't sit there and whisper to somebody else that that tie is really ugly. Get it out in the open and get on with your job.

Jan Kennedy agreed: "Women tend to be kind of backstabbing. I think it's easier to work with men even though I think they're jerks." Women were also described as more likely to carry personal grudges, according to Judy Himle—a characteristic that effectively reduced their ability to cooperate: "Men will let things slide. They'll disagree about something but then get back together and get on track, where women hold this little grudge forever because someone said their hair was out of place or they didn't like the way they picketed or something." Ideally, these women seemed to imply, leadership should be impersonal, direct, objective.

The openness and communication so necessary in informal organizations were hampered in the Support Group, some of the women felt, by an overly emotional environment. Again, this concern was expressed in gender-coded language. If communication were to be conducted in an emotional medium, there was the danger that a misunderstanding or even open conflict would result. According to Michelle Hendrickson, "women have a harder time communicating in the best of times. It's easy to misinterpret what somebody's saying. Men tolerate things more than women do. More patience. Women have the tendency to fly off the handle."

Acting emotionally can, in turn, reinforce the belief that women should not use power because they are subject to control by those emotions. They are too "PMS," too "bitchy": "Anytime you've got women together, there's going to be spats. I think women maybe tend to show their bitchiness more often than men."[33]

Being too emotional also meant not being tough enough. If women are overly sensitive or too easily hurt, the argument went, their effectiveness in working with others is hampered. According to Billie Goodeu, women have to learn to overlook their own tendency to take things to heart.

Women have a harder time overlooking if their feelings are hurt. If my husband's feelings get hurt, he lets them know how he feels and then, if they want to be his friend, he's ready to be friends with them again. If I get my feelings hurt, it takes me a long, long time to get over it. And I don't want anything to do with that person.

In general, as the women criticized their own organizational behavior, "women" were used to describe dysfunctional behavior or abuses of power. A contrast was often made between women's behavior and normal behavior, where "normal" was identified as male. Some of the women said, for example, that they preferred working with men because men were more cooperative, easygoing, and rational in their use of power. These glosses on stereotypical male and female behavior must be read as transitional perceptions reflecting the contradictions in the women's changing environment. Ironically, the more empowered the women became, the more likely they were to critique their own and other women's leadership behavior. This is especially ironic given their dramatically opposite assessment of the Support Group's achievements, which were based on the actual experience of women working successfully together.

WOMEN'S POLITICAL CULTURE: GENDER AND ORGANIZATION

The necessity for a supportive context for change is an often overlooked aspect of personal empowerment. This context is especially important where gender is concerned. In the same way that the women talked in gender-coded language about their struggles over power, they talked about the effectiveness of their new woman-controlled organization in gender terms as well. Historian Sara Evans, in her history of the origins of the contemporary women's movement, documented how women individually and collectively redefined their activities along gender lines in response to the contradictions they encountered between the rhetoric of freedom and the reality of male dominance and sexism in the Civil Rights Movement and the New Left.[34] Many historians of working-class women have noted similar transitions in women taking an active role in labor struggles. Judy Aulette and Trudy Mill's account of the Morenci Copper Strike, for example, noted that the women developed a collective awareness of their own gender-based issues and began challenging male authority as a direct result of their involvement in the strike.[35]

The development of a strong woman's culture in the Support Group contributed significantly to building and maintaining solidarity. The Support Group nourished the women in several ways: it was an environment where they could explore together their changing attitudes and ideas about themselves as women; communication and interaction within the group was highly personal, which encouraged a strong sense of belonging; there was an ethos of mutual respect; there was support from other women as they learned new skills and took up new challenges; and finally, the Support Group gave them an opportunity to work together with other women.

According to Estelle Freedman and many others, a critical factor in women's political empowerment is the amount of control they exercise within an organization.[36] The more separatist a women's organization is, the more successful it will be. Woman-dominated organizations are important, first of all, because they place "a positive value on women's social contributions" and provide "personal support."[37] Historian Diane Balser identified several other reasons why separate organizations are important to women's activism: in their own organizations, women have an opportunity to develop leadership skills, and feel freer to be self-assertive and use their personal powers; and working with other women develops the strong personal ties that contribute to a strong feeling of solidarity.[38] Separate organizations also give women an opportunity to explore how their own values reflect their experiences as women, as mothers, as consumers, as wives of workers, or as workers themselves. In addition, working women's organizations in particular provide women with the opportunity to develop their own economic analysis and create their own working-class agenda.

Historically, women have been most effective in the labor movement when they operated out of women-dominated organizations.[39] In her history of all-women waitress unions in the twentieth century, for example, Dorothy Sue Cobble argued that waitresses were far more effective when they organized in all-women unions rather than mixed-sex unions.[40] In addition to membership in unions, women in the labor movement have a tradition of organizing themselves into auxiliaries like the Support Group. According to historians Guida West and Rhoda Blumberg, these auxiliaries can shift quickly from "service to political roles," and are characterized by a relaxation of role definitions during the time of crisis. The auxiliaries give women ample opportunities to learn new skills, have new experiences, and generally step out of their traditional gender roles.[41]

In the Support Group, the women found a new kind of organizational and social space in which they could explore and initiate new liaisons with other women. The Support Group provided many of the environmental ingredients that Sara Evans felt were necessary for developing group cohesion among women: it was a clearly defined space that was dominated by women; it gave women an opportunity to model activism; it provided an analysis of the power structures in society; it endorsed the individual woman's personal transformation; and it created new communication patterns.[42]

The women in the Support Group were conscious from the very beginning that their group was a "woman's organization." It was important to them to have their own organization and to learn new skills on their own, particularly in the male-dominated world of the labor unions. Barbara Collette, for example, felt she had more opportunities in the company of other women.

I feel good with a group of women. I got a fair shot at being what I wanted to be, or doing what I wanted to do, or being the part that I wanted to be in it. But with men, I think my experience tells me that you don't always have that right to even decide what you want to be. So I'd rather work with women.

Central to any consciousness-raising process is a growing sense of the self as able to be, and act, in an empowered way. Women-dominated organizations like the Support Group give women more opportunities to take on leadership roles. In a supportive environment, women can more easily develop and enhance skills like public speaking and assertiveness. Jane Mansbridge noted in her study of democratic organizations, for example, that "it was the level of verbal self-confidence that most distinguished men from women."[43] In a woman-controlled organization, women have ample opportunities to practice speaking their minds in a supportive environment.

The structure of the Support Group was similar to traditional women's volunteer and self-help organizations. Solidarity was built on close personal bonding. Cheryl Remington described the social climate of the Support Group: "It's the women. There were men in the Support Group, but women just know how to pull a group together and really have strong feelings of friendship and love. That was the strongest part of the Support Group—just everybody pulling together." Friendship was an important organizational ethos. As we have seen, some of the women knew each other before the Support Group began, and those relationships continued and strengthened. Other women met each other as strangers and bonded either as political allies or as deep personal friends. Organizationally, according to Ardis Cameron, this bonding was important for maintaining group identity and cohesion.[44] An important part of bonding is sharing each other's personal lives, emotions, experiences. This takes place, Cameron argues, through "woman talk"—those special patterns of communication and interaction by which women establish intimacy with one another.[45]

WOMEN'S POLITICAL CULTURE: GENDER AND SOLIDARITY

Belonging—the sense of being valued and honored by others—is central to solidarity. Politics became a very personal matter for the women; and feeling oneself to be a part of the Support Group meant having a personal connection with other women. According to Jane Mansbridge, sharing such experiences as "working together under stress, [having] a common 'transcendent' experience, or self-revelation in consciousness raising sessions," all serve as the basis for a strong collective identity.[46] The overall effectiveness of the Support Group was due in large part to the women's skills in creating and maintaining this sense of belonging—of overcoming the sense of isolation. They did this through sensitivity to each other's feelings, by having a similar goal, and by building an alternative community together. According to Susan Benson, the Support Group was effective because women are highly skilled at creating and maintaining these kinds of harmonious and supportive environments.

It's easier for women to change. Women don't have the attitude that they have a right to be what they are. Women are adaptive and doing what is necessary to make things work. I think that's a general attitude. Women have a sense of harmony about them. No matter what situation they're in, they want that harmony. So once you get a woman that is experienced in dealing with other people—or accommodating—and has acquired certain people skills, she's far better than any man could be because she has strived to that point and she's working on it all the time.

To members of the Austin United Support Group, belonging also meant being with other women and believing that other women were supportive of them. This sense of sisterhood—though they did not use this word—empowered them. One woman expressed this feeling as one of comfort: "I would have felt really uncomfortable if the Support Group had been male. I probably wouldn't have been there. The fact that it was mostly women made it easier for me to come to work."[47]

Several women felt that the emotional nature of women's interactions was a positive attribute and contributed to more open, honest working relationships and more direct communication. Where men tend to shun expressiveness, women incorporate it into their interactions, according to Cindi Bellrichard: "Women are more open than men. Men try to hide their feelings. I think when a woman is upset about something, she lets other people know about it. I think that's maybe why women tend to fight with each other more."

Rituals of group maintenance based on mutual respect are important to building and maintaining community and are characterized by attentiveness to learning about one another's lives, listening to one another's ideas, drawing others in, involving people. Belonging was so important in the Support Group that feelings of nonacceptance or alienation caused women to withdraw from the group. Already alienated from the community of Austin, the women had only one another to rely on for support and affirmation. When women left the Support Group, they usually left for these personal—as opposed to ideological—reasons.

The success or failure of community within the Support Group centered in large part on how the women felt they were treated by others in the group. Ensuring that everyone felt involved and appreciated enhanced solidarity and organizational effectiveness. Alienation was described in a variety of ways: being badly treated; a lack of trust; or feelings of rejection. Several women mentioned quitting the Support Group, for example, because they felt like they had been "pushed around," or didn't feel "welcomed."[48] Other women left because they did not feel respected or appreciated: "I felt like I never could do anything good enough. I really felt kind of shoved aside, and I think others probably did, too," and "sometimes I don't think they wanted your input or wanted your ideas or even cared about you" (Anon.). Carol King expected the Support Group to be supportive of her personal growth and aspirations as a woman and as a leader. That was not the case, however.

This disturbance I felt about the inner circle has come from my emerging feeling as a more equal person in society. The first years of my marriage I was Mrs. David King, wife and mom, homemaker. I didn't go out, didn't go back into the workforce. So then when I emerged—I'm not a women's-libber kind, but I feel I'm more equal than women's libbers out in the forefront. So I think maybe that's why that disturbed me. I felt I was as good as anybody. I wasn't any better, but I was as good as. And they never made me feel that I was as good as they were. That bothered me.

Any slight could be perceived as being rejected by the group: "People did ask questions. But anytime a person would ask a question, they were ridiculed or they were come down on—intimidated enough to leave the Support Group" (Anon.). Barbara Collette attributed some of the dropouts to the lack of respect on the part of the leadership for the women who were involved.

There were many people that left the Support Group, who just kind of fell away. I think they felt they weren't heard or understood. I think we did a lot of cruel and mean things to a lot of nice decent people. If I didn't learn anything from those years in the Support Group, I've learned that people are not expendable. I think we thought—or the people with power thought—that people were expendable. I mean, if they didn't agree—"Just get out. If you don't like it, go." A lot of people's feelings were hurt.

When the women became aware that they were the main force in the strike after P-9 was shut down, they realized that the Support Group had power. Appreciation for their efforts as women became the basis of a female solidarity, and their awareness of their collective power as women was celebrated: "Women were the ones that led the meetings almost always; and the times when men spoke, it was by request of the women. The strongest power in the Support Group was the women."[49] The women commented on many occasions about the strength of other women in the Support Group. In fact, "strong" was a commonly used adjective to describe women's activities: "There were some very, very strong women there. Very strong."[50]

Empowerment comes about through a variety of means—some external; some internal to the self. Underlying everything, however, is a sense of expanding or breaking new ground, of becoming more independent. As the women in the

Support Group learned new skills, or exercised old skills in a new arena, they felt the support of other women and the knowledge that they were changing together. Many of the women felt that the Support Group gave them an opportunity to step out of character, out of traditional gender roles. It was acceptable because other women were doing it too—challenging authority; taking risks; being political: "I think it went above and beyond what a woman does and can do. I wasn't afraid to do anything, give anything a try."[51] Many of the women talked about a feeling of independence: "I didn't let anybody tell me what I couldn't do or where I could go."[52] For Susan Benson, an important aspect of that independence was the support of other women: "The experience of the Support Group taught independence in a group. You knew you were supported by others around, and you knew you were offering support. It also made you stronger and more independent to handle things yourself. I felt like I was a more capable person, like there isn't anything that I can't get through."

This newfound sense of empowerment also led women to become more assertive, to speak out publicly. This was a major step for many of the women; and they took it, even when it was painful or difficult: "At times I've had to stand up at the Support Group. Like stopping the Santa's Workshop. Somebody had to do it, so I got up and did it. That was a pretty assertive thing to do; but most of the time, I guess, I was pretty passive and sat and listened."[53]

Working together is still another way for people to know and appreciate one another. They learn to trust one another, rely on one another, gauge one another's skills, talents, personalities. In the Support Group, work was recognized as an expression of women's capabilities and creativity. Jan Kennedy took great pleasure in complimenting women for their special skills in following through and getting things done cooperatively.

I like to work with women. They've got more imagination. If you had left it up to the men, what would they have done? I don't think they would have gotten the picket signs made, they wouldn't have gotten food shelves set up, they wouldn't have gotten clothing drives, they wouldn't have gotten the mailings. There are a few, but I don't think the men would have had enough that would have been able to pull together to do it.

As the women worked together, their appreciation of other women—and women in general—was enhanced: "I think women expect more. They're harder workers, really" (Anon.). They felt that women had special organizational skills: "Women are probably better at organizing some things. Things that men don't think about that are important—home kinds of things."[54] Attention to detail has often been a means of belittling or criticizing women's styles, but clearly it was valued in the Support Group. One woman linked paying close attention to detail with follow-through, and another felt that it served to clear the air and create a more open environment: "With women I think you can get more into details about things and discuss situations more openly, and how to deal with it."[55] Some of the women said that women's attention to detail was just being "picky."

This criticism—couched in gender stereotypes—called into question women's ability to address really important issues that required a broad perspective. Men, as one of the women put it, are not bothered by little things: "I've always found it easier to work with men. They let things slide more—little things. And, 'Who cares?! We're out to do this job. And why worry about this? Why pick, pick at each other? Let's forget it!' "[56] There were good and bad sides to being picky, however.

I hate for this to even go down on record; but generally, women are tougher to work for because they tend to be pretty petty and they tend to look at small things. It's the very makeup of what makes women so special, because they can look at those small things and they do focus on detail and that's what makes life wonderful around them because they're the ones that put that sugar on the cookie—a guy would never do that. They're the ones that polish the shoes Christmas Eve to make the kids look cute the next day. They're the ones that decorate the homes and bring that comfort. They're the ones that actually bring art into daily living. So, it's because of those little things that make women unique. But it's also the thing that is the biggest drawback.[57]

Another important step in the women's expanding political consciousness was the growing awareness that the Support Group women were acting in their own right. Initially, the women saw themselves as supporters of their husbands or of P–9. Identification with the Support Group or with other women was minimal. Over time, however, their perspective shifted. Collective action with other women became an important part of their new identities as military working-class women. This solidarity was based in part on their shared economic agenda and in part on the democratic, participatory nature of the Support Group. Participating with others was in and of itself a highly political action that served to expand the self and, at the same time, integrate the self into the collective body. The organizational dynamic had to hit a balance between cooperation and autonomy; and unity was power.

The women's solidarity with women was especially empowering to them, and probably contributed significantly to the overall solidarity during the strike. Cindi Bellrichard described the transformation the group underwent.

The more I think about it, the more I get confused by the whole thing. I think our main goal in the beginning was to support our husbands. I think, if it hadn't have been for us, they would have fallen apart a lot sooner. We started out as the extension of our roles as women and became the main base, I guess, is how I see it. As I think back, there's a lot of men that maybe wouldn't have been as strong if their wives hadn't been part of the Support Group. Different times people would say things like, "I *couldn't* cross a picket line. My wife would kill me!" I don't think they necessarily had seriously thought about that, but I think they knew that the women were the ones that were the backbone of the whole thing.

At the beginning of the strike, in their role as supporters of their husbands, the women saw themselves as individual women in relation to individual men.

As their level of activity with other women increased, however, the group members gradually shifted their political identity to incorporate a more collective perspective. This collective awareness had two expressions: (1) through identification with the working-class economic agenda of the union, and (2) through solidarity with other women. As this identification with other women in the Support Group solidified, their collective political actions took on greater meaning. They became more conscious of their role as a group in shaping the political reality. They were changed by this self-awareness and sought, in turn, to change the world around them.

As the women moved from their families into the women's community of the Support Group, what began as a traditional supportive role for individual husbands evolved into the defense of their individual families, the striking community, and the whole way of life in Austin, Minnesota. Through their collective efforts to transform themselves and their reality, many of them believed that their work with other women was one of the most profound and deeply satisfying experiences they had ever had. They attributed this success quite consciously to their gender; and as Barbara Collette concluded, "I think a lot of us learned a lot about ourselves and about other women because of the Support Group."

NOTES

1. Marjorie Penn Lasky, " 'Where I Was a Person': The Ladies' Auxiliary in the 1934 Minneapolis Teamsters' Strikes," in *Women, Work, & Protest: A Century of U.S. Women's Labor History*, ed. Ruth Milkman (New York and London, 1987), 183.

2. Jill K. Conway, Susan C. Bourque, and Joan W. Scott, "Introduction: The Concept of Gender," *Daedalus* 116, 4 (Fall 1987).

3. See Guida West and Rhoda Lois Blumberg, "Reconstructing Social Protest from a Feminist Perspective," in *Women and Social Protest*, ed. Guida West and Rhoda Lois Blumberg (New York and Oxford, England, 1990), 21.

4. Ibid.

5. Mary O'Brien, *The Politics of Reproduction* (Boston, 1981), 98.

6. Ibid., 100.

7. Ava Baron, "Gender and Labor History: Learning from the Past, Looking to the Future," in *Work Engendered: Toward a New History of American Labor*, ed. Ava Baron (Ithaca, N.Y., and London, 1991), 1–46.

8. Lasky, "Where I Was a Person," 183.

9. Donna Simon; Dixie Lenz.

10. Susan Benson.

11. Mary Arens.

12. See especially Diane Balser, *Sisterhood and Solidarity: Feminism and Labor in Modern Times* (Boston, 1987); Dorothy Sue Cobble, *Dishing It Out: Waitresses and Their Unions in the Twentieth Century* (Urbana and Chicago, 1991); Estelle Freedman, "Separatism as Strategy: Female Institution Building and American Feminism, 1870–1930," *Feminist Studies* 5, 3 (Fall 1979): 512–29; Temma Kaplan, "Female Consciousness and Collective Action: The Case of Barcelona, 1910–1918," *Signs: Journal of Women in Culture and Society* 7, 3 (Spring 1982): 545–66; Sally Ward Maggard, "Gender

Contested: Women's Participation in the Brookside Coal Strike," in *Women and Social Protest*, ed. West and Blumberg; Ann Schofield, "The Women's March: Miners, Family, and Community in Pittsburg, Kansas, 1921–22," *Kansas History* 7, 2 (Summer 1984): 159–68; E. P. Thompson, "The Moral Economy of the English Crowd in the Eighteenth Century," *Past and Present* 50 (November 1971): 76–136; West and Blumberg, "Reconstructing Social Protest."

13. See especially Martha Ackelsberg, "Communities, Resistance, and Women's Activism: Some Implications for a Democratic Polity," in *Women and the Politics of Empowerment*, ed. Ann Bookman and Sandra Morgen (Philadelphia, 1988); Nancy Cott, "What's in a Name? The Limits of 'Social Feminism'; or, Expanding the Vocabulary of Women's History," *Journal of American History* 76, 3 (December 1989), 809–29; Elizabeth Faue, *Community of Suffering and Struggle: Women, Men, and the Labor Movement in Minneapolis, 1915–1945* (Chapel Hill, N.C., and London, 1991); Susan Levine, "Labors in the Field: Reviewing Women's Cultural History," *Radical History Review*, no. 35 (April 1986): 49–56.

14. See especially Balser, *Sisterhood and Solidarity*; Dana Frank, "Housewives, Socialists, and the Politics of Food: The 1917 New York Cost-of-living Protests," *Feminist Studies* 11, 2 (Summer 1985): 255–86; Maurine Weiner Greenwald, "Working-class Feminism and the Family Wage Ideal: The Seattle Debate on Married Women's Right to Work, 1914–1920," *Journal of American History* 76, 1 (June 1989): 118–49.

15. For an excellent overview of the philosophical and economic problems surrounding the relationship between the household economy and the market economy, see William James Booth, *Households: On the Moral Architecture of the Economy* (Ithaca, N.Y., 1993).

16. Ardis Cameron, "Bread and Roses Revisited: Women's Culture and Working-class Activism in the Lawrence Strike of 1912," in *Women, Work, & Protest: A Century of U.S. Women's Labor History*, ed. Ruth Milkman (New York and London, 1987), 55.

17. Kaplan, "Female Consciousness," 546.

18. Madeline Krueger.

19. Dixie Lenz.

20. Carmel Taylor.

21. Judy Himle.

22. Dixie Lenz.

23. Cheryl Remington.

24. Linda Novak.

25. Barbara Collette.

26. Jean (Vietor) Schiesser.

27. See Jane J. Mansbridge, *Beyond Adversary Democracy* (New York, 1980), 14.

28. Judy Remington, "Women Working Together: How Well Is It Working? Part III: Power and Leadership," *Minnesota Women's Press* (November 23–December 6, 1988): 4–passim.

29. Ibid., 4.

30. Mansbridge, *Beyond Adversary Democracy*, 193.

31. Linda Novak.

32. Remington, "Women Working Together," 5.

33. Cindi Bellrichard.

34. Sara M. Evans, *Personal Politics: The Roots of Women's Liberation in the Civil Rights Movement and the New Left* (New York, 1979).

35. Judy Aulette and Trudy Mills, "Something Old, Something New: Auxiliary Work in the 1983–1986 Copper Strike," *Feminist Studies* 14, 2 (Summer 1988): 258.

36. See Freedman, "Separatism as Strategy."

37. Ibid., 527.

38. Balser, *Sisterhood and Solidarity*.

39. For examples of the effectiveness of women's separate organizations, see Balser, *Sisterhood and Solidarity*; Cobble, *Dishing It Out*; Blanche Wiesen Cook, "Female Support Networks and Political Activism: Lillian Wald, Crystal Eastman, Emma Goldman," *Chrysalis*, no. 3 (1977): 43–61; Cynthia B. Costello, " 'WEA're Worth It!' Work Culture and Conflict at the Wisconsin Education Association Insurance Trust," *Feminist Studies* 11, 3 (Fall 1985): 497–518; Evans, *Personal Politics*; Freedman, "Separatism as Strategy"; Molly Ladd-Taylor, "Women Workers and the Yale Strike," *Feminist Studies* 11, 3 (Fall 1985): 465–89; Mary P. Ryan, "The Power of Women's Networks: A Case Study of Female Moral Reform in Antebellum America," *Feminist Studies* 5, 1 (Spring 1979): 66–85; Louise A. Tilly, "Paths of Proletarianization: Organization of Production, Sexual Division of Labor, and Women's Collective Action," *Signs: Journal of Women in Culture and Society* 7, 2 (Winter 1981): 400–417; plus others.

40. Cobble, *Dishing It Out*.

41. West and Blumberg, "Reconstructing Social Protest," 23.

42. See Evans, *Personal Politics*, 219–20, for a helpful discussion of factors defining collective identity–building.

43. Mansbridge, *Beyond Adversary Democracy*, 192.

44. Cameron, "Bread and Roses Revisited," 55.

45. Ibid., 56.

46. Mansbridge, *Beyond Adversary Democracy*, 243.

47. Julie Wilson.

48. Rietta Pontius; Jan Kennedy.

49. Judy Himle.

50. Carmel Taylor.

51. Rietta Pontius.

52. Mary Arens.

53. Donna Simon.

54. Mary Machacek.

55. Marie Loverink; Judy Kraft.

56. Madeline Krueger.

57. Susan Benson.

CHAPTER 10

"I'd Never Been Radical Before"

What happens to people when the foundations of their culture cave in on them? When they lose their jobs, their faith in the government, their voices in their community? What happens to people when they have to overcome a lifetime of passivity, of comfort, of confidence in the American way of life, and take up a struggle against an array of corporate power just to put food on the table? In Austin, Minnesota, beginning in 1984, the world changed; and the lives of the women and men who participated in the strike against the Hormel Company were transformed. Out of love and anger, passion and commitment, the men and women of P–9 and the Support Group rebuilt their world using their own skills, their own vision. Their struggle is the struggle of all people—the struggle to have a place to live, food enough to eat, good work, and a community of care and of joy.

The story of the Austin United Support Group is the story of one community's response to the economic restructuring of capitalism currently underway in the United States. Transnational corporations all across the land are making an effort to dismantle the American economy as part of a transition to a global market-driven economy built on the foundation of cheap labor. The lower wages and lax environmental regulations in other, poorer countries increasingly make doing business in America appear too costly for those companies concerned with maximizing profits. The American standard of living is eroding as the jobs that have sustained the social and economic life of whole communities are sacrificed to higher corporate profits. Communities all across America are literally being boarded up as companies discard them and the workers who built them.

The Austin Strike was a watershed moment in American economic history— the moment when the national consciousness was first alerted to the systematic dismantling of the economy. Prior to the events in Austin, union struggles were between individual unions and individual companies. Suddenly, in Austin, the pattern became clear. What was happening in Austin had been happening in communities across the United States, and it was here that the contradictions were seen in their sharpest relief. The familiar pattern of abandonment and community destruction emerged: years of threats, coercion, concessions; rising corporate profits accompanied by demands for cheaper labor; accusations that workers were unproductive; new speeded-up technologies introduced; and finally, with the threat to community life itself, open confrontation and battle.

People do not like change, for the most part. Sometimes, however, change is forced upon them. The stimulus for economic change is an especially traumatic occurrence, creating—as it did in Austin—a veritable cultural catastrophe.[1] In response, the men and women who depended on Hormel for their very lives arose to meet the challenge of change. Karl Polanyi argued, in his seminal analysis of the emergence of industrial capitalism, that change generally comes from outside our communities and our families. The response to these external challenges, however, is always an internal social one. Resistance "comes through groups, sections, and classes," and is always, Polanyi argues, initiated in defense of community.[2] In the Austin Strike, change came into people's lives abruptly and totally. Over a few short months, the whole fabric of the community was altered. Nothing remained the same. With the onset of the struggle, the families of striking P–9ers were thrown into a situation where change itself became the reality. From day to day, they were forced to reassess and reinvent everything in their lives: economics, politics, government, family, gender, community. On the personal level, too, people had to reinvent themselves: both men and women were forced to reexamine traditional roles, develop new skills, change their economic lifestyles and learn to make do, meet and interact with a broad diversity of people.

In the end, the battle went to the Hormel Company. But out of that struggle, a new pattern for working people also emerged—a pattern that incorporated women as full partners in the struggle against the loss of community. In Austin, a line was finally drawn; and in response to the threat to their families and their whole way of life, the women of the Austin United Support Group banded together in resistance. In the process they changed, and their world changed as well. This chapter examines the changes they underwent: at the level of personal transformation; at the level of political transformation; and finally, at the level of cultural transformation.

PERSONAL TRANSFORMATION

On the level of personal transformation, the women identified many changes they underwent in the process of becoming more empowered: finding and using their voices to speak out against injustice; developing self-confidence; expanding their worlds; and learning new leadership skills. Over and over the women talked about feeling free to speak their minds—many, for the first time—and then acting on their beliefs. Speaking out was an important act; and as they developed the skills, knowledge, and comfort to stand up in front of a group, they expanded their activism into many public forums. There were many moments of hesitancy and self-consciousness, however, as the women struggled to overcome the culture of silence that women, especially, inhabit.

As far as being active—speaking up and saying what's on your mind, and trying to do something about it—I remember back to the Vietnam War. I felt too old to speak up. But by the time it came down to the strike and the Support Group, my feelings were completely different. I didn't feel like I was too old for anything. I was about the right age for whatever needed to be done![3]

Other women described how the level of frustration became so great that they were compelled to speak out—even when they believed it went against their nature. Anger became a motivating force in their growing activism.

You have a whole change of nature. I did things and I said things that I never in a million years thought I would do or would come out of my mouth. The anger, the frustration, was so great—I don't know, it just changes you completely. It was a real learning experience.[4]

As they moved into new and more public roles, the women found the courage to act more assertively on their beliefs. For Carole Apold, this even included open confrontation.

I'd never been radical before. But once I made up my mind about what I was going to do, nobody could talk me out of it. I'd speak my mind at union meetings. I remember one meeting where Ray Rogers was trying to speak and John Anker disrupted the meeting. He wouldn't let Ray answer. He just walked out. But I went right after him. I mean, I'd get so angry at these people. They'd disrupt the meeting, but they wouldn't listen to the answers. I went right out the front door after him. I never thought of what I was doing or anything—I just did it.

Carol King seemed somewhat amazed at her own transformation into an assertive—even forceful—woman.

If my husband hadn't held me back, I probably would have been a really strong activist. I really didn't know that I was that kind of a person. I got really aggressive, bigmouthed. I guess I just really thought I was kind of a follower, a background person. I think if he hadn't held me back, I would have been a real aggressive person.

As a result of their new assertiveness, many of the women talked about being stronger, about gaining self-confidence and the courage of their convictions. They described themselves as being tougher, less fearful, more direct: "I learned to be tough. To stick up for our rights. I guess that I learned I could voice my opinion even if other people didn't agree'' (Anon.). Another woman agreed: "I'm much tougher, meaner. I'm not afraid anymore to speak up for something. Now I get mad quicker, better, louder."[5] The women did not just become assertive, but aggressively took their beliefs into action, according to Rietta Pontius.

I learned I could speak out if I wanted to. I became a fighter. I didn't think I'd ever be able to stand in line and be able to talk to people and answer questions like I did. But I did it. I'm still fighting for some of the things that I think, and people think I shouldn't think that way.

Learning new skills was another way the women experienced personal growth and transformation. For some, it was the newfound skill of public speaking; for others, it was developing organizational skills. Through her involvement, for example, Barbara Collette experienced two benefits: her self-perception was enhanced; and she had an opportunity to develop many new interpersonal and leadership skills.

What the Support Group did for me is, it really helped my self-image. I had a lot of problems, before then, believing people could like me and that I was worth something. I felt that I was really contributing something and that I was of value and that I was worthwhile. The Support Group fine-tuned some things for me: I think I read people better than I did; I think I see some things more clearly; I think it's easier for me to work with groups than it was; I think I learned to negotiate—which was a skill I didn't have before I got involved.

In many cases, the women brought skills to the group they already had but had never exercised in a collective environment. Sometimes they were simply thrust into new roles and they rose to the occasion, developing into strong leaders.

I probably learned some speaking skills. I would help run meetings. There were times, too, when we went to rallies where I wasn't a speaker but where I went around and talked with people, telling our side of the story, how things were working, and asked for their support. It helped me to learn to speak better, to feel like when you ask for money, or for support, that you aren't begging, that you were asking for their support because you were helping them, too, in the long run.[6]

Sometimes the changes were quite dramatic. Susan Benson recalled her awe and amazement at the changes many of the women underwent.

I saw people that, I swear, wouldn't have gotten up in a group of five people and said anything, and they got up in groups of thousands and told the story. And told it again and again and again and again until they dropped over. And then they got up the next morning and hit the road again and told it again.

Other skills the women talked about included skills in dealing with people, organizational skills, and the skills of care and cooperation mentioned by Marie Loverink: "patience, compassion, unity, strength, and tolerance."

The women also looked deeply into themselves and reexamined long-held personal values. For some, this was an opportunity to look closely at their material existence and decide what was really important to them: "I think we all became better people, in the respect that we learned that a lot of things in life we took for granted were just extra little goodies that we can get by without."[7] For others, it was an opportunity to reflect on their whole lives: "How you really get your head on straight. You think you're a pretty down-to-earth person. But when you have a big trauma in your life, it really makes you stand back and take a look at what your life is."[8] Cheryl Remington reflected on her expanded insights and personal growth.

I probably changed. I got a real good understanding of life. I think I was pretty naive going into it and thought everybody was always happy. My biggest skill was really to be understanding. I really never had to suffer up until that point, so I guess I learned a lot. And I wouldn't trade it for anything.

POLITICAL TRANSFORMATION

At a certain point, however, some of the women were not satisfied with just personal change. What had happened to them was not their individual problem, and the solutions were not individual but collective ones. They learned that their struggle was similar to the struggle of workers in many other places, at many other times in history. As they organized and then acted on their vision of community and on their sense of what was right—in the very process of acting— they themselves became agents of change. Instead of being acted upon, they took control of their own destiny.

The strike radicalized the women of the Support Group. It opened their eyes to the economic and political realities in their community, and in the country. Like many of the women, Barbara Collette went through a long process of questioning her whole reality: her political philosophy, her spirituality, her patriotism.

I never really was Republican or Democrat. I voted for people for reasons at the time— I saw them on TV or read about something in the paper, and voted on that. With the strike, all of a sudden I was forced to really look at it. It was like a mid-life crisis, to be perfectly honest. I had decided I was not going to be either Republican or a Democrat, that I was going to be a Socialist. I really did look into the Socialist Party because at that time we had a lot of Socialists and Communists running around. I decided the Republican/Democrat thing was a lot of garbage and I was not going to be a part of it. I have come back and made different decisions since that time. About the same time, I felt the church—not God, but the church—failed me, so there were some real struggles going on in my life about the things I really believed in. To see what America really was—there were some really tough lessons for me. I really believed that one person could make a difference. When I finally admitted to myself that we lost the fight, it was very, very hard for me. I had given 100 percent—and then to realize that it wasn't enough, that you really couldn't fight city hall in Austin, Minnesota, because city hall was owned by Hormels, and because city hall *was* Hormels. That was difficult for me. There were a lot of things going on in my mind at that time. I could have left the Support Group and gone off in 100 different directions and joined different causes. Until I realized later— much later—that they were somehow all kind of tied up in a little knot together and were really related. So I think I had a real political awakening.

Each woman had to come to peace with her new insights of how the world worked—or didn't work. One of the most important elements in this political transformation was awareness: of how what was happening in Austin connected with the rest of world; of their own values; and of the role of the union in their lives.

The women were also radicalized by their activism, as we have already seen. Doing empowers people. When people take their beliefs and visions into the streets, these ideas become more real, as they become grounded in individual acts and in the community of activists. Finally, in addition to awareness and activism, the women's political transformation was also characterized by a grow- ing tolerance of other people and other perspectives. In short, their world view expanded and became more inclusive.

For the most part, people in Austin before the strike were indifferent to the analysis of broader economic issues. Insulated and isolated by a comfortable standard of living and generations of labor union–company peace and mutual prosperity, the residents of Austin paid little attention to the striking mineworkers in Appalachia or to the civil rights protests in New York City. The Hormel/P– 9 Strike changed all that. As they looked back on their political transformation, the women felt they had expanded their political vision and sharpened their skills in political and economic analysis. The strike opened their eyes and connected their experience to other people's experiences: "It was my first realization about civil disobedience. The shell you put around yourself—until you have something happen like it did here. Then you see it's happening all over" (Anon.). Women like Billie Goodeu saw themselves acquiring new political depth and maturity.

I think we've become better people for the simple reason that there isn't a situation I see on TV where some group is taking a stand where I don't sit and try to think through, "What is the meaning? What is this group trying to tell us?" You look past the media, past the cops dragging them to the paddy wagons, and think, "Well, what are they trying to do? Do they have a purpose? You just think more deeply. You pay closer attention. You buy American-made things.

They also came to know some of these stories firsthand, according to Judy Himle.

I gained insights into government and law procedures that I was not aware of. I also learned the value of our constitutional rights. During rallies, we often housed people in our home from all parts of the country and all walks of life. We also traveled to some meetings and rallies. We feel we have expanded our views and, in sharing our story, have heard others who have also had worse strifes in their lives.

For some individuals, the transformation was dramatic. They were forced to reexamine old prejudices as they encountered new experiences, new people. These new experiences resulted in new insights into the nature of oppression.

It was a horrible time, but it was the best of times. I think we grew a lot as people; we got to understand a lot. I don't know if my husband would appreciate me saying this or not, but—he probably grew a lot more than I did because he got out. I think a lot of the men that went out on the road—they went out a bunch of packinghouse rednecks, so to speak, and came back completely different people. They saw what was going on in the world, and they didn't like it. My husband came back, and he didn't like what he was seeing as far as people that were being oppressed. We grew.[9]

This expanded awareness created a certain openness to new experiences generally. Carole Apold described it this way: "It made me more open to what was going on around me. Seemed like I was closed up—not closed up exactly, but I guess my mind was just a little bit more closed." An appreciation for diversity was not always easy to achieve, even with political allies. Sometimes the women were uncomfortable.

There was one guy who stayed at our house—it was a last-minute thing. He came out here. I mean, he was dirty. He wanted to stay up all night and talk about his political interests, but I wasn't interested in communism, exactly. It's okay, though. I mean, as far as I'm concerned, it doesn't hurt you to be a friend of people like that. I think that helps broaden your scope. (Anon.)

Although race was not a factor in the strike, several of the women talked about how events forced people in Austin to reexamine their beliefs on cultural diversity. Coalition building with African Americans, Native Americans, and Hispanic people opened the P–9 families up to new worlds, new perspectives. Susan Benson, for example, described how she came to understand and appreciate that people are alike despite cultural differences.

A highlight for me was when Jesse Jackson came. I was impressed, I was motivated, I was moved. And I learned something—when you start singing those gospel songs, you realized that little Midwestern folks don't know the words, and it's like you've got a different church down there that's a little more vocal. And all the different people we met throughout the land—that expanded our viewpoint of people. Other communities, other lifestyles—I felt fortunate to have met some of the people that came in to help us.

It was not just a matter of becoming more accepting or tolerant of differences. Susan also described how, prior to the strike, her family's world had been impoverished by the absence of encounters with different people.

I had worked with people and gone to school with people of other races, so I was open to that; but my husband was not—until the strike. We had different people stay in our home, and we stayed in theirs and talked with them. And it opened up him and our whole family. We used to argue about racial things and prejudice, and his bigotry was a source of irritation that no longer exists because his mind was open and he saw that people are people wherever you go. All of a sudden he realized there were a whole lot more similarities. It helped all of us as a family—opened us up.

Susan also talked about how politically naive she had been.

And I thought how closed my world had been until this point—how safe it's been all these years—and then I'd hear these people who have struggled and struggled and struggled. Histories of struggle for them—coal mines, different strikes. It was mind opening to experience that; and I think it expanded us, and it got us over a lot of prejudices.

Barbara Collette, too, began making important connections between the strike and acts of resistance generally in the United States.

I got rid of a lot of prejudices at that time. Because for the first time I realized that, if this could happen to me as an average middle-class white American woman who was Protestant, then some of the things I saw on television probably weren't true either. I had to go back to the sixties in my mind and remember the Watts riot and the things I saw on TV, and—seeing what the television did with what was happening for us—all of a sudden I realized those same things probably happened in the sixties when blacks were trying to make people understand their oppression.

Vickie Guyette's contact with a wide diversity of people was an occasion for deep personal changes in both perception and action: "I've learned that everybody's different and that's okay. I've also broadened my perspective on listening to different points of view and not being so judgmental. I've grown as a person because I've learned this."

During the strike, the women had an opportunity to explore both economic and gender issues. Their experience is invaluable because it is often difficult to discern where class issues end and gender issues begin.[10] The boundary is blurred not because the actors are uncertain about what is motivating their behavior, but because gender and class are interdependent systems of oppression. This becomes more clear when we see that a central issue in gender struggles is the distinction between public and private. The contemporary women's movement understood this contested ground and staked a claim to the public arena for women in its call to bring the personal and the political together in one praxis action. The challenge for women in articulating an economic agenda is to find the best way to bring their concerns into the public arena. Motivation for women involved in labor struggles is twofold, and both are grounded in women's personal experiences. First, as members of the working class, they bring to their politics a belief in the need to work collectively with others. Second, as women, their economic and political agenda is shaped by the spheres of family, of gender, and of community. In short, to understand the motivations and actions of the women in the Support Group, we need to appreciate the many "communities" that influenced their actions. Only by understanding the context of their experiences are we able to understand their actions.[11]

A new or strengthened consciousness of class was probably the most powerful motivator for the women's political transformation. Their political analysis identified the primary oppression as economic, not genderic. It was not male power, but the economic power of the Hormel Company that most strongly influenced the course of their personal and collective lives. Although the women had some minor encounters with the male-dominated union, in general the men were not the primary problem. The few attempts made to control the women by shaming them for acting like men or by appealing to traditional gender roles and stereotypes did not deter the women. They moved quickly and comfortably into new expanded roles in the strike and, in the process, redefined both gender and labor movement boundaries. The women and men in Austin were, after all, on the same side; and some of the women took pains to point that out. Donna Simon, for example, felt that gender was not the basis for her actions; "union" was.

I'm not a woman's libber. I'm very happy to be a woman. I have no intention of competing in a man's world. I can't lift 100 pounds of potatoes. Whether I was a man or a woman I still would've done what I could do, because I have always been very strong union.

Although they did not identify gender as a primary point of conflict, the women were nevertheless highly sensitive to the fact that they were acting both individually and collectively as women—defending their families, their class, and their community.[12]

Another major political transformation some of the women underwent was a renewed appreciation of labor unions and union solidarity. Sometimes those insight were bittersweet, according to Shirley Heegard.

Even though we didn't so-called "win" the strike—if you don't obtain the goal that you set out to win, you have to pick another thing that you have won—and I think that we did win. We still hear from people how proud they were that the P–9ers hung in like they did—other union people. We gave strength to other unions; that was the big thing that this strike did. I understand now even the UFCW is using our tactics in some of their strikes.

Even though she grew up in a strong union family, Jeannie Bambrick, too, changed her perception of unions and the role they play in people's lives.

When I was little, my dad was in the union—and here I lived in a union town—and I didn't even realize what unions were. You heard so much talk about the unions and the Mafia image they had. But it's not like that at all. It really taught me a lot about what people in unions are really all about. It's not machine guns; it's just working people that are out there wanting to make a better life for themselves and their families.

Billie Goodeu said that her activism grew out of her family's union allegiance: "I guess because of the fact that I was a wife and a mother—because of my son-in-law and my husband [P–9ers]—I guess that's why I became so strong politically." For Billie, being "union" meant connecting her experience with the experience of working people everywhere. It meant solidarity with all working people, not just P–9; and it meant incurring an obligation to care for others, as well.

I remember driving by some poor picketers out on the line in Red Wing—it was a trucking company. So I swung in there, and it was cold, and I went and bought them some rolls, and I told them, "If there's anything I can do, let us know." At one time, I wouldn't have done that. I wouldn't have been thoughtful enough. I don't think people are thoughtful until you experience something like this.

Solidarity came to have a deeper meaning, beyond support or commitment to a cause. It meant taking action together. Their sudden transition from the relatively passive private sphere to the role of militant activist on the front lines of a major labor struggle had a profound impact on many of the women. Prior to the strike, very few of the women had been involved in political activism. There had not been a strike since 1933; local politics was quiet and stable; and in general, the Austin political scene was dominated by men. Radical politics such as the Civil Rights Movement, the Women's Movement, the Anti-war Movement, the Environmental Movement—all were distant and threatening events. Individuals, of course, were touched by those movements and changed by them; but the community as a whole had little experience in social-change activism. Social change happened in other places, but not in white, working-class, patriotic, rural Austin, Minnesota. As a result, the women were amazed at themselves as they became political activists.

The times that we would banner and mass picket really stick out in my mind. I'm a person who would never do it, would never get involved like that, and I really felt that it was right. So that really sticks out—that I really do have it in me that, when times get tough, I can do something about it.[13]

Through their activism, the women gained new insights into political power. Their activism also changed their political behavior; they learned that politics is a collective activity. Judy Himle, for example, saw for the first time the power of collective action and solidarity.

I never had been involved with anything political. I guess one of the things that was a real learning experience was the insight that, when we grouped together, we could change some things politically. I can remember going to some of the Democratic caucuses—I'd never gone before, or been involved in any kind of government things. We realized—or felt—that a lot of our issues were politically motivated, and they were also things that were probably handed down because big government was involved politically in a lot of those issues. We felt it was important for us to group together and get involved in some of those things, to try and change how some of those laws and how some of those things came about.

It was not easy to make the transition to activism—even for women like Barbara Collette who had been involved in other social issues. What made the difference was believing in what she was doing and having the support of other women.

I've always been involved in what I would call "causes." I guess I've always been a kind of fighter. There were lots of things I thought about before speaking out and becoming active in the Support Group, but I never verbalized them. I guess I hoped that other people were thinking about it and they'd have the courage to do it—which would give me the courage to do it. It wasn't easy going door to door and talking, or explaining, or asking for money. Demonstrating was not easy for me. Carrying a banner was not easy for me.

For Barbara, the decision to become an activist meant that every facet of her life would undergo change. To speak out was to risk losing everything. Taking action had profoundly personal consequences.

It's real difficult to take a public stand, because you realize that some people may never talk to you again. And maybe that was part of it in the beginning—I worried about my job, I worried about my family, I worried about my kids in school and what kind of reaction they would get from their teachers.

Though some of her fears were realized, in the end she felt she had made the right decision.

I think I worried that I'd never get a job again, which pretty much came true. I never did feel free to speak my mind—I just did it. Because my name was in the paper for being arrested, I lost my job. And there was a real sense of embarrassment because my family didn't really understand. My youngest daughter, my parents—that was sometimes hard, being labeled a "radical" or a "fool." Going public with anything presents some problems, and yet it didn't diminish the power I felt. My husband was really supportive—more than I thought he would be. I think there was even a sense of pride, of really standing up for what I believed in to the point of going to jail. All of that still gives me a sense of power today. The whole thing gave me a sense of self-esteem that I maybe didn't possess then. Knowing that I could do something like that made me feel good—knowing that if I'm ever called to do it again, or ever feel like I need to do it again, I can. The fear will still be there, and all the other things; but I believe in that sense of power—the boost in your self-esteem—just seeing yourself a little differently will also be there.

CULTURAL TRANSFORMATION

The women in the Support Group were very sensitive about being labeled "radicals." In the anti-labor political climate of conservatism in the 1980s, their activism came under fire as excessive and un-American. They did not consciously identify and promote a radical agenda or develop a comprehensive critique of capitalism or the nation state. While they might listen to the Socialist party or Communist party analysis and position, for example, only a few women took up a revolutionary—or even a social-change—agenda. In fact, they went to some lengths to disavow that label of "radicalism," and they were indignant when radical labels were applied to them. Historian Lawrence Goodwyn attributes this reluctance to claim radicalism and radical terminology to deference by working-class people to the dominant capitalist hegemony.[14]

But they were radicals—in essence, if not in name. Their analysis was radical; their decision to confront the power of the Hormel Company and the forces of authority in the larger community was radical. They were radical because they understood the profound implications of their actions on the economic, political, and social life of their community. According to Goodwyn, a radical community can be characterized by three qualities: (1) a collective sense of purpose; (2) an analysis of the power structure; and (3) confrontation with that power structure. On all three counts, the Support Group could be defined as a "radical organization."

Certainly, the women in the Support Group had a collective sense of purpose that they expressed through collective action. It was shaped around care and concern for their families and their community, and a strong sense of justice. Together they challenged the corporate and community institutions that stood in the way of those objectives; and in the process, they shaped a new collective cultural awareness that was embodied in the strike culture they formed. Goodwyn hesitated to call this collective awareness a "class consciousness," preferring the term "collective self-confidence . . . a new way of looking at society, a way of thinking that represented a shaking off of inherited forms of deference."[15] A similar consciousness undergirds E. P. Thompson's definition of an emerging collective awareness: "Classes do not exist as separate entities. . . . On the contrary, people find themselves in a society structured in determined ways . . . [in which] they experience exploitation . . . , they identify points of antagonistic interest, they commence to struggle around these issues and in the process of struggling they discover themselves as classes."[16] Collective awareness and the culture that sustains it, according to Thompson, emerge out of a given historical context.

Moreover, the Support Group had a well-developed analysis of the power structure in the town of Austin—both economically and politically. They developed a critique of capitalism, though they never called the dynamic between Hormel and the workers by that term. Their analysis of the local economic power structure was sound, and their own experience with the Hormel Company taught them the classical dialectic between the capitalist and the worker.

In other ways, however, the Support Group did *not* develop a radical ideology: for example, the women did not challenge the government or the idea of private property, nor did they call for the destruction of the market economy or industrial capitalism as a whole. Their focus was on the immediate economic crisis in their own community. Rather than calling for the destruction of the Hormel Company, or the appropriation of the means of production, they hoped—and then demanded—the company would see that paying a fair and decent wage was in the interest of the community as a whole. They appealed to corporate responsibility—not realizing that, even though the Hormel Company had a history of close ties to Austin, the company did not see its corporate activities as being part of the community or responsible to the community. The women never really challenged the existing political and economic structures, although, when they saw how power really operated in their community, their faith in those structures was so shaken that the sense of alienation they feel is probably permanent. Despite these insights, they never articulated the overthrow of those structures, or even suggested reforming them.

The most radical act of the Austin United Support Group was its establishment of a model participatory democratic community. In his study of nineteenth-century Populism, Lawrence Goodwyn described the process a community underwent as it formed a participatory democratic culture. The first step was the formation of an autonomous organization, followed by efforts to recruit and involve people. As we have seen, the Support Group followed this same process—establishing its identity, its goals and objectives, and then reaching out to involve people from the union families and the broader community. A third and very critical step was self-education. Early on, one of the major objectives of the Support Group was to educate itself and the community—particularly when members believed that the whole community would join them in their efforts. Self-education, and the dissemination of information, continued throughout the strike and beyond. It involved communicating through external and internal media to a national audience. Finally, according to Goodwyn, democratic community is born with the establishment of a new institution to implement a new political vision. The vision of the Support Group articulated confrontation and need: a moral economy where basic human needs for survival are met; a nonrepressive government; new roles for women; and most importantly, fairness and justice.[17]

There were other organizational elements marking the Support Group as a democratic community: the high degree of participation in decision-making; the decentralization of decision-making and managing; the high level of activism, which empowered people to influence and control their environment; the creation of a democratic economy with its emphasis on sharing, in such programs as the

Food Shelf, Santa's Workshop, and Adopt-a-Family; the establishment of its own informal governance structure; and consensus on an ethical framework. These participatory and democratic elements stood in sharp contrast to the repressive, controlling, and exploitive corporate and governmental hegemony of the dominant culture. The Support Group also provided leadership opportunities for the women involved, and a way to become equal participants in the democratic process. As women, the members went through a painful but meaningful process learning how to be participatory. Even the internal conflict was beneficial. Open democratic decision-making processes require a high degree of interaction; and even though dialogue and discussion became heated and contentious, the process remained open to all points of view.

It takes more than organization, however, to create and sustain democratic community. It takes individuals with a strong sense of self-esteem and self-confidence. According to Goodwyn, "Democratic movements are initiated by people who have individually managed to attain a high level of personal political self-respect."[18] Similarly, a maxim of the women's movement has always been, "The personal is the political"—to which we can add, "And it equals democracy." It was at the personal level that the Support Group was most effective. The environment created an opportunity for personal transformation, and it was because of this environment that women were able to empower themselves as women. The better they felt about themselves and their skills, the more able they were to participate fully in creating and maintaining their democratic community.

Creating this alternative democratic community was a radical action. It was also a very quiet action. As radical tactics, demonstrations and civil disobedience confrontations tend to be sporadic and incident specific. They are flashy, they are important—especially in this era of the mass media. But real change—at the root, the radical—takes place at the personal and community level.

THE PRICE OF THE STRIKE

The economic impact of the strike was devastating both to the striking families and to the community of Austin as a whole. Patricia Higgins summed it up well.

Many people lost their homes. Austin became, for a while, a ghost town. People didn't shop here; they didn't come into the community. When you have 1,500 people that are out on strike, and most of them were married and had children—so we are probably talking about 5,000 people, out of a community of 26,000, who were affected. So it had to have a huge economic effect on the community.

People working at other businesses were laid off from their jobs, hours were cut, storefronts emptied.[19] Even after the strike was "settled," according to Vickie Guyette, businesses suffered: "When the Hormel Company hired the people from Iowa and out of town—they don't spend their money here." The real estate market was seriously depressed as many families lost their homes: "They were talking about $8.25 an hour. What type of home could you buy with that kind of money? Even in Austin, with real estate prices being low, you could probably only afford something in the twenties, two bedroom."[20] Individual families suffered serious financial losses: "We sold our house and lost $20–25,000 on it over what the market value had been previous to the strike."[21] Other people were forced to migrate permanently from the area in order to find work.

We moved out of the area in 1988, and I haven't been to Austin all that much since. It really bothers me to go back there. There is so much hurt in that town, so many bad feelings. I was born and raised there and know many people there, but to go and visit is emotionally hard for me. It brings back a lot of anger—anger I don't think will ever go away. So many people gave so much of themselves for that community and for the strike, and it seemed wherever we turned, whatever we did, we were stepped on by big business. I still have a strong emotional tie with certain people. But as for Austin, it's not my home anymore.[22]

Some families simply walked away, leaving empty houses and unpaid mortgages. Others who still remain in Austin would like to start over in another place, but can't leave because they can't sell their houses. There were many stories of economic hardship when families were forced to leave.

We have three houses—two by choice and one not by choice. Al's son had to leave town to find work and they couldn't buy a house because they had their loan here, so we paid off the loan and gave him the balance of the house's value for a down payment on a house there. So we acquired a third house. But we're renting it out to one of the good Ottumwa workers.[23]

Many of the women wept during the interviews. Although it had been years since the strike, the pain was still raw and fresh, the sense of loss and sorrow profound. Despite their tears, however, they were still able to glean positive insights from the experience.

It gets easier as time goes by. I hate to think that I needed people, but I think I did. And the bitterness has gotten better. In our family, we want to put it behind us. We've lived through this, we've made it, we'll never forget it, we've learned a lot from it. But it's kind of like we need to go on. I'm trying to keep the tears from flowing down—they don't flow as often and it isn't as emotional. So, time does heal. It doesn't make it go away, but it softens it.[24]

Some of the women talked about the deep personal losses they experienced as their lives were forced in new directions. They missed friends and family who were forced to move away. Some felt that the stresses from the strike had caused the early deaths of friends (Anon.). While the strike served to strengthen some marriages, others ended in divorce.[25] Sometimes, lifestyles were altered dramatically.

It's still really emotional. When I start to talk about it, it's like it just happened yesterday. Before the strike, my husband had the job of his dreams. He had a day job. Our life was perfect. We're still suffering from the strike. He's on nights now; we never see each other. He lived away from home for a year. The real personal things that happened to me weren't covered in the interview. It's really hard. I could just about sit here and cry when I think about the time that was lost with my husband. We still don't spend a lot of time together, because of his hours and mine. So many people are still suffering, and it still hurts a lot.[26]

The strike is deeply embedded in the women's psyches. The memories come flooding back. They remember the little funny things, and the dark things, all in the same moment.

I was usually angry most of the time during that time. I'll remember how I survived on dried beans and commodity cheese! Even today, on foggy days I can see the National Guard standing out in front of the plant—and that's real eerie. I still don't feel good when I go by there.[27]

Anger and bitterness still lie close to the surface for many of the women. For some, the emotional price was high.

And I guess the biggest lesson for me was that, when you take a stand for something and really believe in it, it's going to cost you. You don't think it will, but it's gonna cost you. I'm not talking just money and stuff. You've got to be prepared. I wasn't prepared for all it could cost you to take a stand.[28]

The aftermath of the strike was especially difficult for Vickie Guyette: her marriage ended, and she found herself back in school learning a new profession. Emotionally, she had a unique burden.

It was harder for me, I think, because I'm going to counseling now to try to work everything out. I still have a lot of hate, and I want to get rid of that. I don't want to carry that around with me forever. And because Jim always told me that I wasn't to cry, I wasn't to be like everybody else. Because I had to be strong, because people look at me like I knew more than the normal rank-and-file, because Jim was my husband. If I started crying and confiding in anybody, he was afraid that they would feel like we were losing. What he wanted people to get from me was strength and not to blend. So that was hard, because a lot of times I needed someone to just sit down and talk to me, and I couldn't do that. It was also hard to see him take the blame for what were really rank-and-file decisions. And it was hard to see my children get ragged on at school because of who their dad was. Yeah, it was hard.

The most lasting impact, however, may be memory itself. The collective memory is long. One woman talked about the strike as something that people would carry to their graves; another simply said, "You can't forget. It isn't something you forget" (Anon.).

After all is said and done, what happened to the community of Austin? Years after the strike officially ended, Austin is still a divided town and probably will be for at least a generation. Hundreds of workers are still "out" and waiting to be called back. Others have given up and left town. The Support Group continues to meet in a rented space within sight of the plant, and functions as a social club and a support group for those people still waiting to go back to work. Hormel "sold" the hog-kill portion of the business, and the new owners lowered the wages, impoverishing the community still further.

The strike still impacts the social life of the community in many little ways. Some people who dropped out of their churches have stayed away permanently. People still boycott certain businesses and Hormel products: "I recently took my ten-year-old grandson out to breakfast in Austin. And when he ordered breakfast, we checked if it was a Hormel product he had ordered. It was, so I changed his breakfast—he couldn't order that."[29]

Austin was changed forever. People made permanent enemies; lines were drawn that can never be crossed. Even the Hormel Company is aware of the divided nature of the town since the strike. In a recent public relations piece celebrating 100 years of operation, the writer commented on one obvious legacy of the bitterness: "Where once the company's union and management workers shared favorite restaurants and after-work hangouts, now purposeful segregation occurred."[30]

A MESSAGE FROM AUSTIN

What happened in Austin is important for everyone, but especially for women. Although many articles and books have been written about those events in the mid–1980s, each and every one of them overlooked the major contributions made by the women. It is important that the roles women play in political and economic struggles be recognized and appreciated. Women have a stake in community issues, and their perspective must be incorporated in all actions shaping economic, political, and social change.

The women in the Support Group developed a model for that activist role, and other women can replicate that model. The Support Group women thought through and developed points of view on all the significant issues of our time: in economics, they developed positions on a just wage, the standard of living, the nature of economic power; in politics, they debated tactics, established a women's role in the labor movement, and learned about the power of women in social change. They showed us that women have major contributions to make to the political and economic survival of their communities.

The Austin Strike also alerted the labor movement to a major flaw in modern labor-movement theory: the arbitrary separation of the productive and reproductive economies—the workplace, and the family and community. This rift is a result of the gendering of work, which is shaped by the sexism deep in our culture. The working-class men and women in Austin learned that women have a revolutionary role to play in radicalizing everyday life and implementing social change in their communities. The women in the Support Group created one of the finest contemporary examples of women organizing, demanding, and making their community responsible for major social transformation. As the experience of P–9 and the Support Group has shown us, creating a new world requires the skills and talents of all—both men and women.

The Support Group also has a message for America about work and community. The message to the labor movement from the Support Group is that unions need to stop seeing labor struggles as power struggles or contests played between groups of men for individual workers' rights. The issues of labor are the issues of community and survival, of economics and democracy. The context of labor issues is critical, and labor will not achieve its goals without understanding the connection between wages and the deep structures of political and social life.

According to political theorists Peter Bachrach and Aryeh Botwinick, political struggle that begins in the workplace has an important role to play in making fundamental changes in the structure of American democracy as it operates in community.

The objective of participatory democracy is thus not just to democratize the workplace for its own sake, but to have the workplace emerge as a point of leverage from which to achieve a more egalitarian redistribution of power, leading to a greater democratization of the entire political process.[31]

In their arguments for a participatory democracy, Bachrach and Botwinick are attempting to expand the concept of class beyond its classic Marxist economic configuration, to incorporate a broader analysis of conflict between groups in society.[32] With this expanded definition of "class" and "class struggle," the full magnitude of what took place in Austin becomes apparent. What was at stake in Austin was the idea of democracy itself. Democracy on the shop floor translated into democracy in the community as a whole. Out of the confrontation with Hormel, democratic principles were articulated, experienced, and reaffirmed. According to Bachrach and Botwinick,

working class struggle can contribute to democracy . . . by nurturing democratic attitudes and values in working men and women, including a sense of group empowerment, and concurrently engendering a growing awareness and understanding that the idea of democracy is more than an abstraction, that it can play an important role in the improvement of the quality of life for working people and their communities.[33]

The labor movement agenda needs to be broadened to incorporate and respond to these issues of community economics and democratic political power—for as we lose control of our work cultures, we run the risk of losing democracy as well.

The story of the strike in Austin is only the beginning of a new phase in the struggle of the American worker. The genie will never go back in the bottle. Like many Americans, the striking families in Austin have been radicalized. Their political consciousness has been permanently raised, and only a spark may be needed to ignite their political passions again. The American Dream of a comfortable middle-class lifestyle is still the standard for the American labor movement—in Austin and everywhere. As the economic situation in the United States worsens, the message from Austin is that the working class will not go down without a fight, and women will have a key role in defining that struggle, leading it, and shaping the aftermath. The Austin Strike is a warning and a lesson, a plan and a dream.

The story of the Support Group is a special part of a larger story of hope and potential. The women learned that we all have culture-building skills within us, and that, given the opportunity, we have the power to take control of, and change our lives. They learned that people can struggle for economic justice and defend their values; that people can come together in community to support one another and recreate culture; that they can recreate democratic structures to achieve collective goals. Despite their valiant efforts, however, P–9 and the Support Group lost. They were outmaneuvered, outfinanced and outgunned at every turn. But from another perspective, they won. They were right and they knew it, and history will bear out the justice of their struggle.

The Support Group still meets in Austin, and its persistence continues to remind the community of the power of working people to confront corporate power. On the individual level, the women struggle to heal—to learn to live on less money; to mend fences with family and friends; to bring their shattered lives back together. And as one woman predicted, the struggle will continue: "I think you're going to hear about the Hormel strike, the P–9ers, and the Support Group for years and years to come."[34]

NOTES

1. I am indebted to Karl Polanyi for this phrase. See Karl Polanyi, *The Great Transformation: The Political and Economic Origins of Our Time* (Boston, 1957).
2. Ibid., 152
3. Madeline Krueger.
4. Billie Goodeu.
5. Mary Arens.
6. Judy Himle.
7. Jeannie Bambrick.
8. Carol King.
9. Shirley Heegard.
10. See Ava Baron, "Gender and Labor History: Learning from the Past, Looking to the Future," in *Work Engendered: Toward a New History of American Labor*, ed. Ava Baron (Ithaca, N.Y., and London, 1991).
11. See Susan Levine, "Labors in the Field: Reviewing Women's Cultural History,"

Radical History Review, no. 35 (April 1986): 56: "Women's culture, to be a meaningful category of analysis, needs to be carefully situated in time and place, and needs to be discussed in the context of a particular culture or class."

12. See Nancy Cott, "What's in a Name: The Limits of 'Social Feminism': or, Expanding the Vocabulary of Women's History," *Journal of American History* 76, 3 (December 1989): 809–29. Cott is anxious to explore the relationship between gender and social group as it affects women's movement into the public arena. She identifies a "communal consciousness" that is "based on solidarity with men and women of the same group, local or global—for one's own 'group' may be defined in class, ethnic, racial, geographical, religious, or national terms. Women's communal consciousness ought to be explicitly recognized for its role in women's self-assertions, even while those self-assertions are on behalf of the community that women inhabit with their men and children," 827. See also Maurine Weiner Greenwald, "Working-class Feminism and the Family Wage Ideal: The Seattle Debate on Married Women's Right to Work, 1914–1920," *Journal of American History* 76, 1 (June 1989): 118–49, for a discussion of the relationship between gender and class; and Elizabeth Faue, *Community of Suffering and Struggle: Women, Men, and the Labor Movement in Minneapolis, 1915–1945* (Chapel Hill, N.C., and London, 1991), for her argument for a community-based unionism that reintegrates the reproductive and productive economic agendas, and the traditional separate men's and women's spheres into the idea of "community."

13. Cheryl Remington.

14. Lawrence Goodwyn, *The Populist Moment: A Short History of the Agrarian Revolt in America* (Oxford, England, 1979).

15. Ibid., 33.

16. E. P. Thompson, "Eighteenth-century English Society: Class Struggle without Class?" *Social History* 3, 2 (1978): 149.

17. Goodwyn, *Populist Moment*.

18. Ibid., xix.

19. Barbara Collette.

20. Madeline Krueger.

21. Carol King.

22. Marie Loverink.

23. Donna Simon.

24. Mary Machacek.

25. Cheryl Remington.

26. Cheryl Remington.

27. Jan Kennedy.

28. Billie Goodeu.

29. Madeline Krueger.

30. Doniver Adolph Lund and V. Allan Krejci, *The Hormel Legacy: 100 Years of Quality* (Austin, Minn., 1991), 186.

31. Peter Bachrach and Aryeh Botwinick, *Power and Empowerment: A Radical Theory of Participatory Democracy* (Philadelphia, 1992), 12.

32. Ibid., 149. Class, the authors argue, is a "power relation between those who dominate and those who are dominated."

33. Ibid., 31–32.

34. Billie Goodeu.

Selected Bibliography

Ackelsberg, Martha. "*Mujeres Libres*: Community and Individuality: Organizing Women in the Spanish Civil War." *Radical America* 18, 4 (July/August 1984): 7–19.

———. " 'Separate and Equal'? Mujeres Libres and Anarchist Strategy for Women's Emancipation." *Feminist Studies* 11, 1 (Spring 1985): 63–83.

———. "Communities, Resistance, and Women's Activism: Some Implications for a Democratic Polity." In *Women and the Politics of Empowerment*, edited by Ann Bookman and Sandra Morgen. Philadelphia: Temple University Press, 1988: 297–313.

Ackelsberg, Martha A., and Kathryn Pyne Addelson. "Anarchist Alternatives to Competition." In *Competition: A Feminist Taboo?* edited by Valerie Miner and Helen E. Longino. New York: Feminist Press, 1987: 221–33.

Alexander, Sally, Anna Davin, and Eve Hostettler. "Labouring Women: A Reply to Eric Hobsbawm." *History Workshop: A Journal of Socialist Historians*, No. 8 (Autumn 1979): 174–82.

Armitage, Susan H. "The Next Step." *Frontiers* 7, 1 (Fall 1983): 3–8.

Aulette, Judy, and Trudy Mills. "Something Old, Something New: Auxiliary Work in the 1983–1986 Copper Strike." *Feminist Studies* 14, 2 (Summer 1988): 251–68.

Avery, Michael, Brian Auvine, Barbara Streibel, and Lonnie Weiss. *Building United Judgment: A Handbook for Consensus Decision Making*. Madison, Wis: Center for Conflict Resolution, 1981.

Bachrach, Peter, and Aryeh Botwinick. *Power and Empowerment: A Radical Theory of Participatory Democracy*. Philadelphia: Temple University Press, 1992.

Balser, Diane. *Sisterhood and Solidarity: Feminism and Labor in Modern Times*. Boston: South End Press, 1987.

Barnes, Donna A. "Organization and Radical Protest: An Antithesis?" *Sociological Quarterly* 28, 4 (December 1987): 575–94.

Baron, Ava. "Gender and Labor History: Learning from the Past, Looking to the Future." In *Work Engendered: Toward a New History of American Labor*, edited by Ava Baron. Ithaca, N.Y., and London: Cornell University Press, 1991: 1–46.

————, ed. *Work Engendered: Toward a New History of American Labor*. Ithaca, N.Y., and London: Cornell University Press, 1991.

Baxandall, Rosalyn Fraad. *Words on Fire: The Life and Writing of Elizabeth Gurley Flynn*. New Brunswick, N.J., and London: Rutgers University Press, 1987.

Bayard, Charles J. "The 1927–1928 Colorado Coal Strike." *Pacific Historical Review* 32, 3 (August 1963): 235–50.

Beaton, Lynn. *Shifting Horizons*. London: Canary Press, 1985.

Benello, C. George, and Dimitrios Roussopoulos, eds. *The Case for Participatory Democracy*. New York: Viking Press, 1971.

Beneria, Lourdes, and Gita Sen. "Accumulation, Reproduction, and Women's Role in Economic Development: Boserup Revisited." *Signs: Journal of Women in Culture and Society* 7, 2 (Winter 1981): 279–98.

————. "Class and Gender Inequalities and Women's Role in Economic Development." *Feminist Studies* 8, 1 (Spring 1982): 157–76.

Berman, Hyman. "Education for Work and Labor Solidarity: The Immigrant Miners and Radicalism on the Mesabi Range." Unpublished article in Minnesota Historical Society.

Betten, Neil. "Strike on the Mesabi—1907." *Minnesota History* 40, 7 (Fall 1967): 340–47.

————. "Riot, Revolution, Repression in the Iron Range Strike of 1916." *Minnesota History* 41, 2 (Summer 1968): 82–93.

Blantz, Thomas E. "Father Hass and the Minneapolis Truckers Strike of 1934." *Minnesota History* 42, 1 (Spring 1970): 5–15.

Bloor, Ella Reeve. *We Are Many*. New York: International Publishers, 1940.

Blum, Fred H. *Toward a Democratic Work Process: The Hormel-Packinghouse Workers' Experiment*. New York: Harper and Brothers Publishers, 1953.

Boggs, C. "Revolutionary Process, Political Strategy, and the Dilemma of Power." *Theory and Society* 4, 3 (Fall 1977): 359–93.

Bookman, Ann, and Sandra Morgen, eds. *Women and the Politics of Empowerment*. Philadelphia: Temple University Press, 1988.

Booth, William James. *Households: On the Moral Architecture of the Economy*. Ithaca, N.Y., and London: Cornell University Press, 1993.

Boris, Eileen. "The Power of Motherhood: Black and White Activist Women Redefine the 'Political.' " *Yale Journal of Law and Feminism* 2, 25 (Fall 1989): 25–49.

Bourque, Susan C., and Kay B. Warren. "Technology, Gender, and Development." *Daedalus* 116, 4 (Fall 1987): 173–97.

Bridenthal, Renate. "The Dialectics of Production and Reproduction in History." *Radical America* 10, 2 (March/April 1976): 3–11.

Brissenden, Paul F. *The IWW: A Study of American Syndicalism*. New York: Russell & Russell, 1957.

Bronner, David G. "Changes and Trends in Labor–Management Relations at the Geo. A. Hormel & Company, Austin, Minnesota." M.A. Thesis, Mankato State University, 1968.

Buechler, Steven M. *Women's Movements in the United States*. New Brunswick, N.J., and London: Rutgers University Press, 1990.

Burrows, Edwin G. "The Transition Question in Early American History: A Checklist of Recent Books, Articles, and Dissertations." *Radical History Review*, No. 18 (Fall 1978): 173–90.

C. George Benello on the Liberation of Work. Special issue of *Changing Work*, No. 7 (Winter 1988).

Cahill, Tom. "Co-operatives and Anarchism: A Contemporary Perspective." In *For Anarchism: History, Theory, and Practice*, edited by David Goodway. London and New York: Routledge, 1989: 235–58.

Cameron, Ardis. "Bread and Roses Revisited: Women's Culture and Working-class Activism in the Lawrence Strike of 1912." In *Women, Work, & Protest: A Century of U.S. Women's Labor History*, edited by Ruth Milkman. New York and London: Routledge and Kegan Paul, 1987: 42–61.

Canning, Kathleen. "Gender and the Politics of Class Formation: Rethinking German Labor History." *American Historical Review* 97, 3 (June 1992): 736–768.

Cantarow, Ellen, with Susan Gushee O'Malley and Sharon Hartman Strom. *Moving the Mountain: Women Working for Social Change*. Old Westbury, N.Y.: Feminist Press and McGraw-Hill, 1980.

Case, John, and Rosemary C. R. Taylor, eds. *Co-ops, Communes, and Collectives: Experiments in Social Change in the 1960s and 1970s*. New York: Pantheon Books, 1979.

Cassel, Joan. *A Group Called Women: Sisterhood and Symbolism in the Feminist Movement*. New York: David McKay, 1977.

Caudwell, Christopher. *Illusion and Reality*. New York: International Publishers, 1977.

Chambers, Clarke A. "The National Cooperative League of the United States of America, 1916–1961: A Study of Social Theory and Social Action." *Agricultural History* 36, 2 (April 1962): 59–81.

Chernick, Jack. *Economic Effects of Steady Employment and Earnings: A Case Study of the Annual Wage System of Geo. A. Hormel & Co*. Minneapolis: University of Minnesota Press, 1942.

Clark, Christopher. "The Household Mode of Production." *Radical History Review* No. 18 (Fall 1978): 166–72.

Cloward, Richard A., and Frances Fox Piven. "Hidden Protest: The Channeling of Female Innovation and Resistance." *Signs: Journal of Women in Culture and Society* 4, 4 (Summer 1979): 651–69.

Cobble, Dorothy Sue. *Dishing It Out: Waitresses and Their Unions in the Twentieth Century*. Urbana and Chicago: University of Illinois Press, 1991.

Cockburn, Cynthia. "When Women Get Involved in Community Action." In *Women in the Community*, edited by Marjorie Mayo. London: Routledge & Kegan Paul, 1977: 61–70.

Cohen, Yolande, ed. *Women and Counter Power*. Montreal and New York: Black Rose Books, 1989.

Conde, Carole, and Karl Beveridge. *First Contract: Women and the Fight to Unionize*. Toronto: Between the Lines, 1986.

Conlin, J. R. *Bread and Roses, Too: Studies of the Wobblies*. Westport, Conn.: Greenwood Publishing, 1969.

Conway, Jill K., Susan C. Bourque, and Joan W. Scott. "Introduction: The Concept of Gender." *Daedalus* 116, 4 (Fall 1987): 21–29.

Cook, Blanche Wiesen. "Female Support Networks and Political Activism: Lillian Wald, Crystal Eastman, Emma Goldman." *Chrysalis*, No. 3 (1977): 43–61.

Costello, Cynthia B. " 'WEA're Worth It!' Work Culture and Conflict at the Wisconsin

Education Association Insurance Trust." *Feminist Studies* 11, 3 (Fall 1985): 497–518.

Cott, Nancy. "What's in a Name? The Limits of 'Social Feminism'; or, Expanding the Vocabulary of Women's History." *Journal of American History* 76, 3 (December 1989): 809–29.

Cotter, John J. "Ethics and Justice in the World of Work: Improving the Quality of Working Life." *Review of Social Economy* No. 40 (December 1982): 393–406.

Curl, John. *History of Work Cooperation in America: Cooperatives, Cooperative Movements, Collectivity, and Communalism from Early America to the Present.* Berkeley, Calif.: Homeward Press, 1980.

Dannenbaum, Jed. "The Origins of Temperance Activism and Militancy among American Women." *Journal of Social History* 15, 2 (Winter 1981): 235–52.

Davis, Angela Y. *Women, Culture, and Politics.* New York: Random House, 1989.

Deslippe, Dennis A. " 'We Had an Awful Time with Our Women': Iowa's United Packinghouse Workers of America, 1945–75." *Journal of Women's History*, 5, 1 (Spring 1993): 10–32.

Diacou, Zoë. "An Interview with Anne Kanten: 'I'm a Farmer, I'm a Woman, and I'm Angry.' " *World Women News* 1, 2 (Winter 1989): 1–passim.

Dietz, Mary G. "I. Citizenship with a Feminist Face: The Problem with Maternal Thinking." *Political Theory* 13, 1 (February 1985): 19–37.

diLeonardo, Micaela. "Women's Work, Work Culture, and Consciousness." *Feminist Studies* 11, 3 (Fall 1985): 491–95.

District 65/*Heresies.* "Union Women on Feminism." *Heresies* 3, 1, No. 9 (1980): 83–87.

Divine, Robert C. "Turmoil in Austin: Hormel Strike of 1985–86." M.B.A. Thesis, Mankato State University, 1988.

Dobbs, Farrell. *Teamster Rebellion.* New York: Monad Press, 1972.

Dolgoff, Sam. *The Anarchist Collectives: Worker Self-management in the Spanish Revolution 1936–39.* Montreal: Black Rose Books, 1974.

Dougherty, Richard. *In Quest of Quality: Hormel's First 75 Years.* St. Paul, Minn.: North Central Publishing, 1966.

DuBois, Ellen Carol, and Vicki L. Ruiz, eds. *Unequal Sisters: A Multicultural Reader in U.S. Women's History.* New York and London: Routledge, 1990.

Dubofsky, Melvyn. *We Shall Be All: A History of the IWW.* New York: New York Times Book Company, 1969.

Dunayevskaya, Raya. *Women's Liberation and the Dialectics of Revolution: Reaching for the Future.* Atlantic Highlands, N.J.: Humanities Press International, 1985.

Dye, Nancy Schrom. "Feminism or Unionism? The New York Women's Trade Union League and the Labor Movement." *Feminist Studies* 3, 1/2 (Fall 1975): 111–25.

Ehrlich, Howard. "How to Get There from Here—Building a Revolutionary Transfer Culture." *Social Anarchism* 2, 2 (1982): 3–21.

Engelmann, Larry D. " 'We Were the Poor People'—The Hormel Strike of 1933." *Labor History* 15, 4 (Fall 1974): 483–510.

Erickson, Herman. "WPA Strike and Trials of 1939." *Minnesota History* 42, 6 (Summer 1971): 202–14.

Evans, Sara M. *Personal Politics: The Roots of Women's Liberation in the Civil Rights Movement and the New Left.* New York: Alfred A. Knopf, 1979.

Ewen, Linda. *Which Side Are You On?* Chicago: Vanguard Books, 1979.

Fahey, Michael T. *Packing It In! The Hormel Strike, 1985–86: A Personal Perspective.* St. Paul, Minn.: Kirwin and Sons Publishers, 1988.

Fanon, Frantz. *The Wretched of the Earth*, translated by Constance Farrington. New York: Grove Press, 1963.

Faragher, John Mack. "History from the Inside Out: Writing the History of Women in Rural America." *American Quarterly* 33, 5 (Winter 1981): 537–57.

Faue, Elizabeth. *Community of Suffering and Struggle: Women, Men, and the Labor Movement in Minneapolis, 1915–1945.* Chapel Hill and London: University of North Carolina Press, 1991.

Fink, Deborah. *Open Country, Iowa: Rural Women, Tradition, and Change.* Albany: State University of New York Press, 1986.

Fisher, Marvin. "The Iconography of Industrialism, 1830–1860." In *The American Culture*, edited by Hennig Cohen. Boston: Houghton Mifflin, 1968: 228–45.

Fitz, Don, and David Roediger, eds. *Within the Shell of the Old: Essays on Workers' Self-organization.* Chicago: Charles H. Kerr, 1990.

Flynn, Elizabeth Gurley. *The Rebel Girl: An Autobiography.* New York: International Publishers, 1973.

Folbre, Nancy. "Families of the World Unite." *Zeta Magazine* 1, 12 (December 1988): 31–36.

Folsom, Franklin. *Impatient Armies of the Poor: The Story of Collective Action of the Unemployed 1808–1942.* Niwot: University Press of Colorado, 1991.

Frank, Dana. "Housewives, Socialists, and the Politics of Food: The 1917 New York Cost-of-living Protests." *Feminist Studies* 11, 2 (Summer 1985): 255–86.

———. "Gender, Consumer Organizing, and the Seattle Labor Movement, 1919–1929." In *Work Engendered: Toward a New History of American Labor*, edited by Ava Baron. Ithaca, N.Y., and London: Cornell University Press, 1991: 273–95.

Freedman, Estelle. "Separatism as Strategy: Female Institution Building and American Feminism, 1870–1930." *Feminist Studies* 5, 3 (Fall 1979): 512–29.

Freeman, Jo. "The Tyranny of Structurelessness." *MS* 11, 1 (July 1973): 76–passim.

Garland, Anne Witte. *Women Activists: Challenging the Abuse of Power.* New York: Feminist Press at the City University of New York, 1988.

Golod, Fluffy. "Power: What *Should* Women Want?" *Soil of Liberty* 6, 3 (November 1980): 2-passim.

Goodwyn, Lawrence. *The Populist Moment: A Short History of the Agrarian Revolt in America.* Oxford, England: Oxford University Press, 1979.

Green, Hardy. *On Strike at Hormel: The Struggle for a Democratic Labor Movement.* Philadelphia: Temple University Press, 1990.

Green, Jim. "Culture, Politics, and Workers' Response to Industrialization in the U.S." *Radical America* 16, 1–2 (January/February, March/April 1982): 101–28.

Greenwald, Maurine Weiner. "Working-class Feminism and the Family Wage Ideal: The Seattle Debate on Married Women's Right to Work, 1914–1920." *Journal of American History* 76, 1 (June 1989): 118–49.

Griffin-Pierson, Sharon. "Achievement and Competitiveness in Women." *Journal of College Student Development* 29, 6 (November 1988): 491–95.

Hage, Dave, and Paul Klauda. *No Retreat, No Surrender: Labor's War at Hormel.* New York: William Morrow, 1989.

Hahn, Steven, and Jonathan Prude, eds. *The Countryside in the Age of Capitalist Trans-*

formation: Essays in the Social History of Rural America. Chapel Hill: University of North Carolina Press, 1985.

Hall, Jacquelyn Dowd. "Disorderly Women: Gender and Labor Militancy in the Appalachian South." *Journal of American History* 73, 2 (September 1986): 354–82.

Halstead, Fred. *The 1985–86 Hormel Meat-packers Strike.* New York: Pathfinder Press, 1986.

Heresies Editorial Collective. "Editorial." *Heresies* 2, 3 (Spring 1979): 3–passim.

———. "True Confessions." *Heresies* 2, 3 (Spring 1979): 93–96.

Hobsbawm, Eric. *Primitive Rebels: Studies in Archaic Forms of Social Movements in the Nineteenth and Twentieth Centuries,* New York: Norton, 1955.

———. "Man and Woman in Socialist Iconography." *History Workshop Journal* No. 6 (Autumn 1978): 121–38.

Hobsbawm, Eric, and Terence Ranger, eds. *The Invention of Tradition.* London: Cambridge University Press, 1983.

Holloway, Mark. *Heavens on Earth: Utopian Communities in America 1680–1880.* New York: Library Publishers, 1951.

Hooks, Bell. *Feminist Theory: From Margin to Center.* Boston: South End, 1984.

Hormel, Geo. A., & Company. *Notice of Annual Meeting of Stockholders.* Austin, Minn., January 3, 1991.

Horowitz, Roger. "Behind the Hormel Strike: The Fifty Years of Local P–9." *Against the Current* 1, 2 (March 1986): 13–18.

Huck, Gary, and Mike Konopacki. *Bye! American: The Labor Cartoons of Gary Huck and Mike Konopacki.* Chicago: Charles H. Kerr Publishing, 1987.

Hyman, Paula. "Immigrant Women and Consumer Protest: The New York City Kosher Meat Boycott of 1902." *American Jewish History* 70 (Summer 1980): 91–105.

Illich, Ivan. *Shadow Work.* Boston and London: Marion Boyars, 1981.

James, Selma. *The Global Kitchen.* London: Housewives in Dialogue, 1985.

Jameson, Elizabeth. "Imperfect Unions: Class and Gender in Cripple Creek, 1894–1904." *Frontiers* 1, 2 (Spring 1976): 89–117.

Jansen, Sue Curry. "Collapse of the Public Sphere and Information Capitalism." *INQUIRY: Critical Thinking across the Disciplines* (November 1991): 8–23.

Jones, Mary Harris. *Autobiography of Mother Jones,* edited by Mary Field Parton. Chicago: Charles Kerr, 1925.

Jordan, Myron Leonard. *The Second Generation of the George A. Hormel Company, 1929–1954.* Austin, Minn.: Myron Leonard Jordan, 1965.

Kahn, Douglas, and Diane Neumaier, eds. *Cultures in Contradiction.* Seattle: Real Comet Press, 1985.

Kamerman, Sheila B. "Work and Family in Industrialized Societies." *Signs: Journal of Women in Culture and Society* 4, 4 (Summer 1979): 632–50.

Kanovsky, Eliyahu. *The Economy of the Israeli Kibbutz.* Cambridge, Mass.: Harvard University Press, 1966.

Kanter, Rosabeth Moss. *Commitment and Community: Communes and Utopias in Sociological Perspective.* Cambridge, Mass.: Harvard University Press, 1972.

Kaplan, Temma. "Female Consciousness and Collective Action: The Case of Barcelona, 1910–1918." *Signs: Journal of Women in Culture and Society* 7, 3 (Spring 1982): 545–66.

Kerber, Linda K. "Separate Spheres, Female Worlds, Woman's Place: The Rhetoric of Women's History." *Journal of American History* 75, 1 (June 1988): 9–39.

Kercher, Leonard C., Vant W. Kebker, and Wilfred C. Leland, Jr. *Consumers' Cooperatives in the North Central States.* Minneapolis: University of Minnesota Press, 1941.

Kessler-Harris, Alice. *Out to Work: A History of Wage-earning Women in the United States.* New York: Oxford University Press, 1982.

———. "Problems of Coalition-building: Women and Trade Unions in the 1920s." In *Women, Work & Protest: A Century of U.S. Women's Labor History*, edited by Ruth Milkman. New York and London: Routledge and Kegan Paul, 1987: 110–38.

Kingsolver, Barbara. *Holding the Line: Women in the Great Arizona Mine Strike of 1983.* Ithaca, N.Y.: ILR Press, 1989.

Koppel, Barbara. "A Company Town Decays." *Progressive* 53, 2 (February 1989): 12–13.

Kopple, Barbara, producer. *Harlan County U.S.A.* 16-mm Color Film, 103 min. 1976.

———. *American Dream.* 16-mm Color Film, 1991.

Kornbluh, Joyce L., ed. *Rebel Voices: An IWW Anthology.* Ann Arbor: University of Michigan Press, 1964.

Kovel, Joel. *History and Spirit: An Inquiry into the Philosophy of Liberation.* Boston: Beacon Press, 1991.

Kramer, Dale. "The Dunne Boys of Minneapolis." *Harper's Magazine* 184, 1102 (March 1942): 388–98.

Krimerman, Len, Frank Lindenfeld, Carl Korty, and Julian Benello, eds. *From the Ground Up: Essays on Grassroots and Workplace Democracy by C. George Benello.* Boston: South End Press, 1992.

Kropotkin, Peter. *Mutual Aid.* Boston: Porter Sargent, 1973.

Ladd-Taylor, Molly. "Women Workers and the Yale Strike." *Feminist Studies* 11, 3 (Fall 1985): 465–89.

Lasky, Marjorie Penn. " 'Where I Was a Person': The Ladies' Auxiliary in the 1934 Minneapolis Teamsters' Strikes." In *Women, Work & Protest: A Century of U.S. Women's Labor History*, edited by Ruth Milkman. New York and London: Routledge and Kegan Paul, 1987: 181–205.

Lawson, Ronald, and Stephen E. Barton. "Sex Roles in Social Movements: A Case Study of the Tenant Movement in New York City." *Signs: Journal of Women in Culture and Society* 6, 2 (Winter 1980): 230–47.

Leacock, Eleanor. "History, Development, and the Division of Labor by Sex: Implications for Organizations." *Signs: Journal of Women in Culture and Society* 7, 2 (Winter 1981): 474–91.

Lears, T. J. Jackson. "The Concept of Cultural Hegemony: Problems and Possibilities." *American Historical Review* 90, 3 (June 1985): 567–97.

Lerner, Michael. *Surplus Powerlessness: The Psychodynamics of Everyday Life . . . and the Psychology of Individual and Social Transformation.* Oakland, Calif.: Institute for Labor and Mental Health, 1986.

Le Sueur, Meridel. "The Fetish of Being Outside." *New Masses* (February 26, 1935): 22–23.

———. "I Was Marching." In *Salute to Spring.* New York: International Publishers, 1940, 1977: 159–71.

————. *The Girl*. New York: West End Press, 1978.

Leval, Gaston, *Collectives in the Spanish Revolution*. London: Freedom Press, 1975.

Levine, Susan. "Labors in the Field: Reviewing Women's Cultural History." *Radical History Review*, No. 35 (April 1986): 49–56.

Lewin, Ellen. "Feminist Ideology and the Meaning of Work: The Case of Nursing." *Catalyst* 10–11 (Summer 1977): 78–103.

Lewis, Helen Matthews, Linda Johnson, and Donald Askins. *Colonialism in Modern America: The Appalachian Case*. Boone, N.C.: Appalachian Consortium Press, 1978.

Lewis, Helen, and John Gaventa. *The Jellico Handbook: A Teacher's Guide to Community-based Economics*. New Market, Tenn.: Highlander Center, 1988.

Long, Priscilla. "The Women of the Colorado Fuel and Iron Strike, 1913–1914." In *Women, Work, & Protest: A Century of U.S. Women's Labor History*, edited by Ruth Milkman. New York and London: Routledge and Kegan Paul, 1987: 62–86.

Lund, Doniver Adolph, and V. Allan Krejci. *The Hormel Legacy: 100 Years of Quality*. Austin, Minn.: Geo. A. Hormel & Company, 1991.

Lynd, Staughton. "Solidarity Unionism." *Zeta Magazine* 1, 3 (March 1988): 85–91.

————. "The Genesis of the Idea of a Community Right to Industrial Property in Youngstown and Pittsburgh, 1977–1987." *Changing Work* 9 (Spring 1989): 14–19.

MacKinnon, Catharine A. *Toward a Feminist Theory of the State*. Cambridge, Mass., and London: Harvard University Press, 1989.

Maggard, Sally Ward. "Women's Participation in the Brookside Coal Strike: Militancy, Class, and Gender in Appalachia." *Frontiers* 9, 3 (1987): 16–21.

————. "Gender Contested: Women's Participation in the Brookside Coal Strike." In *Women and Social Protest*, edited by Guida West and Rhoda Lois Blumberg. New York and Oxford, England: Oxford University Press, 1990: 75–98.

Maglin, Nan Bauer. "Visions of Defiance: Work, Politics, Commitment, and Sisterhood in Twenty-one Works of Fiction, 1895–1925." *Praxis* 1, 3 (1976): 98–112.

Mansbridge, Jane J. *Beyond Adversary Democracy*. New York: Basic Books, 1980.

May, Martha. "The Historical Problem of the Family Wage: The Ford Motor Company and the Five Dollar Day." *Feminist Studies* 8, 2 (Summer 1982): 399–424.

Merrill, Michael. "Cash Is Good to Eat: Self-sufficiency in the Rural Economy." *Radical History Review*, No. 16 (Winter 1977): 42–71.

————. "So What's Wrong with the 'Household Mode of Production'?" Radical History Review, No. 22 (Winter 1979/80): 141–46.

Milkman, Ruth, ed. *Women, Work & Protest: A Century of U.S. Women's Labor History*. New York and London: Routledge and Kegan Paul, 1987.

————. "Women Workers, Feminism, and the Labor Movement since the 1960s." In *Women, Work & Protest: A Century of U.S. Women's Labor History*, edited by Ruth Milkman. New York and London: Routledge and Kegan Paul, 1987: 300–322.

Miner, Valerie, and Helen E. Longino, eds. *Competition: A Feminist Taboo?* New York: Feminist Press, 1987.

Moberg, David. "Experimenting with the Future: Alternative Institutions and American Socialism." In *Co-ops, Communes, and Collectives: Experiments in Social*

Change in the 1960s and 1970s, edited by John Case and Rosemary C. R. Taylor. New York: Pantheon Books, 1979: 274–311.

———. "Austin City Limits, Strikers on Guard." *In These Times* (January 29–February 4, 1986): 3, 8.

Morris, David, and Karl Hess. *Neighborhood Power: The New Localism*. Boston: Beacon, 1975.

Morrison, Roy. *We Build the Road as We Travel*. Philadelphia: New Society Publishers, 1991.

Mumford, Lewis. *The Story of Utopias*. New York: Viking, 1962.

Naftalin, Arthur. "A History of the Farmer-Labor Party of Minnesota." Unpublished Ph.D. Thesis, University of Minnesota, 1948.

Nelson, Bruce C. *Beyond the Martyrs: A Social History of Chicago's Anarchists, 1870–1900*. New Brunswick, N.J., and London: Rutgers University Press, 1988.

Neunsinger, Gerald Francis. "A Study of Management's Attitude toward Labor in Two Minnesota Packinghouses." M.S. Thesis, Mankato State University, 1961.

Noy, Danny. "The Kibbutz as an Open Social System." *Kibbutz Studies* 14 (August 1984): 13–29.

O'Brien, Mary. *The Politics of Reproduction*. Boston: Routledge and Kegan Paul, 1981.

Ostreicher, Richard. "From Artisan to Consumer: Images of Workers 1840–1920." *Journal of American Culture* 4, 1 (Spring 1984): 47–64.

Papanek, Hanna. "Family Status Production: The 'Work' and 'Nonwork' of Women." *Signs: Journal of Women in Culture and Society* 4, 4 (Summer 1979): 775–81.

Papanikolas, Zeese. *Buried Unsung: Louis Tikas and Ludlow Massacre*. Lincoln and London: University of Nebraska Press, 1991.

Pateman, Carole. *Participation and Democratic Theory*. Cambridge, England: Cambridge University Press, 1970.

Paules, Greta Foff. *Dishing It Out: Power and Resistance among Waitresses in a New Jersey Restaurant*. Philadelphia: Temple University Press, 1991.

Pellis, Richard H. *Radical Visions and American Dreams*. New York: Harper and Row, 1973.

Polanyi, Karl. *The Great Transformation: The Political and Economic Origins of Our Time*. Boston: Beacon Press, 1957.

Puette, William J. *Through Jaundiced Eyes: How the Media View Organized Labor*. Ithaca, N.Y.: ILR Press, 1992.

Pym, Denis. "The Other Economy as a Social System." In *Why Work: Arguments for the Leisure Society*, edited by Vernon Richards. London: Freedom Press, 1983: 137–49.

Raboy, Marc. *Movements and Messages: Media and Radical Politics in Quebec*, translated by David Homel. Toronto: Between the Lines, 1984.

Rachleff, Peter. "The Hormel Strike: Turning Point for the Rank-and-file Labor Movement." *Socialist Review* 16, 5 (September/October 1986): 71–98.

———. "Turning Points in the Labor Movement: Three Key Conflicts." In *Minnesota in a Century of Change: The State and Its People since 1900*, edited by Clifford E. Clark, Jr. St. Paul: Minnesota Historical Society Press, 1989: 195–222.

———. "Art and Activism in the American Labor Movement." *Artpaper* 10, 8 (April 1991): 12–13.

———. *Hard-Pressed in the Heartland: The Hormel Strike and the Future of the Labor Movement*. Boston: South End Press, 1993.

Randall, Adrian. *Before the Luddites: Custom, Community, and Machinery in the English Woollen Industry, 1776–1809*. Cambridge, England: Cambridge University Press, 1991.

Rapp, Rayna. "Family and Class in Contemporary America: Notes toward an Understanding of Ideology." In *Rethinking the Family: Some Feminist Questions*, edited by B. Thorne and M. Yalom. White Plains, N.Y.: Longman, 1982: 167–87.

Remington, Judy. "Women Working Together: How Well Is It Working? Part III: Power and Leadership." *Minnesota Women's Press* (November 23–December 6, 1988): 4–passim.

Riker, David. "The Struggle against Enclosures in Jay, Maine: An Account of the 1987–88 Strike against International Paper." *Midnight Notes: The New Enclosures*, No. 10 (Fall 1990): 42–53.

Rothschild-Whitt, Joyce. "Conditions for Democracy: Making Participatory Organizations Work." In *Co-ops, Communes, and Collectives: Experiments in Social Change in the 1960s and 1970s*, edited by John Case and Rosemary C. R. Taylor. New York: Pantheon Books, 1979: 215–44.

Rowbotham, Sheila. *Women, Resistance, and Revolution: A History of Women and Revolution in the Modern World*. New York: Vintage, 1972.

Ruddick, Sara, and Pamela Daniels, eds. *Working It Out*. New York: Pantheon, 1977.

Russ, Joanna. "Power and Helplessness in the Women's Movement." *Sinister Wisdom* 43/44 (Summer 1991): 146–54.

Ryan, Mary P. "The Power of Women's Networks: A Case Study of Female Moral Reform in Antebellum America." *Feminist Studies* 5, 1 (Spring 1979): 66–85.

Salerno, Salvatore. *Red November Black November: Culture and Community in the Industrial Workers of the World*. Albany: State University of New York Press, 1989.

Schleuning, Neala. *I Always Believed It Was a Beautiful Town*. Videotape. Mankato, Minn., 1987.

Schofield, Ann. "Rebel Girls and Union Maids: The Woman Question in the Journals of the AFL and IWW." *Feminist Studies* 9, 2 (Summer 1983): 335–58.

———. "The Women's March: Miners, Families, and Community in Pittsburg, Kansas, 1921–22." *Kansas History* 7, 2 (Summer 1984): 159–68.

———. "An 'Army of Amazons': The Language of Protest in a Kansas Mining Community, 1921–22." *American Quarterly* 37, 5 (Winter 1985): 686–701.

Schwartz, Michael, Naomi Rosenthal, and Laura Schwartz. "Leader–Member Conflict in Protest Organizations: The Case of the Southern Farmers' Alliance." *Social Problems* 29, 1 (October 1981): 22–36.

Seddon, Vicki, ed. *The Cutting Edge: Women and the Pit Strike*. London: Lawrence and Wishart, 1986.

Seeger, Peter, and Bob Reiser. *Carry It On: A History in Song and Picture of America's Working Men and Women*. New York: Simon and Schuster, 1985.

Sen, Gita. "The Sexual Division of Labor and the Working Class Family: Toward a Conceptual Synthesis of Class Relations and the Subordination of Women." *Review of Radical Political Economics* 12, 2 (Summer 1980): 76–86.

Service Employees International Union, AFL-CIO, CLC. *Americans Deserve a Living Wage: Minimum Wage*. Washington, D.C.: SEIU, 1988.

Sinclair, Upton. *The Jungle*. New York: Penguin, 1990.

Somplatsky-Jarman, William. "Bringing Home the Bacon: The Real Hormel Story."

Christianity and Crisis: A Christian Journal of Opinion 46, 1 (March 3, 1986): 56–58.

Songs of the Workers to Fan the Flames of Discontent. Chicago: Industrial Workers of the World, 1974.

Stephenson, Charles, and Robert Asher, eds. *Life and Labor: Dimensions of American Working-class History*. Albany: State University of New York Press, 1986.

Strom, Sharon Hartman. "Challenging 'Woman's Place': Feminism, the Left, and Industrial Unionism in the 1930s." *Feminist Studies* 9, 2 (Summer 1983): 360–86.

Support Report, newsletter of the Austin United Support Group, Austin, Minn., 4 vols., 1986–90.

Taft, Philip. "The IWW in the Grain Belt." *Labor History* 1, 1 (Winter 1960): 53–67.

The Anti-Mass: Methods of Organization for Collectives. Anonymous, c. 1970.

"The History of Our Union from 1933–49." *Unionist*, Austin, Minn. (May 7, 1971): 2.

Thomas, Sherry. "Digging beneath the Surface: Oral History Techniques." *Frontiers* 7, 1 (1983): 51–55.

Thompson, E. P. *The Making of the English Working Class*. New York: Vintage, 1966.

———. "The Moral Economy of the English Crowd in the Eighteenth Century." *Past and Present* 50 (November 1971): 76–136.

———. "Eighteenth-century English Society: Class Struggle without Class?" *Social History* 3, 2 (1978): 133–65.

Tilly, Louise A. "The Food Riot as a Form of Political Conflict in France." *Journal of Interdisciplinary History* 2, 1 (Summer 1971): 23–58.

———. "Paths of Proletarianization: Organization of Production, Sexual Division of Labor, and Women's Collective Action." *Signs: Journal of Women in Culture and Society* 7, 2 (Winter 1981): 400–417.

Tocqueville, Alexis de. *Democracy in America*, edited and abridged by Richard D. Heffner. New York: New American Library, 1956.

Trimble, Steve. "1934 Teamsters Strike." *Scattered Seeds* 2, 2 (1975): 50–53.

Tuan, Yi-Fu. "The Significance of the Artifact." *Geographical Review* 70, 4 (October 1980): 462–72.

Vazquez, Adolpho Sanchez. *Art and Society: Essays in Marxist Aesthetics*. New York and London: Monthly Review, 1973.

Veblen, Thorstein. *Absentee Ownership and Business Enterprise in Recent Times: The Case of America*. Boston: Beacon Press, 1967.

Veysey, Laurence. *The Communal Experience: Anarchist and Mystical Communities in Twentieth-century America*. Chicago and London: University of Chicago Press, 1978.

Walker, Charles R. *American City: A Rank and File History*. New York: Farrar and Rinehart, 1937.

Wallace, Anthony C. F. *Rockdale: The Growth of an American Village in the Early Industrial Revolution*. New York: Knopf, 1980.

Ward, C. Osborne. *The Ancient Lowly: A History of the Ancient Working People from the Earliest Known Periods to the Adoption of Christianity by Constantine*, Vols. 1 and 2. Chicago: Charles H. Kerr, 1907.

We Are Strong: A Guide to the Work of Popular Theatres across the Americas. Mankato, Minn.: Institute for Cultural Policy Studies, 1983.

West, Guida, and Rhoda Lois Blumberg. "Reconstructing Social Protest from a Feminist

Perspective." In *Women and Social Protest*, edited by Guida West and Rhoda Lois Blumberg. New York and Oxford, England: Oxford University Press, 1990: 3–35.

———, eds. *Women and Social Protest*. New York and Oxford, England: Oxford University Press, 1990.

Wetzel, Tom. "On Organization." *Ideas & Action* 9 (Spring 1988): 6–8.

———. "Origins of the Spanish Collectives." *Ideas & Action* 9 (Spring 1988): 16–17.

White, Deborah Gray. "Female Slaves: Sex Roles and Status in the Antebellum Plantation South." In *Unequal Sisters: A Multicultural Reader in U.S. Women's History*, edited by Ellen Carol DuBois and Vicki L. Ruiz. New York and London: Routledge, 1990: 22–33.

Whyte, William Foote, and Kathleen King Whyte. *Making Mondragon: The Growth and Dynamics of the Worker Cooperative Complex*. Ithaca, N.Y.: ILR Press, 1988.

Wilson, Michael, and Deborah Silverton Rosenfelt. *The Salt of the Earth*. Old Westbury, N.Y.: Feminist Press, 1978.

With Babies and Banners: The Story of the Women's Emergency Brigade. Motion Picture. Women's Labor History Film Project. Directed by Lorraine Gray, Produced by Anne Bohlen, Lyn Goldfarb, and Lorraine Gray. New Day Films, Franklin Lakes, N.J., 1978.

"Women Working Together." Special Issue of *Heresies* 2, 3 (Spring 1979).

"Women's Time Is Not Money." Special issue on "Women and Work." *Connexions* 30 (1989): 2–3.

Women's Work Study Group. "Loom, Broom, and Womb: Producers, Maintainers, and Reproducers." *Radical America* 10, 2 (March/April 1976): 29–45.

Yeghissian, Patricia. "Emergence of the Red Berets." *Michigan Occasional Papers* 10 (Winter 1980): 27 pages.

Zerzan, John, and Paula Zerzan. *Industrialism and Domestication*. Detroit: Black Eye Press, 1979.

Index

Blum, Fred, 3, 5
Boycott, 23, 124; of Austin businesses, 29–31, 211; of Hormel products, 23–24, 26, 31, 55, 69–70, 107, 124, 132, 136, 138, 211; secondary, 9
"Boycott Hormel: Live from Austin,"114
Boyle, Peter, 55
"Bread and roses," 95, 130
Brookside Coal Strike (1963), 135, 140
Brother Paul's Mission, 127
Burnout, 157–58
Butts, Jan, 130, 151, 159, 160, 161

Cameron, Ardis, 175, 186
Capitalism, 5, 90, 195, 196, 207. *See also* Class
Cardel, Eide, 107
Caudwell, Christopher, 116
Chamber of Commerce, 27, 28, 29, 30, 57–58. *See also* Haugen, Larry
Cheeta, Tom, 74
Chernick, Jack, 16
Children, 48, 92–93, 176, 208; and activism, 86; impact of strike on, 68–69, 210; women and care of, 174, 175. *See also* Family; Santa's Workshop
Churches, 19, 48, 66, 101, 116, 135, 178, 211; failure to support strike, 49–52, 60, 67, 199
Civil disobedience, 10, 11, 45, 47–48, 51, 55, 122–23, 132, 134, 135–38, 139, 178, 179, 200, 208. *See also* Demonstrations; Picketing
Civil Rights Movement, 184, 200, 204
Class, 21–22, 99, 103, 113, 118, 202, 206; consciousness, 91, 100, 203, 206; gender and, 202; intra-class tensions, 24, 67, 77; within Support Group, 152, 154. *See also* Working class
Clothing Exchange, 122, 132
Cobble, Dorothy Sue, 185
Collective memory, 201
Collette, Barbara, 19, 25, 35, 37, 43, 44, 45, 48, 51, 53, 64, 65, 83, 86, 88, 93, 94, 103, 105, 107, 128, 137, 139, 150, 151, 152, 153, 158–59, 160, 162,

167, 174, 178, 186, 188, 191, 198, 199–200, 202, 205, 208
Colorado Coal Strike (1927–28), 134
Commitment, 84–86, 101, 105, 171; time, 85, 154, 157
"Communal unionism," 91
Communism, 83, 199, 201, 206
Community: business, in Austin, 27–31; definition of, 17–18, 131; economic survival of, 102, 196, 211, 212; moral economy and, 89–94; radical, 100–101, 200, 206; in Support Group, 82–84, 103–4. *See also* Austin, Minnesota; Government; Strike culture
Company town, 6, 8, 18–19, 20–27, 33, 55, 57, 91, 92. *See also* Small town
Concessions, 7, 8, 10, 12, 14, 26, 94
Conflict: gender and, 156; in organizations, 149, 155–56; in Support Group, 150, 155–63, 168, 181, 183, 208
Constitutional rights, 42–43, 48, 60, 113, 201
Consumer politics, 20, 29. *See also* Boycott
Conway, Jill, Susan Bourque and Joan Scott, 171
Cooper, Jake, 126
Corporate Campaign, 8, 9, 10, 20, 21, 42, 81, 123–24, 151. *See also* Rogers, Ray
Corporate paternalism, 24, 33, 35, 36, 88
Corporate responsibility, 94, 207
Criminal activities, 45, 82, 103. *See also* Civil disobedience; Law enforcement; Violence
Cripple Creek Strike(s), 90, 109, 135
"Cultural catastrophe," 196

Deindustrialization, 1
Democracy, 60, 135, 212; democratic decision-making, 15, 145–50, 208; economic, 141, 207; participatory, 145–50, 155–56, 190, 207, 212; in Support Group, 145–50, 152, 207; workplace, 4–5. *See also* Conflict; Government; Leadership
Demonstrations, 9, 10, 11, 45, 87, 108,

About the Author

NEALA J. SCHLEUNING, Ph.D. American Studies, is a member of the National Coalition of Independent Scholars. She is the author of *Idle Hands and Empty Hearts: Work and Freedom in the United States* (1990), *America—Song We Sang without Knowing: The Life and Ideas of Meridel Le Sueur* (1983), and many journal articles.